Police Dogs
of Trinidad and Tobago

"Dogs in Our World" Series

Canine Crania: Your Dog's Head and Why It Looks That Way
(Bryan D. Cummins with Kaelyn Racine, 2024)

*The Peace Puppy: A Memoir of Caregiving
and Canine Solace* (Susan Hartzler, 2024)

My Broken Dog: Living with a Handicapped Pet
(Sandy Kubillus, 2024)

Canine Agility and the Meaning of Excellence
(Beth A. Dixon, 2024)

We Saved Each Other (Christopher Dale, 2024)

*Police Dogs of Trinidad and Tobago:
A 70-Year History* (Debbie Jacob, 2024)

*The Force-Free Dilemma: Truth and Myths
in Modern Dog Training* (Nicola Ferguson, 2024)

*Dogs of the Railways: Canine Guardians, Companions
and Mascots Since the 19th Century* (Jill Lenk Schilp, 2023)

Horror Dogs: Man's Best Friend as Movie Monster
(Brian Patrick Duggan, 2023)

*I Know Your Dog Is a Good Dog: A Trainer's Insights on Reactive,
Aggressive or Anxious Behavior* (Linda Scroggins, 2023)

*The Most Painful Choice: A Dog Owner's Story
of Behavioral Euthanasia* (Beth Miller, 2023)

Your Service Dog and You: A Practical Guide (Nicola Ferguson, 2023)

*Dog of the Decade: Breed Trends and What They Mean
in America* (Deborah Thompson, 2022)

*Laboratory Dogs Rescued: From Test Subjects
to Beloved Companions* (Ellie Hansen, 2022)

*Beware of Dog: How Media Portrays
the Aggressive Canine* (Melissa Crawley, 2021)

*I'm Not Single, I Have a Dog: Dating Tales
from the Bark Side* (Susan Hartzler, 2021)

*Dogs in Health Care: Pioneering Animal-Human
Partnerships* (Jill Lenk Schilp, 2019)

*General Custer, Libbie Custer and Their Dogs:
A Passion for Hounds, from the Civil War to Little Bighorn*
(Brian Patrick Duggan, 2019)

*Dog's Best Friend: Will Judy, Founder of National Dog Week
and* Dog World *Publisher* (Lisa Begin-Kruysman, 2014)

*Man Writes Dog: Canine Themes in Literature,
Law and Folklore* (William Farina, 2014)

*Saluki: The Desert Hound and the English Travelers
Who Brought It to the West* (Brian Patrick Duggan, 2009)

Police Dogs of Trinidad and Tobago
A 70-Year History

DEBBIE JACOB

DOGS IN OUR WORLD
Series Editor Brian Patrick Duggan

McFarland & Company, Inc., Publishers
Jefferson, North Carolina

ISBN (print) 978-1-4766-9406-1
ISBN (ebook) 978-1-4766-5190-3

LIBRARY OF CONGRESS AND BRITISH LIBRARY
CATALOGUING DATA ARE AVAILABLE

Library of Congress Control Number 2024009027

© 2024 Debbie Jacob. All rights reserved

No part of this book may be reproduced or transmitted in any form or by any means, electronic or mechanical, including photocopying or recording, or by any information storage and retrieval system, without permission in writing from the publisher.

Front cover image: Malissa Narine and Adina on the training field in Cumuto (photograph by Miquel Galofré, May 22, 2016).

Printed in the United States of America

*McFarland & Company, Inc., Publishers
Box 611, Jefferson, North Carolina 28640
www.mcfarlandpub.com*

For Geoffrey Hospedales and Patsy Joseph, the superintendents
of the Trinidad and Tobago Mounted and Canine Branch
who made this history possible.

And in memory of my dad, Paul J. Bowman, who loved all animals,
and Leonard Dyer, who led me to the dogs' history.

Table of Contents

Acknowledgments	ix
Preface	1
Introduction. Trinidad: An Island of Beauty, an Island in Crisis	7
1. Dog Days	11
2. Backtracking: Bruno	16
3. Along Came a Spider	21
4. Shah: King of the Dogs	28
5. Ralph and Rex	34
6. Dreams, Nightmares and Other Business	42
7. Sheba and Sheba	49
8. Carlo	54
9. Panther	60
10. Adolph, ANZAC, and Bullet	64
11. Trigger	73
12. Shep	78
13. Black Power, Daemon and Rex	81
14. Murder in St. Vincent	90
15. Dyer Memories	97
16. Inside the Caroni Kennels	100
17. Jango and Strike	105
18. A Line in the Sand	110
19. The Piegaro Team	116

Table of Contents

20. Ambush and Kidnappings	125
21. Springing into Action	132
22. Dog Days Two	136
23. Where the Air Is Rare	140
24. A Woman's Touch	145
25. Tobago Tales	151
26. Starring: The "M" Dogs	160
27. Training Days	169
28. What the Future Holds	174
Appendix A: Thomas's Final Report on Bruno	183
Appendix B: Panther's Veterinary Report	186
Appendix C: Privy Council Summary of Junior "Spirit" Cottle Case	188
Chapter Notes	193
Bibliography	207
Index	215

Acknowledgments

I AM INDEBTED TO ALL the canine police officers who offered continuous support above and beyond the call of duty—especially former superintendents of the Mounted and Canine Branch Patsy Joseph and Geoffrey Hospedales, Cpl. Shane Chase, Cpl. Premnath Maharaj, Cpl. Akil Bernard and the late PC Sherwin Cedeno.

Getting unrestricted access to police dogs' files and police officers to write a book required the help of special people. Former canine police inspector Michael Roban facilitated permission from acting police commissioner James Philbert; retired prison commissioner Sterling Stewart got permission from acting police commissioner Stephen Williams and Supt. Hospedales procured permission from the current acting police commissioner Erla Harewood-Christopher. Thanks to these police commissioners for realizing the importance of having a book about the police dogs' history.

Invaluable editing came from Anu Lakhan, Austin Fido, Susan Al-Jarrah and Justice Kathy Ann Waterman-Latchoo. Judy Raymond's final edit shaped this book before it went to the publisher and made it better.

I thank the *Trinidad Express* and *Trinidad and Tobago Newsday* for their support. *Newsday* granted permission to use photographs by Sureash Cholai, Roger Jacob and Angelo Marcelle.

Independent photographer Miquel Galofré from Barcelona, Spain provided stunning pictures and the book trailer for this project.

A book comes to life with unexpected discoveries and the most memorable one for me was Austin Fido finding out that Spirit was

Acknowledgments

still alive in St. Vincent. Nazma Muller tracked him down for me to interview.

Thanks to Asst. Commissioner of Police (Ret.) Joanne Archie and PC Darrius Allen of the police communications department for their invaluable assistance and to Aisha Baptiste, Library Assistant at the West Indiana & Special Collections department of the Alma Jordan Library at the University of the West Indies St. Augustine Campus for the picture of the first four canine officers as they arrived in Trinidad.

My gratitude extends to canine officers I never met. Theophilus Thomas tops the list. There would be no books without the police dogs. Finally, they have their voice in history. No words can convey my gratitude to McFarland for publishing this book.

Preface

GROWING UP ON A REMOTE dairy farm in Lexington, Ohio, gave me the patience and the appreciation of solitude that would be necessary for writing about the Trinidad and Tobago police dogs. My education and work experience provided the skills to recognize the canine police section's history as an unusual and important angle in understanding how crime developed in a Caribbean nation just seven miles from Venezuela.

It has been quite a journey to get to this book. After earning my BA in anthropology from Ohio State University in 1974, I moved to Mountain View, California, to pursue graduate work in anthropology at California State Hayward. There, I learned of the Trinidadian Nobel laureate, V.S. Naipaul. His literature put Trinidad on the map for me.

Three years later, I moved to Seattle, Washington, where working at The Boeing Company provided experience in putting mounds of information together into cohesive documents.

In 1983, I moved to Trinidad and lived with a friend in Warrenville, a village in central Trinidad carved out of a sugarcane field, which felt much like the wheat and corn fields I knew growing up on a farm. Becoming a journalist at the *Trinidad Express* in Port of Spain in 1984, was my ticket to follow my curiosity. Every day on my way to work I passed through Caroni, the headquarters for the canine police section.

In 1992, I wrote my first feature on police dogs. The story stuck with me—even when I left my full-time job in journalism to start the English department for the International School of Port of Spain. There, I got a master's degree in international education from

Preface

Framingham State University, taught English and ancient world history, completed a certificate in library science from Indiana State University, and became the head librarian.

All the tools to work on this book were now in place. I had the blueprint for fitting into another country gleaned from studying anthropology; interviewing skills honed in my journalism, which I continued part-time; and research skills developed in both disciplines and library science.

About 80 percent of this book is based on primary sources, mostly information from police dogs' files and interviews with canine officers sanctioned by three police commissioners and three superintendents of the Mounted and Canine Branch. Interviews over a 14-year period mainly took place at the canine section's headquarters in Caroni; Chaguaramas, in the western part of the island; Cumuto in the east, and in Tobago.

No civilian ever had access to the police dogs' files or spent such an extended period of time with police officers. This meant I had no one else's research to point me in any other direction. Some dogs had scanty files; some files were missing. Strict gag orders normally imposed on public servants created a communication barrier that had to be broken. Selecting officers who worked from the 1960s to the present was a challenge, but the rewards of original research far outweighed the challenges.

History is not information confined to the past. It lives in the present by showing us how we got to a particular place in time. This book uses a methodical, thematic approach placing police dogs' stories at the center of 70 years of Trinidad and Tobago's history. Undoubtedly, that creative decision is rooted in my life on a dairy farm long ago where animals provided invaluable lessons about trust, love, perseverance, and the natural wisdom of following instincts.

Police Dogs of Trinidad and Tobago is for high school and university classes on crime, policing, Caribbean history, anthropology, and immersion journalism or for anyone who simply enjoys history, stories about crime, Caribbean culture, or police dogs. Follow the dogs wherever they lead you.

Preface

Trinidad: An Island of Beauty, an Island in Crisis

I was in the Arena forest in Cumuto with the canine police and wondering if I would cross paths with a howler monkey, ocelot or poisonous mapepire snake when Prime Minister Keith Rowley announced a state of emergency in an effort to control the Covid-19 pandemic. That drastic measure would begin the following day, on May 15, 2021.[1] The country's borders had been closed since March 23, 2020, and violating the law that you must wear a mask already meant a fine of up to TT$3,000.

Such strict measures formed a stark contrast to the picture-postcard image of carefree Trinidad and Tobago, but these southernmost islands in the Caribbean (Trinidad is just seven miles from Venezuela) form a land of contrast. It's a birdwatchers' paradise, with over 470 species, including many South American ones.[2] Some of its beaches have deceptive currents, but some are welcoming spots for endangered sea turtles to come ashore and lay their eggs here.

The dark presence of blue devils with pitchforks in hand ushers in J'Ouvert morning, followed by the "pretty mas" (masquerade) of Carnival, played in the blazing sun. French settlers brought Carnival to a British-controlled Trinidad, and the African population added another dimension to the festivities with calypso featuring double entendres that Europeans couldn't comprehend and costumes like the Dame Lorraine, which poked fun at proper European women's way of dressing. Carnival's Panorama, a festival of steelbands for the steeldrums, originated on this island.

But there's also Hosay, a Shi'ite Muslim commemoration of the martyrdom of the prophet Mohammed's grandsons Hassan and Hussein, which takes place in St. James and Cedros. The battle of Karbala in ancient Iraq is acted out with tassa drummers beating different rhythms, which evoke a call to assemble, march, go to battle and mourn. Tadjahs (replicas of mosque-shaped tombs) are pushed through the streets, and men take off their shoes to convert a main road to a sacred space as they balance two heavy replicas of crescent moons on their backs, a green one for Hassan and a red one for

Preface

Hussein. The handmade tassa drums, traditionally fashioned from clay structures with a goat skin stretched over the top are held with a rope around the neck. It is a predominantly Indo-Trinidadian observance, but tassa sides (groups) accept drummers from any religion or race.

Trinidad is a mosaic of religions and cultures: Catholics and Protestants—including Presbyterians, Seventh-Day Adventists and Anglicans—Hindus and Muslims, Shouter/Spiritual Baptists. Native peoples, Spanish, Portuguese, French creoles (local white people, traditionally an elite, who may have some mixed-race ancestry), Syrian and Lebanese, Chinese and the vast majority whose ancestors originally came from Africa or India live on this island.

This is not your typical tourist destination. It's an industrialized island with oil, natural gas, and a pitch lake that holds an estimated ten million tons of natural asphalt. In 1595, nearly a century after Christopher Columbus first spotted the Trinity Hills that give the island its name, English explorer Sir Walter Raleigh learned of the Pitch Lake in La Brea and caulked his ship on a trip back from the Orinoco River in Venezuela.[3] Countries around the world now make roads from natural asphalt originating from the Pitch Lake.

Some of the best and most sought-after flavoring cocoa, which gives chocolate bars their distinct taste, comes from Trinidad. In 1830, Trinidad was the third highest producer of cocoa, after Venezuela and Ecuador, and produced 20 percent of the world's cocoa.[4] These days artisan chocolates made at Cocobel rival any foreign hand-made chocolates, and chocolates representing various cocoa estates offer a taste of sweet Trinidad. Renowned local singer Machel Montano produces his own brand of chocolate bars.

There are unexpected historical links to the U.S. as well. Trinidad has a history in sugarcane, slavery and indentureship. Rarely does anyone mention tobacco from Trinidad, but Virginia credits English explorer Sir Walter Raleigh with introducing tobacco plants from Venezuela and Trinidad to that U.S. state. Native Americans grew tobacco for 3,000 years before this, but the crop never took root in Virginia until Raleigh's discovery.[5]

Skip ahead to the 19th century with two key connections relating

Preface

to the British invasion of the U.S. during the war of 1812–14. A number of black marines who gambled on siding with the British ended up on the losing end of the war and 700 of them were resettled by the British in Trinidad.[6] They were called Merikins, and they showed up for a most unusual burial in Port of Spain on August 24, 1819.

U.S. naval hero Oliver Perry, most famous for his battle of Lake Erie in the war of 1812, had sailed to Venezuela to meet with Simón Bolívar about the pirate problem in the Caribbean. Perry became ill while traveling down the Orinoco River on his return voyage and died of yellow fever. His crew took his body to the British colony of Trinidad, where he was buried at the Lapeyrouse cemetery in Port of Spain. In 1826, the U.S. government brought Perry's body home for re-interment in his birthplace, Newport, Rhode Island.

Trinidad's fortunes changed in 1857, when the Merrimac Company dug the first oil well near the Pitch Lake. Walter Darwent hit his first successful well in 1866.[7] Oil changed the fortunes of Trinidad and put it on the world stage with other oil-producing nations.

But this land of racial, cultural and religious contrasts, with a well-educated and literate population, struggles with poverty. A 2012 study said an estimated 21 percent of the population lived below the poverty line, even though the country is oil-rich.[8] The culture of poverty and crime go hand in hand. Trinidad feels and looks like a microcosm of the world with all its problems: illegal drugs, kidnappings, murders and gun violence. Crime fighting tactics change, but police dogs remain a constant force in that battle.

At the end of the day, Arci the police dog and canine officers emerged from the forest. I didn't spot any forest creatures, but we did hear a howler monkey as we drove away. Back in Camp Cumuto, barking puppies welcomed the police officers back to this training facility. The police canine section was closing in on its 70th anniversary and taking a page from its own history.

Introduction

A NEWSROOM IN THE 1990s felt like a beehive, and there is no way ever to forget its energy or promise. Journalists—even me, a rather timid worker bee among a swarm of seasoned journalists—chased after that ever-elusive, "perfect" story. Never good at finding an empty desk so I could tap out my story on a clunky old computer, I darted about the *Trinidad Express* office looking for a place to land. The clock ticked. Deadlines loomed. In one hand, I held a sweating bottle of Coca-Cola purchased in Viet Nam, the bar across the street where customers ducked bottles flying through the air. My free hand snatched a ringing phone from its cradle.

I had no idea this was *the* call—the one we all waited for, but never expected to get. On May 3, 1992, Cpl. Leonard Dyer committed an unspeakable act when he dialed the *Express* office in Port of Spain. The desperate canine police officer defied the public-service gag order. I listened to his plea, grabbed my notebook and pen; jumped in a taxi to central Trinidad, and headed for a story that would haunt me for decades and ultimately change my life. In all my excitement, I forgot to ask for a photographer.

In the warm breeze of the Caroni plains, in central Trinidad, Cpl. Dyer sat on a gray metal chair outside the annex at the Caroni Canine headquarters, situated in a sugarcane field. His disarming smile, brassy voice, and percolating exuberance initially hid his concern. Constable (PC) Stephen Mahabir walked across the compound with Bonnie, a sleek yellow police dog twirling in her Labrador dance.

"She's something else," said Dyer.

Bonnie, a drug detection dog, reigned as the Canine Section's

Introduction

undisputed star during the early 90s. Over three years, Police Dog #204 had sniffed out cocaine and marijuana worth a street value of TT$3 million. Her closest rivals in the Canine Section had just crossed $1 million in drug finds.[1]

"That makes us the unheralded branch of the police service," said Dyer.

His pride, then concern, spilled out of him.

"Just the presence of dogs on police patrols decreases crime. Criminals have suspicious behavior that these dogs sense instantly. The dogs rarely make mistakes, but the heat is a big stress factor for these dogs, and we transport them with open Land Rovers in the hot sun. That's bad. These dogs should be going to work in air-conditioned vans. When they're exposed to plenty of heat, they pant too much and don't rely on their noses. Then stress affects them, and they die at alarming rates."

Something caught Dyer's eye and he chuckled. Nine-month-old yellow Labrador puppies loped across the grass behind Corporal Khairool Khan. Ace leaped up and rested his front paws on Dyer's lap; then dipped into the annex, sniffed around, and scratched madly at the stainless-steel table leg where Dyer had hidden a training device for marijuana detection.

"Good boy!" Dyer shouted.

He doled out hugs and hearty pats on the puppy's back.

"They say a dog handler should be able to win an Academy Award for his acting," Dyer laughed.

With tails wagging, puppies Action and Aurora arrived for their performance.

"Don't worry. The dogs don't come in contact with drugs or get hooked on marijuana or cocaine. They just sense one or more of the components inside a training device," Dyer said.

"Drug dealers try all kinds of tricks to mask the odor of their drugs: perfume, coffee, rasta oil, paint. But if a dog has a nose like Bonnie..."

Back at the newspaper office, I tapped out a story about Bonnie, the police puppies, and the need for air-conditioned vehicles, but I couldn't shake off something Dyer had told me.

Introduction

"The police dogs have files—just like police officers—and they date back to the first four dogs in 1952."

He had pointed to gray metal cabinets in the anteroom of the annex where the puppies had searched. Crime stories in the media rarely mentioned police dogs' work. I thought: this could be a fresh new angle for a journalist to explore. What secret world of crime did these dogs work in? What did they know about crime that people did not know? How could the dogs help us to understand the history of crime in Trinidad and Tobago? How could I get to those secret police files?

Bonnie's story began on the front page of the *Trinidad Express* on Tuesday, 12 May 1992.

> Drug Lords' Worst Enemy
> Bonnie is a sleek blonde bitch who has stolen more than $3 million from Trinidadian drug lords.
> "She's something else," Corporal Leonard Dyer says with a smile that rivals Dick Tracy's whenever Breathless Mahoney crosses his mind.
> "She's on her way to the airport," her police partner, Stephen Mahabir says.
> Dyer flashes a wry smile. Before the day's finished he's sure a drug dealer somewhere in the country will say, "You're a dog, Bonnie."
> The drug lord would be absolutely right..."[2]

The graphic artist drew a black-and-white smile-worthy picture of Bonnie standing upright on shapely legs in high-heeled shoes. The story haunted me. I stopped flitting around like a bee in the newsroom and became dogged in my quest to see those dog files. The breakthrough came in 2006, when canine police inspector Michael Roban got that permission from Acting Police Commissioner James Philbert.

I headed back to those filing cabinets in Caroni, still in the same spot where I had first spotted them while interviewing Dyer. Here, I would return to my training in anthropology, be tossed into history from half a century ago, and be propelled into the heady experience of immersion journalism.

A senior officer and I opened two filing cabinets and found six drawers of dog files. The officer carried the brittle brown files outside to wipe off the covers so we could read the dogs' names. I felt the

Introduction

adrenaline rush that came from discovering information no other civilian had ever seen. The canine officer stacked the dusted files on a desk so I could read and transcribe the handwritten reports inside.

The dogs in the kennels had been fed, so they settled into sleep. A cool breeze gently rustled through the sugarcane. A fleeting memory of Ace, Action, and Aurora dashing about this room crossed my mind. The canine officer chuckled and gently laid a thick file in front of me.

I looked down and gasped.

The file read: "Dog #1, Bruno."

Chapter 1

Dog Days

September 25, 1952

Four Trinidadian police officers, accompanied by their newly acquired Alsatians,[1] had no idea of the fate awaiting them as they boarded the ship that would carry them home. They had just completed a three-month course at the Metropolitan Police Training Centre in the UK. Cpl. Theophilus Thomas, Cpl. Carlyle Piggott; Sgt. Hamilton Bridgeman, and Police Constable (PC) George Alexis must have felt excited about the new venture awaiting them in the British colony of Trinidad and Tobago. Quite possibly, they were unaware of a storm brewing in the Atlantic.

Storms in the Caribbean can take unexpected turns and curl towards any island—especially during the hurricane season from June through November. On September 25, meteorologists in Florida noted an easterly wave that showed signs of intensifying over the Atlantic, about 700 miles east of the Lesser Antilles. Aircraft scanning the area encountered squalls of 68 knots over a considerable distance. Reports noted 100-mph winds. A hurricane appeared to be forming, but no closed center of circulation could be found. The sea appeared rough and unpredictable.[2]

At around 8 a.m. that day the four officers, "justly proud of these dogs with which they were trained" (as Thomas would later write in Bruno's file), arrived in Port of Spain. Thomas and his dog Bruno; Piggott with his dog Winston; Bridgeman and Shah; and Alexis, with Carlos, landed in Trinidad without any recorded fanfare. The four officers, dressed in suits, ties, and the fedoras of the day, posed for a picture on the deck of the ship. With heads held high, the four dogs sat at their handlers' feet.[3]

Police Dogs of Trinidad and Tobago

The first four police canine officers and their police dogs arrive in Trinidad on September 25, 1952. From left: Cpl. Theophilus Thomas, Bruno, Cpl. Carlysle Piggott, Winston, Sgt. George Alexis, Carlos, PC Hamilton Bridgeman and Shah (photograph by a *Port of Spain Gazette* photographer, from the Eustace Bernard Photograph Collection, SC.30 Box 1 Folder 6, Alma Jordan Library, University of the West Indies, St. Augustine, Trinidad).

The first official notation of the dogs' presence in Trinidad came from a note Thomas wrote in Bruno's file: "Bruno, Carlos, Shah, and Winston arrived in the Colony on September 25, 1952, and were taken on the strength of the force and posted to the Depot (DP 9031)." There the dogs would await their first duties.

On September 27, the Florida Met Office watched the weather pattern that had formed just before the officers' arrival and finally assigned a name: Hurricane Dog.[4] Thomas, Piggott, Bridgeman, and Alexis escaped that storm, but they would face unimaginable danger in the future while making history as the first four Trinidadian canine police officers.

The new, uncharted territory of the Dog Section came under the British colony's paramilitary force led by Col. Eric Hammet Fairfax Beadon from 1949 until independence in 1962. The officers'

Chapter 1. Dog Days

pioneering efforts brought fame to one of the officers and a horrifying end to another's career. The other two canine officers quietly slipped into history.

Thomas would advance to the position of superintendent of the Mounted and Dog Branch and eventually become an assistant commissioner of police (ACP). He would champion the police dogs' cause for the rest of his life. His stories, often dramatic—especially when it came to his dog Bruno—sounded like passages from a novel rather than official police reports, but the stories proved necessary for the survival of the Dog Section in those early days. Without Thomas's dramatic flair, the dogs' stories might have slipped into oblivion.

Expectations grew high for Bruno, a sable Alsatian with a black face, and his working partner, Shah, a black-and-gray Alsatian with black-and-gray legs and a tan-and-black face. Trained as tracker dogs, Bruno, Shah, Winston, and Carlos were off and running. Their files recorded the dogs' every move.

Jail Break
19 December, 1952
The call came to the Northern Division requesting the services of two dogs in connection with a jailbreak at the Royal Gaol on Frederick Street, Port of Spain. Cpl. Theophilus Thomas, with dog Bruno, and PC Bridgeman, with Shah, immediately headed for the gaol.[5]

On their arrival, Thomas and Bridgeman met three superintendents and a few detectives from police headquarters, headed by Supt. Carr.

> We were at once given a verbal detail of the two escaped convicts and were shown to the cells in which they were last kept. We took the blanket in which the prisoner slept. We were also told that one of [the prisoners] had been recaptured in hot pursuit, therefore we had only the other man to contend with. The blanket was taken with us to the entrance of the prison where the prisoners were said to have escaped from a vehicle while being ushered into the jail.

The prisoners had pounced upon an opportune moment to escape, after a court appearance, when they were being shuffled back to prison. Bruno took a sniff of the blanket and Thomas gave him the signal to track the escaped convict.

Police Dogs of Trinidad and Tobago

> [Bruno] quickly took on the scent and headed down the pitched road south along Frederick Street. He turned east and continued onto Charlotte Street where he had a bit of confusion with traffic and pedestrians. Bruno picked up the scent again, crossed the street, and continued eastbound to Belmont Circular Road.
>
> Bruno reached a bridge crossing the East Dry River[6] in Belmont, and again had difficulties. After several futile efforts ... he eventually took up the scent again. This time he continued South along the bed of the said river to about fifty yards from the Observatory Street Bridge when he, on his own initiative, jumped onto the bank on the Eastern side and continued into a yard and finally came out on Observatory Street.

An audience swelled along the route as curious onlookers witnessed a police search never before seen in Trinidad.

> All this time [Bruno] kept his nose turned to the ground and I, having a thorough knowledge of his reactions, was quite certain that he was on the trail. By then the crowd was getting thicker and the police men available had great difficulty in keeping them from crowding the dog and me.... The dog sniffed around in a desperate effort for some time.

Meandering from one street to the next, Bruno ended up on the Park Street bridge, where he sniffed and jumped up on the western bank of the river.

> I assisted him up. He took up the scent again and came out through a hole in a fence, large enough for a man to pass. The crowd was terrible and uncontrollable. The police managed to keep them back a bit. The dog again made a gallant effort, but this time he failed to get any scent and therefore went no further. He was tired and taken off [the trail] to the agreement of Supt. Neish who was present all along.
>
> It is my opinion, sir, that the dog was right all along and had it not been for the confusion of picking out the scent from the many of the crowd gathered, he might have gone that way where the escaped convict was actually resting in a house a little beyond Park Street.[7]

At the end of the report, Thomas made a parenthetical note. "(When the criminal was apprehended he did say that he went that route.)"

Early the following day, Thomas noted that the police had arrested the escaped convict about five miles away in San Juan, a town east of Port of Spain, which had served as the Spanish island's capital from 1592 to 1783.

From that first report, Thomas established himself as Bruno's

Chapter 1. Dog Days

biggest defender. From 1952 until 1960, Thomas worked alongside Dog #1 and recorded every detail of Bruno's working life. Bruno's files are possibly the best chronicle of crime in those eight years of Trinidad and Tobago's waning era as a colony. To Thomas, Bruno always appeared to be on the right track.

Chapter 2

Backtracking: Bruno

January 4, 1953: "I received a telephone message from Belmont police requesting the services of a dog in connection to a report of larceny in a dwelling house. I was immediately dispatched from the Depot Kennels at the Mounted Branch headquarters with Bruno to report to the Belmont Police Station for duty."

On my arrival at the said station, I was handed a portion of a man's jersey and told certain facts. I was also directed to a house at Number 21 Jerningham Avenue, Belmont where I met Sgt Balfour and Cpl. Beckles who were investigating. They told me that a thief was seen in the said house by the owner. The thief, on being discovered, ran out of the home. He was chased by the owner who got near enough to grab him, but he managed to escape by the jersey he was wearing being torn and the part in which I got from the station vicinity was left in the owner's hand.

I was then shown the direction in which the man ran and after giving Bruno a sniff of the piece of the jersey directed him to the area. He quickly took up the scent, which he followed at a fast pace. The track led along the pitched street then down into a paved canal for a distance of about 300 yards and then onto the road again, this time on Belmont Circular Road near the corner of St. Francois Valley Road.

He, Bruno, had a bit of confusion there, but quickly got back on scent and went directly in a shoemaker's shop in the area. Not being sure of his movements, I pulled him back and started him off from the Road. He again followed the scent back to the shoemaking shop.

Cpl. Beckles, who accompanied me along the way, and I made inquiries from a shoemaker who was there working and he bluntly denied knowing anything about what we were talking. This shoemaking shop is in a front room of a small house and has a door connecting it to other rooms. A young boy came out from the back room. He was questioned and he too denied knowing anything about the matter. The owner of the house from which the culprit was chased was also present, but he said neither of the two questioned was the culprit. I took Bruno to the back of the house and

Chapter 2. Backtracking: Bruno

to likely areas in the vicinity, but he failed to pick up any further scent therefore he was taken off.

On the next day, I saw Cpl. Beckles and he informed me that the dog Bruno was right that he received information from other persons that the young man as described, including his manner of dress, did go into the shoemaker's shop and quickly came back out and caught a passing taxi. He further stated, however, that he had also got a good idea who the culprit is and is making all efforts to find him.

From the manner in which Bruno did the track I was almost certain that he was right and had it been that we had the full co-operation of the shoemaker, who of course is a known scamp in the district, the culprit might have been held on the said night.[1]

On March 21, 1953, Thomas with Bruno and Bridgeman with Shah worked together to track down a thief attempting a house break-in. Transportation problems (no police vehicle was available) caused them to arrive in San Juan three hours late, but they found the culprit had left his gym boots at the scene of the crime when disturbed in the act of stealing. Thomas reported that the ground felt dry and the dogs tracked for about 300 feet, around many houses in the area.

> The people ... crowded on the roads and kept running in front and around the dogs along the way in spite of all the efforts made by the few policemen available to keep them back. Therefore the dogs were compelled to work under confusing circumstances, which to my opinion was the cause of their failure.[2]

Next, Bruno investigated a theft at the tobacco factory in Champs Fleurs, just east of San Juan. A thief had ransacked the offices and stole Anchor Special cigarettes.

> August 3, 1953
> ...footprints were discernible in certain places in the offices and store room from which the cigarettes had been stolen. These prints were believed to be those of the intruders. I caused Bruno to sniff at these footprints and when I observed that he had a scent, directed him to follow.
>
> He did follow for some time inside the building and then attempted to jump through a window on the Eastern side of the building. This window was open and there were markings on the wall and sill indicating someone had climbed through recently. I helped Bruno through the window and he immediately got back on the scent which he followed briskly.[3]

Bruno crisscrossed an area outside the factory and led Thomas to a hole cut in a wire fence.

Without encouragement, Bruno went through the hole. I followed him, he continued to a clump of bushes about twelve feet from the fence where I saw seven large cardboard cartons of Anchor special cigarettes. Bruno recovered cigarettes valued at $840, which was the said amount missed.[4]

Thomas and Bruno investigated a report of shooting with intent at a sugar estate in Cunupia, central Trinidad. Thomas captured the excitement of Bruno's chase in this report:

August 19, 1953

I was given particulars of the crime as follows: That at around 8 p.m. on August 19, the victims were driving along the estate road returning home. Mr. Rohett was driving and his wife was seated next to him. Just as they turned off the road to enter the driveway to their home, they heard the discharge of a gun and realized that they were shot at. Mrs. Rohett managed to see a man running away from a spot at the side of the estate. The shot was discharged after they had stopped the car and removed a log which was across the road and got back into their car.

The spot from which the alleged assailant was seen running was pointed out to me. He had left nothing there but footprints that could be seen as the ground was somewhat muddy. I caused Bruno to sniff at the footprints and he at once took the scent which he followed at a brisk pace in the direction the man was seen running. He followed for about one mile along the railway line and then on a dirt road, but finally came to stop on the doorstep of a room of a barrack for employees of the said estate. Seeing that Bruno started clawing at the door, I with the assistance of Constable Brathwaite, one of the investigators, caused the occupants to open to us.

An old East Indian man came to us, and he said that he and his family lived there and that they were asleep. All this time Bruno kept straining on his lead. Upon our request he woke a young nephew who came to us. I at once observed that he still had mud on his feet. As he approached the door, Bruno made a sudden go for him, but I held him back. The young man appeared to be terribly frightened. He was questioned extensively and the account he gave us was very unsatisfactory.[5]

Thomas took Bruno back to the scene of the crime to see if Bruno would retrace his tracks.

This time he followed at a faster pace and ended on the steps of the same room. Having in view to locate the gun I urged him on this time. He sniffed his way to the latrine at the back of the yard. It is impossible to see in the cesspit as same was full of water due to heavy rains.

Immediate enquiries were made in the vicinity and from information

Chapter 2. Backtracking: Bruno

received the same man was detained pending further enquiries. Bruno followed the scent as well as can be expected. From the actions of Bruno when the man came out of the room, I am confident that the man whose scent Bruno followed is the culprit. But in spite of our combined efforts the gun was never found. Further enquiries were made by Cunupia police but conclusive evidence against the man was not obtained and he was allowed to go.

Bruno's assistance proved invaluable to the police investigating a break-in at the home of a Dr. Hosein on Estate Road, Couva.

October 7, 1953

The facts in brief are that a masked man entered the home with a revolver in hand, held up a servant and demanded to be shown where the family kept their money and to be told where Mrs. Hosein was.

Mrs. Hosein was at the time in another room and heard the commotion. She made an alarm and the gunman ran out of the house and then out of the premises into a cane field across the road. She quickly telephoned the police and reported the matter. They quickly arrived on the scene and their efforts arrested the man from under a bed of a house about two miles from the scene, but he had time to hide the gun and mask which it was alleged he had.

Nothing was left at the scene. Neither was any footprints discernible there, but among the cane through which he was seen to have entered footprints were seen. I caused Bruno to take a good sniff and he followed the scent nicely. The trail led through the full extent of the cane field from North to South into a track then turned West and took me to an old abandoned track where he started sniffing at an old box. I checked and found a wooden pistol so designed that it appeared to be real. That was seized.

Bruno continued on the scent, this time along the muddy banks of a river. After covering about 150 yards we came upon a side of crepe-soled shoe, which Bruno sniffed at considerably. That too was seized. It was later discovered to be belonging to the accused. Bruno still continued along the track and came up to the house in which the man was held. On reaching, Bruno jumped through the window of the bedroom. Muddy footprints were seen on the sill. Bruno went under the bed and started sniffing around. On examination a cloth mask was seen tucked away in a corner under the bed.[6]

Note in red on top of the file: *Case made and man convicted.* After one year in Trinidad, Dog #1 had his first conviction. Meanwhile, criminals became bolder.

Police Dogs of Trinidad and Tobago

November 21, 1953

One Gladstone Gibson of Jerningham Junction Cunupia whilst riding his push bicycle along the Cunupia Saddle Road was on his way from work to home bounced into a piece of wire which was stretched across the road. As he fell off his bicycle two men one armed with a knife rushed up to him, threatened him with the knife and started beating him. He tried to fight back and eventually had to give up and pretend to be dead. He got up after assailants had gone and realized he was wounded on the hand and $27 in cash stolen from his trouser pockets. He proceeded to the police station, reported the matter, but was unable to identify either of the men. Nothing at all was left on the scene by the culprits.[7]

Bruno was made to sniff about a spot pointed to by the investigators which they believed must have been trampled by the culprits. He took up a scent, which he followed for a little distance up the road. He was taken with the investigators on enquiries but without success.

In a surprising and uncharacteristic entry at the end of Bruno's report, Thomas wrote, "General notes: Shah works hard too."

Chapter 3

Along Came a Spider

Theophilus Thomas, PC # 4138, honed Bruno's tracking and interdiction skills at a particular time and place when the newly-emergent steelband movement lapsed easily into gang violence, and some bands moved through the city like invading armies looking for a fight. "And then when two bands clash, Mama, if you see cutlash," calypsonian Carlton "Blakie" Joseph sang in his 1954 Road March, "Steelband Clash" (the most played song on the road during Carnival Monday and Tuesday). Lord Blakie later led San Juan All Stars into its infamous 1959 clash with Port of Spain–based Desperadoes.

"Steelbands were part of the musical development of the African diaspora in Trinidad from the percussion instruments made from bamboo and pounded on the turf before the 1930s to the first iron bands made from any piece of iron and then the steelbands later made from oil drums," said steelband historian Kim Johnson.[1]

It was a cultural evolution that coincided with the emergence of labor unions, and it fit in with the island's changing musical tastes from Spanish music with guitars and quatros to American jazz with its rhythm, sliding melodies and improvisations.

"The generation that created the first iron bands, all metal percussion ensembles—not yet pans [steel drums]—had never played bamboo," said Johnson. "The group that came up with the first pans was the first generation cut off from the lingua franca, which until then was French patois. They only spoke English."[2]

"They were cut off from the working-class folk culture of their parents' generation, and they realized you could beat some iron and get a sound from it. Once they discovered you could get different tones, pan evolved where they could play notes—not just rhythm.

Police Dogs of Trinidad and Tobago

The steelbands became competitive, playing on the streets, often in front of the police headquarters in the 50s, and the fighting, often referred to as gang warfare, wasn't like the gangs of today. It came from the musical competitiveness combined with profound gang loyalty. You fight someone in my band and my whole band will fight you."[3]

Bitter fights broke out on the streets of Port of Spain.

"People feared the steelbands—even the police dared not accost them alone,"[4] said Johnson.

But police dogs often dealt with the clashes. They also broke up wappie (an illegal card game) and dice gambling in front of cinemas.

One day, Thomas and Bruno, working out of the Besson Street police station and traveling east down old St. Joseph Road, Laventille, spotted four men crouching in front of the door of the Rio Theatre. Sighting the police, the men ran off in different directions.

> March 9, 1955
> I quickly jumped out from the back of the vehicle with dog Bruno and sent him after one of the men running down Esprit Street. Up to that time, I did not know what the men were actually doing. I ran and caught up to Bruno in the backyard of a house.
> I quickly ran around and with the aid of my torchlight saw the man lying on the ground with Bruno standing very near to him growling threateningly. I called him off, took the man into custody and took him back to Cpl. James at the vehicle. We then went to the spot where we saw them and there on the ground directly in front of the door of the theatre, we found playing cards strewn about. We examined the door of the theatre and found it to be intact and so we came to the conclusion that the men were gambling.
> The men were found guilty of gambling and given a fine of $5.00 or 14 days in jail.
> In this case, Sir, I think that Bruno did a good job of the chase. It is difficult to state whether Bruno threw the man down or he fell, but I must state that from the lane I sent him off, he went about it with more zeal.[5]

Routine patrols often turned up suspicious characters, as Thomas showed in a report written after he accompanied officers from the Besson police station in Port of Spain working in the hilly section "Behind the Bridge" from the Laventille Road extending to and including Oxford, Charlotte, and Observatory Streets.

Chapter 3. Along Came a Spider

March 23, 1955
    Whilst patrolling along the East Dry River, Port of Spain, I saw a man with a basket in hand trotting down the said street toward us from the opposite direction. He reached the corner of Lubin Lane which was between us and he hurriedly turned into the lane. From where we were the same corner was blind to us and so being suspicious of his demeanour we hurried to the corner. On reaching, I observed that the man was then running at top speed and was near to the other end of a fairly short lane.
    I sent the dog Bruno after him and started the chase followed by the other two constables. The dog caught up with the man as he was turning into another lane and when we did reach to that corner I was only able to catch a glimpse of the dog and man turning another corner. We continued but was only able to keep on the trail by hearing the mixed growling and barking of the dog. I saw neither the dog nor the man again until I got to Observatory Street when I saw both dog and man still running turn North into Charlotte Street.
    Constable Pierre went off at a terrific burst of speed and was gaining rapidly on the men and the dog when they turned East into Oxford Street. When I reached the corner I saw Constable Pierre assisted by two young men holding the man which Bruno stood by. I at once observed that the man hadn't the basket with him. I also noticed that the pants he had on had been torn in several places and they appeared to be freshly torn and so I concluded that the dog tore them in his attempt to stop him.
    The man denied having the basket that he ditched. After questioning he led police to a house where he pointed out some bleach and clothes on a line. The man was charged with larceny of clothing.
    It is my opinion, Sir, that in spite of the fact that Bruno failed to stop the man or prevent him from giving us such a long chase, Bruno's efforts must be considered as being useful because had it not been for his presence the man would have surely eluded us in the maze of short narrow lanes in the area.[6]

In red at the top of the page Thomas wrote: "Case made out and defendant convicted."

    A few months later, Bruno was on patrol duty in central Trinidad and working out of the Caroni Police Station.

October 5, 1955
    Whilst on patrol duty in that district with other policemen we saw and chased a jitney carrying stolen motor car parts and three men. The jitney eventually crashed on the Caroni bridge and the three men made good their escape, but with the aid of the dog in tow three men were arrested after fishing them out, one from the river and the other from a cane field

150 yards away. These men have since been convicted and sentenced to imprisonment.[7]

Note in red: "Case made and conviction obtained."

House break-ins were on the rise. Often homeowners had already chased intruders down the street before Bruno arrived on the scene. Liquor shops were popular targets and women were often victims of crime. Thieves grabbed women's handbags and jewelry as they walked home from work in the dim night light.[8]

In 1955, Bruno's notable cases included the arrest of a small-time gambler and the recovery of another stolen basket of laundry. The following year, Thomas filed more reports of armed robberies and fewer petty larceny cases. On October 17, 1956, Bruno found a suspect hiding in the bushes; fished a radio out of a river; and recovered stolen clothes on October 25, 1956.

Then came the case Thomas never imagined.[9]

On November 25, 1956, Thomas loaded revolver number 4 with six rounds of live ammunition, grabbed the station torchlight number 3, and led Bruno out of the St. Joseph police station at 10:52 p.m. Bruno and Thomas headed towards the railway line at the back of the police station, where they joined police looking for a "suspicious-looking man seen leaving the Eastern Main Road in the vicinity of St. Joseph Hospital where he walked along the railway line and disappeared into the bushes with a parcel."[10]

November 25, 1956
Knowing the area well, I at once thought that a man bent on evading the police will ... cut across the open Savannah shielded by the thick bushes at the side of the line from anyone on the line, get out on the Farm Road along which he can make his way unnoticed towards the Southern Main Road, Curepe.
In view of these deductions, about which I informed Const Arneaud, I told him to remain where he was and left with the dog walking along the Farm Road in a southerly direction in the same cautious manner and without using my torchlight.
On reaching a point about three hundred yards south of the railway crossing and on the same road, I observed the dog was acting strangely. He had become alert and excited about something ahead. Not wanting to flash my light too quickly, I moved in briskly, but silently as possible. Just then I heard a shuffling noise in the grass of the savannah on the Eastern

Chapter 3. Along Came a Spider

side of the said Farm Road. I quickly flashed my torchlight in the direction and saw a man running across the savannah. I quickly released the dog with the order "Get him boy" and that dog shot off after the man. I too joined in the chase.

The terrain was very soft—with concealed holes, mud and water holes which caused me to fall down on three occasions leaving my shoes along the way. Of whilst yet running, I heard the dog barking furiously ahead of me and knew he had cornered the man. I hastened on in that direction. There are tall bushes there and my view of the dog and man was obstructed. It was near to the railway line.

On reaching the bush, I forced my way through and had to jump a canal with water and more mud. As I did so, I saw by my torchlight that the man was lying on his back in the canal with water about five feet from me. The dog was practically standing on him. Just then I saw him raise his hand with a revolver holding and pointing toward me. The dog at once grabbed at the hand, and I heard a shot discharge. I then quickly took out my revolver and discharged a shot at his left side saying, "I have one too, you better keep yourself quiet." Then I saw his hand go limp and the revolver fell out of his hand into the water. His head, which was then raised, fell back into the water which covered his face.

Thinking him to have become unconscious, I quickly lifted him from the water and dragged him across the mud onto a bank and started shouting for the other policemen to come.

After about two to three minutes Cpl. Beckles and Const Arneaud followed by the civilians came. I quickly told them what happened. It was then I observed the man was bleeding on his left shoulder and appeared to be still unconscious. I went back in the water where the man was and searched with my hand until I found the revolver which I handed to Cpl. Beckles. It was a small black revolver and there was a shot protruding from the muzzle. I further retained a side of the man's crepe sole shoes from the mud. The distance covered during the chase was about 150–200 yards.

Cpl. Beckles, Const Arneaud, assisted by two civilians, lifted the man and took him away to the hospital leaving me in the area with the dog. I made a further check in the area but found nothing. Shortly after Cpl. Beckles and Const Arneaud returned with the police car and I went with them to the police station where on reaching, I learnt the man was suspected to be from his resemblance to Festus Lewis alias "Spider" the wanted murderer from Grenada.

At the time I saw the man bleeding on his left shoulder I thought that he was shot by his own revolver judging from the angle it was turned when the dog grabbed at his hand, but after further investigations coupled with the doctor's report, it was discovered that the wound was caused by the shot I discharged from my revolver .45.[11]

The next morning, Thomas and Bruno returned to the scene of the crime and found a khaki jacket, a matchbox, razor blades, and matches.

> The dog led us to these things and from the excited manner he exhibited I am strongly of the opinion that they fell from the man during the chase. I handed them over to Cpl. Beckles. I did not find the other side of my shoes. Further enquiries were made about the man by members of the Criminal Investigation Department, and it was established beyond doubt that the man is indeed Festus Lewis, alias "Spider" the wanted man from Grenada.[12]

This would be Bruno's most famous case, and it would make him a legend.

By the middle of 1958, Thomas and Bruno closed in on six full years of service together. They had tracked gamblers, thieves, and murderers. A small slip of paper in the middle of Bruno's file dated June 1958 shows that Bruno received his first official police commendation. It reads, "Police Dog Bruno is commended for the part he played in assisting in the recapture of an escaped prisoner." Bruno's second commendation reads: "Police Dog Bruno is commended for prompt action which led to the arrest and subsequent conviction of Clifford Lopez for robbery with violence." Bruno's third commendation said: "Police Dog Bruno is commended for good work done in the capturing of a wanted man [Festus Lewis]."[13]

Thomas penned lofty, long reports about Bruno's exploits. A note from police headquarters shows his superior's reaction to these reports: "I wonder if these long statements from dog handlers are necessary?" For the most part, Thomas ignored his superior's question, but occasionally he did file pithy reports when Bruno's tracking proved unsuccessful. Bruno couldn't solve a case on August 2, 1959, when someone ambushed and shot to death an East Indian man while he and his wife pushed a cart along Red Hill Road, D'Abadie, or when Bibaki, a shopkeeper in Curepe, faced thieves as he closed for the night on September 12, 1959. On September 24, 1959, Bruno couldn't find the man responsible for an attack on a couple in Lover's Lane at the old American base in Wallerfield. Someone shot the man to death, stabbed the woman, and left her for dead.[14]

Thomas wrote that "The day was a very hot one and the dog

experienced difficulty to keep his nose down when the heat from the ground was most terrible."[15]

For Thomas, Bruno's efforts counted as much as his successes. But on this day, something was clearly amiss. Thomas wrote, "Vet advises a warm enema, follow with one tablespoon liquid paraffin, followed by soft foods, no biscuits." On the following day, a long report from the Depot Kennels said, "I have to report for your information that at around 2:40 p.m. on Tuesday, July 26, 1960, Police dog Bruno died at his Kennel at the Mounted Branch. The Veterinary officer Dr. Khan had not long left. He had given him two injections and taken a sample of his blood for tests. The doctor was unable at the time of examination to diagnose his complaint."[16]

Thomas was by Bruno's side when he died. In Bruno's last report (featured in Appendix A) Thomas revealed some of the abuse Bruno met in his work and chronicles his desperate bid to diagnose Bruno's cause of suffering and save him. Bruno tried to work and please Thomas to the very end of his life. Thomas attended his dog's necropsy and took copious notes. Days later, he collected a note from the government veterinarian, A. Khan. Bruno's necropsy showed he died from severe gastritis and peritonitis.

News of Bruno's death appeared in the official police orders. In the end, Bruno's story consisted of three fat brown folders filled with reports in Thomas's meticulous handwriting. No other police dog's work would ever be recorded in such detail. Thomas would reminisce about Bruno for the rest of his life.

The ink on Bruno's files faded and the paper turned brittle and brown; the edges crumbled when touched. Bruno's and the other dogs' files remained in that unlocked filing cabinet in Caroni until a flood on October 22, 2018, destroyed the canine section's historical records.

Chapter 4

Shah: King of the Dogs

Bruno's bulging files suggest that he had emerged as the star of the original police dog pack of four, but Carlos, Shah, and Winston made their marks in the early days of the Dog Section as well. Thomas noted that Dog #2, Carlos, and his handler, Cpl. George Alexis, stationed at Cunupia police station, between Caroni and Chaguanas, performed the same duties as the other dogs and handlers, "mainly patrols and attending to calls for the dogs' specialized services, viz. tracking down wanted culprits, searching in bushes or cane fields for culprits in hiding or for hidden stolen property or weapons; escorting or guarding dangerous prisoners; accompanying investigators on the execution of search warrant."[1]

Carlos showed great promise. An entry in his file with no date said, "Following a report of housebreaking in St. Clair police dogs, Shah and Carlos tracked down a man to La Seiva about three miles away shortly after 12:30 p.m. yesterday. The dogs picked up the trail from a pair of shoes that were reported to have been left behind by the suspect."[2] But Carlos had little time to establish a career. He died of cancer and was "struck off the record" on April 24, 1954.[3] Alone now, with no dog partner, Alexis remained stationed at Cunupia Police Station in the Central Division until August 8, 1954.

Then there was Shah, who often appeared in an offhand note in Bruno's file. On a few occasions, Thomas wrote that Shah "showed promise." Dog #3 didn't get all the credit he deserved. Never prone to spinning elaborate stories about his dog, Sgt. Hamilton Bridgeman wrote concise reports about Shah's duties and exploits. Most interestingly, he gave Shah credit for arrests as one would give a police officer credit, noting in his dog's file: "Shah made the arrest."

Chapter 4. Shah: King of the Dogs

Shah, a black-and-grey Alsatian with a black-and-tan face, and sinewy black-and-grey legs, had grown from an eight-month-old gangly puppy with a champion grandfather to a 26½-inch intimidating police dog who loved to give chase.[4] "Shah was one of the biggest Alsatians I have ever seen," said retired canine officer Hector "Pee Wee" Lewis, who entered the Dog Section in the 1960s.[5]

Born on November 3, 1951, and enlisted in the Dog Section on September 25, 1952, when the four dogs arrived in Trinidad, Shah, a feisty, fearsome dog, covered every district in Trinidad and even worked in Tobago. He came to Trinidad with the Persian name for a king, undoubtedly earned from his commanding demeanor. When Bridgeman submitted stark reports on Shah's cases, Thomas, always realizing the importance of publicity, sometimes lent a helping hand by highlighting attention-grabbing details and sending action-packed reports to seniors—even if the case had not been made.

On one exercise in November 1954, Bridgeman and Shah were on mobile patrol along Old St. Joseph Road. Thomas saw the report and wrote a letter to his superintendent, "When they reached about 30 yards from the shop of Lee Wai Yin, three men were seen trying to break into the shop. On seeing the police car, the men ran, leaving the implements behind. Dog Shah gave chase and held one of the men. He was arrested and charged and the case was dismissed in the Port of Spain Court."[6] Why the magistrate dismissed the case when Shah reportedly caught the accused red-handed is not recorded.

Bridgeman and Shah carried on with their duties. Sometimes Shah seemed to be starring in an episode of Keystone Cops. Take the escapade on August 22, 1955, when Shah and Bridgeman patrolled the Southern Main Road, Caroni, and encountered police from the San Juan Station searching for three men who had escaped after a police chase. Bridgeman assisted in the search. Not seeing the men, he continued his patrol. Bridgeman wrote in Shah's file, "About two hours later, whilst proceeding along Warren Road, two men hailed the car [used by Bridgeman].[7] The driver stopped and it was observed that those were the wanted men. They ran. Dog Shah gave chase and held one of the men who gave his name as [X]. He was subsequently convicted and sentenced to two years hard labour in the PoS Assizes."[8]

As the anniversary of Carlos's death approached in September, Thomas and Bridgeman built their cases for a successful Dog Section. Little did they know that September 1955 would prove to be the worst month ever in the Dog Section's history. News reached the police that a minor, imprisoned in the Youth Training Centre (YTC) for killing his father, had escaped from Arouca. Cpl. Carlyle Piggott and his dog Winston rushed to Kelly Village, near the Piarco airport. Piggott and Winston were in hot pursuit of the teenager.

"Winston and Piggott spotted him near Seu Tong's shop opposite Hydraulic Road in Kelly Village, and the boy started to run," said retired canine officer Winston Matthews, who worked in the 1960s and had been recruited by Thomas. Piggott let go of Winston and the dog went for the teenager's gun. "While Winston ran, Piggott shot at the suspect and he fell to the ground. Piggott ran to the boy, and Winston ran away when he heard the gunshot. The teenager turned on the ground and shot Piggott dead with a sawed-off shotgun."[9]

This was the story passed down among police officers over the decades. Matthews and Cpls. Dyer, Lewis and Khan, all tell the same story about Piggott's murder, but no two stories match when it comes to what happened to Winston after Piggott died. "I understand the dog went out of his mind with grief when Piggott died, and they had to put him to sleep," said Lewis. Other stories said Winston was shot and killed on the spot because he went crazy when he realized Piggott was dead, or that he died of grief in the Caroni kennels, or he had to be euthanized in the kennels because he never recovered from the trauma of that day.[10] All of the speculations about Winston turned out to be untrue.

A note in one of Thomas's administrative files said that Thomas found a home for Winston with a Mr. Tench from Besson Street, Port of Spain, a place that canine officers knew well from their work apprehending gang members attached to steelbands. Winston lived out his days serving as a guard dog and pet. His career is confined to his lost file, which would have been pulled for the teenager's court

Chapter 4. Shah: King of the Dogs

case. Winston is mentioned only one other time in one of Thomas's official reports of the dogs' major successes.

The Dog Section regrouped. Bridgeman filled Shah's file with concise reports, all of which give Shah—not Bridgeman—credit for arrests. Thomas relayed these reports to their superiors. The police were discovering new and innovative ways to use the dogs. An entry in Shah's file on May 13, 1956, showed police laid a trap at Invaders Bay, Woodbrook. Bridgeman wrote, "About 10:20 p.m. four men fell into the trap. After being given a signal the men ran, Shah gave chase and arrested one [X] who was charged with assault with intent to rob. He was convicted and sentenced to four years hard labor at the Port of Spain Assizes." Suddenly, Shah's files became action-packed narratives.

> On Wednesday November 14, 1956, Cpl. Bridgeman with dog Shah rushed to Couva a distance of thirty-two miles in search of a man who snatched $200 and other documents from a woman. He (Shah) ran through a field of canes. The dog arrived on the scene two hours after the offense was committed and immediately went into action. After traveling some distance in the canes, he arrested the man who was charged with the offense. He was convicted and sentenced to four months HL [hard labour].[11]

Still going strong in the new year, Shah received a commendation on January 14, 1957, for his work in apprehending a thief, who was later convicted. By all appearances, Shah enjoyed chasing culprits. Newspaper stories showcased the dramatic descriptions of the dogs' escapades.

Police Dogs Track Down Suspect
SHAH GETS HIS MAN

Trinidad Chronicle, November 16, 1956, by *Chronicle* reporter.

Police Dog Shah made a thirty-two-mile dash and cornered a snatch-and-grab thief in a Chaguanas canefield on Wednesday night. The man, police said, had grabbed a wallet with $200 and some documents from Rampersad Maraj, a taxi-driver of Espinet Street, Laventille.

Shortly after the report was made, Shah and his trainer Bridgeman were called from the St. James Barracks. They rushed to the scene in a police vehicle and a couple of hours later the man they searched for was found crouching in the cane. Everything in the wallet was intact. Maraj said he had picked up the man at Marabella. His taxi stalled at Chaguanas and the man helped him to push the vehicle off the road, then snatched the wallet.[12]

The depot superintendent expressed his pleasure with the newspaper story. "Good work. File this [story] in [Shah's] file," he wrote. Shah was a testy dog, too, as a report shows:

> October 14, 1957
> At around 7:55 p.m. on Monday whilst on my way to Besson Street with Shah, the vehicle stopped at the traffic lights at the corner of Charlotte Street and Marine Square. A woman who gave her name as Edith De Four passed very close to the vehicle. The dog made a snatch at her and caught her on the right shoulder giving her a small bite. I got out of the vehicle and invited her to the Port of Spain General Hospital for attendance, but she refused saying she will go by herself. I encouraged her to go to the Besson Street Police station where I will put the dog down and send her to the hospital.[13]

Shah continuously lived up to his name. Brave and tenacious, he never cared if the enemy outnumbered him. On November 12, 1957, Bridgeman and Shaw ambushed 14 gamblers in possession of whe whe marks [an illegal numbers game] in San Juan. Shah caught one of the gamblers trying to escape.[14]

By the end of the following year, a new crime began to appear in the dogs' records: stealing copper wiring. It would keep police dogs busy and provide Thomas with another challenge: training dogs outside the police force. The first report of such a crime came from Bridgeman, who wrote in Shah's file that on July 15, 1958:

> Shah and I saw a suspicious-looking man walking along the southern pavement with a bag on his head which appeared to be heavy laden.
> We followed the man with the police vehicle, and when the man ran, Shah chased him into a clump of bushes and apprehended him. He was taken to the bag and an examination of a quantity of pipe fittings and copper wire was found within.
> He made no reply when questioned about the same. He was arrested and taken to the Besson Police Street Police station where a charge of unlawful possession was referred against him. He was eventually convicted and sentenced to six months hard labour.[15]

Shah continued to improve his tracking skills, impressing both Bridgeman and Thomas. It seemed no one could intimidate Shah,

Chapter 4. Shah: King of the Dogs

and it would take more than a common criminal to get the better of him.

On August 16, 1958, Bridgeman wrote to the Depot Commandant that Shah had been given a shirt to sniff in the hopes of recovering $8,000 hidden by a thief somewhere in the bush. Shah led the police to a mangrove tree and freshly pulled weeds thrown on the ground. After digging down about one foot, the police found an enamel pot containing a number of paper notes, copper, and silver coins.[16]

The Dog Section expanded modestly. In that first decade, there had been only 12 dogs. The First Nominal Roll of Police Service Dogs (by enlistment numbers) appears in Thomas's administrative files.

1. Bruno died on July 26, 1960
2. Carlos died on April 24, 1954
3. Shah struck off (the service record) on September 1, 1962
4. Winston struck off (the service record) on September 28, 1955
5. Ralph
6. Minnie
7. Bruce
8. Rex
9. Satan
10. Flash was destroyed on February 2, 1960
11. Prince
12. Butch

With its usual financial constraints, the Dog Section crept forward.

Chapter 5

Ralph and Rex

THE UNTIMELY DEATH OF CARLOS meant Handler No. 4034, Cpl. George Alexis, could not make a defining mark in the initial stages of the Dog Section, but he would eventually push forward with Police Service Dog #5 Ralph.

On November 26, 1955, Ralph and Minnie arrived from the UK through the Commissioner of Police, Colonel Eric Hammet Fairfax Beadon. Superintendent Frisby presented Dog #7, Bruce, a donated dog, to the police force on October 12, 1956. The police commissioner bought Dog #8, Rex, from the St. Vincent police on April 30, 1957.[1] Rex's chicken-chasing shenanigans in St. Vincent were so notorious it seems the police wanted to expel him from the country. Rex terrorized chickens in Trinidad as well.[2]

Ralph and Rex would become the Bruno/Shah combination of the second stage of the Trinidad and Tobago Dog Section. They proved a comical pair, often frustrating the canine police with their embarrassing antics. A letter from the assistant superintendent of the Southern Division noted the presence of Ralph and Rex assigned to South Trinidad on June 17, 1957.

By August 23, the two dogs were in trouble. Assistant Superintendent of Police (ASP) Duke from the Southern Division wrote:

The dogs and handlers have been detailed daily for duty and have been working good, except for the incident which I mention below:

(1) At 10 am on 19.6.57 whilst Const Alexis and Figaro were on a tracking exercise at Marabella with dogs Ralph and Rex, Rex suddenly came upon a ewe goat which was tied and grazing nearby and bit the goat. The owner Lal Seelachan was not pleased about this, and he complained to the Supt of the Division who paid him a bag of feed for compensation.

(2) On 26 June, 1957 Detective Const No 3364 Brooks spotted a noted

Chapter 5. Ralph and Rex

fowl thief, selling dead fowls to a restaurant owner. Brooks went up to him, and the thief ran, leaving his hat. The hat was taken and brought to the station, and Const Alexis with dog Ralph went with Const Brooks on enquiries. The hat was given to Ralph to smell and some time later the same day whilst Ralph was with the police in the car on Mucurapo St. the policemen saw the foul thief walking towards them. They went out and held him but the dog never moved or acted in any manner which indicated he recognised the smell of the thief whose hat was still in the car.

(3) On 25.7.57 Detective Sgt John and Const Alexis with dog Ralph were on patrol along San Fernando Bye Pass in a car in the vicinity of Trinidad Major Market when they saw four young men with their bosoms very bulky. They stopped the car and got out, but the men ran into the bushes. Const Alexis told the dog to get them, but the dog ran back in the car and remained there unnoticed by Alexis who began to run after the men. He soon fell, and on getting up, looked for the dog and saw him in the car alone, though all the other occupants were engaged in running after the men, who eventually escaped. It is believed that those men had "fished" groceries out through the expanding door of the Major Market.

The handlers have been and are still working well and are also co-operative.

Nothing outstanding was done by the dogs since their arrival here, but I believe their presence serves as a preventative measure.[3]

The depot commandant wrote back with great concern.

August 26, 1957

Many thanks for the report submitted on dogs Rex and Ralph. As dog Shah, handled by Sgt Bridgeman, is the only trained dog left in Port of Spain, it will not be possible for me to make a change as far as Rex is concerned immediately. I will, however, bear your report in mind and as soon as one of the younger dogs is fit for outside work I will effect a change over.

I was extremely disappointed to hear of the behaviour of Ralph in Para. 3. I have personally always harboured the opinion that Const Alexis is inclined to be too rough with his dog, Ralph at one time was very bold in his outlook and attitude and I noticed particularly that some time later he had become a little cowed. I think it would be wise at this stage to point out to Const Alexis that the reactions of this dog are due entirely to the method of its training, and that I was not at all pleased to hear of Ralph's reaction in the face of practically no opposition.[4]

Depot Commandant

Desperate for dogs, police officers pondered the best way to use Rex. In September 1957, Alexis informed the depot commandant that "the

Police Dogs of Trinidad and Tobago

dogs have done nothing spectacular" and suggested transferring Rex to town because of his chicken-and-goat-chasing problem. Two years later, on October 19, 1959, Rex finally utilized his chicken-chasing skills in the call of duty.

> Some time between 1 p.m. and 5 p.m. Cpl. Ashby and Const Edwards were on mobile patrol in the district when they saw a man carrying two fowls. They drove up to him and after he discovered it was a police car he dropped the fowl and ran away. In his haste, he dropped his cap but did not turn back.
> On arrival on the scene, Rex was given a sniff from the cap and immediately followed a trail where we discovered a box containing a quantity of fowls thirty yards away with their legs tied. We collected the fowls and followed the trail for about 250 yards where the trail ended at a river's edge.
> This was a very good track because the dog followed the track all the way with its nose on the ground and the quantity of stray dogs passed on the trail did not hamper the situation.
> Case determined. The accused was sentenced to four months hard labour for unlawful possession on 21/10/59.[5]

Given Rex's obsession with chickens, it is puzzling that Alexis even considered his dog would be distracted by other dogs.

Meanwhile, the Dog Section hoped that police dog recruits would come from Minnie's pups. On April 15, 1957, Minnie had a litter of seven puppies, but Thomas wrote in his administrative file that "fate struck another blow as Minnie died after her first litter."[6] He wrote that Superintendent Frisby's wife, Mrs. A Frisby, cared for the orphaned puppies and fed them powdered milk, oatmeal, and glucose syrup. Only two puppies, Flash and Satan, made it as police dogs.[7]

A puppy named Prince came to the unit in exchange for a pup from Shah, who had better luck after his first disastrous encounter with an aggressive bitch. Mr. Benson of the Agricultural Department presented Prince to the police, while Butch entered the force on October 8, 1957, and died two years later, on July 4, 1959. The police acquired a black Alsatian, Jett, bought from Mr. S. Hamid of Valsayn Park, a posh suburb of Port of Spain, on September 21, 1959.[8]

The Dog Section began experimenting with Doberman Pinschers, a personal favorite of Thomas, "who often went to the market

Chapter 5. Ralph and Rex

with his Dobermans," said retired canine officer Cpl. Dunstan Harry.[9] Thomas wrote that:

> it is interesting to note that over the years, the only other breed of dogs used by the Trinidad and Tobago Police Force were two Doberman Pinschers, two Labradors, one yellow and the other black, and one half-breed Collie Alsatian. They have in fact contributed largely to the creditable record attained, but the Alsatians have proven themselves to be the more dependable, controllable and versatile workers. This observation by no means discredits the Doberman as a good police dog. He is in fact very good, but his duties cannot be generalised as that of an Alsatian. It is hoped to acquire at least two of them for service in the Force.[10]

Four dogs worked out of the Depot Kennels, which still serves as the headquarters of the Mounted and Canine Branch of the Police Service, on Long Circular Road, St. James, and four dogs worked out of Northern Division police stations. Thomas noted concerns in his administrative files as well. One note said, "Although all the dogs had been trained in all aspects of police work, it was necessary to continue further training with a view of having them acclimatized and familiar with local conditions."

The Dog Section operated in a shifting political landscape. The West Indies Federation proposed under the British in January of 1958 to unite the Caribbean politically and economically, collapsed on May 31, 1962, and on August 31, Trinidad and Tobago became an independent nation. Thomas took stock of the Dog Section. He created a list for his administrative file of some of the most outstanding cases and noted the dogs that broke with the traditional police dogs of choice, German Shepherds, most often called Alsatians. It is the only place where Winston's work is officially documented.

1. Arrest of the Grenadian murderer Festus Lewis alias Spider—Bruno
2. Recovery of $8,000 in cash snatched from a bank employee—Shah
3. Arrest of a man for grocery-breaking and larceny—Winston
4. Led to the recovery of stolen property—store-breaking and larceny—Carlo

5. Arrest of a dangerous gun-man—Bruno, Jett
6. Arrest of a motorcar thief—Prince (Doberman Pinscher)
7. Arrest of a man on attempted murder charge—Ralph
8. Arrest of a man for larceny from Pick-n-Pay grocery—Bobby
9. Arrest for shooting with intent—Caesar
10. Arrest of two men for armed robbery—Chag
11. Arrest of a man for factory breaking and larceny—Panther (black Labrador)
12. Led search party and found man lost in the forest—Carlo
13. Recovered stolen property—a purse with valuable documents—Ben (yellow Labrador)

Thomas reported that "court convictions were secured in the cases concerned with each of the incidents mentioned in the over-leaf and the sentences varied from six months to seven years of hard labour." Dogs that did not make the grade as police dogs were sold. A bull fetched $45 and a bitch fetched $35.

AP Christie, the Assistant Estate Superintendent of police, wrote to Major GTW Carr, Acting Commissioner of Police, on November 27, 1958, asking for two dogs. The Shell Oil company wanted to buy Bruce and Flash for two estate policemen, Cpl. A Moore and PC L Paul, selected to be trained by Thomas as handlers. Estate police expressed interest in dogs to serve as a deterrent for thieves who had identified a gold mine in stealing copper wiring.

Internal problems plagued the police as the battle between the station police and the Dog Section heated up. Dog handlers complained about the treatment of the dogs at police stations. Bitterness seethed particularly at the St. Joseph police station. Police there resented the dogs' presence and made no bones about their feelings—even when the dogs solved cases.

On July 10, 1960, Dog #13, Jett, accompanied a search party into the forest as they tracked a man wanted for several shooting incidents and shooting a policeman on July 8, 1960. Jett spotted the suspect hiding in the bushes before the police did.[11] This find failed to

Chapter 5. Ralph and Rex

mitigate the St. Joseph police officers' resentment. Canine officer PC Hicks finally had enough and wrote to Thomas.

11 July, 1960
    Sir, I have to report for your information, working conditions under which the police handlers and their dogs are subjected to at St. Joseph Police Station. The SPO, Sgt Gill, who from all appearances seems not in favour of the dogs and handlers, has gone so far as to say that they are a waste of taxpayers' money and that he thinks that they should be kept at Port of Spain [and] is exercising no discretion in his method of fixing duties for the dogs and handlers.
    The whole trouble is sir, because of the unreasonable manner in which the dogs are worked and in spite of repeated suggestions made by me he insists that the dogs must be worked as he directs as long as they are at his station.
    I suggested to him that the dog patrols should be done early on mornings or late in evenings, making allowances for proper cleaning of the kennels, grooming and exercising of the dogs but he arranges his duties such as 9 a.m., 11 a.m ... and 2 p.m. and 4 p.m. when the sun is the hottest and which is difficulty and punishment to the dogs, the paved roads at such times are terribly hot and the dogs actually do a hopscotch whilst walking along. After a short period, the dogs are very much spent from the terrible heat of which dog Jett suffers particularly due to his colour.
    It has also happened quite frequently the dogs after working the evening patrols as stated are called upon to do four hours again from 7 p.m. [...].
    I have also asked the SPO that we should be exempted at least one day each week from the daytime patrol to enable some general practices which are necessary to keep the dogs in proper working conditions. This he refuses to do and states that the dog handlers do not want to do any work.
    Some time about a week ago during the interview with the Supt of Northern Division, I mentioned to him about the duties as mentioned above, he said that he would not interfere with the manner in which the sergeant runs his station.
    In view of these facts, sir and because No. 5007 Charles and I, the handlers are in fear that it will be finally believed that we do not want to work as Sgt Gill states, which is very untrue, also with a view of having the dogs at St. Joseph station kept in a fit state of health and proper working form to be a credit to the section and the police force I respectfully ask sir, that enquiries be made to verify this my report of conditions as they are present. Constable Hicks[12]

Thomas would not tolerate such disrespect for his officers and their dogs. He wrote a long letter to the superintendent of the Mounted Branch and Dog Section on September 30, 1960, and attached Hicks' report about the St. Joseph police treatment of Satan and Jett. Thomas wrote that he had experienced the same conditions while working there.

> Working the dogs during the time of day when the sun is hot does more injury to them than help for the purpose such patrols are intended. [...] It is noticeable that Alsatians are easily overcome by the tropical heat, and they should be spared at such times whenever possible....
>
> It has been very noticeable sir, that in recent times the dogs at St. Joseph fail to retain good health in spite of the fact that their food and treatment are the same as those at the main kennels. It is my opinion, sir, that the hot sun patrols are partly responsible for this. In the interest of the dog section sir, I respectfully ask that the attached report be considered for further enquiries into the matter.[13]
>
> Submitted please.
> Corporal Thomas

Chag, Dog # 23, a mixed-breed that Khairool Khan said "looked like a wolf," didn't help matters when he escaped from his kennel and held St. Joseph Police Station officers hostage for a day. Only his handler, Horace Hicks, could control Chag, and Hicks hadn't returned from court. An angry report filed by the station's sergeant said that no one could enter or leave the police station in the meantime. Police climbed onto the counter or hid in other rooms while the dog roamed the station, keeping everyone at bay.[14]

Meanwhile, in South Trinidad, where the dogs were always well appreciated, a senior officer begged for police dogs. On March 10, 1961, the senior superintendent of the Southern Division wrote to the assistant commissioner of the Police Mobile Unit.

> I have to report that within recent times there had been incidents of shooting and other crimes which necessitated the use of a police dog. As a result messages had to be sent to Port of Spain to get a dog by which time we were unable to conduct our enquiries efficiently. I may mention two incidents of note, one at Texaco, Pointe-a-Pierre, where an Estate Constable was shot at around 11:40 p.m. on 6/3/61 and the other where a police patrol stopped a man at about 4:10 p.m. on 10/3/61 carrying a bag of split peas. The man threw the split peas on the police, whipped out a cutlass

Chapter 5. Ralph and Rex

and made good his escape. The police fired a round from a revolver but it did not succeed in stopping the thief.

It is apparent from the facts mentioned that had there been a dog in the division, it would have been easily collected and within seconds it would have been on the scene with the hope of catching the thief.

In the circumstances I recommend that immediate action be taken in having a dog posted to the division. In addition it will well serve the south-western division.[15]

Cromwell St. Louis
Senior Superintendent
Southern Division

On March 15, 1961, the superintendent of the Mounted Branch sent his regrets that the request could not be accommodated.

> At present we have four dogs only which can be considered as trained. They are Jett, who is posted to the Northern Division at St. Joseph, Ralph, who is in the Central Division, Shah who is handled by Sgt Bridgeman, the Snr. dog handler who I need at my headquarters and I am afraid that Shah has long passed his best, and it would serve no useful purpose to send him down to Southern Division. The remaining dog, Satan which was posted to Southern Division was withdrawn by me and brought to the Depot. He has been on the sick list for quite a while. He is slowly getting better, but I personally feel that he will be no longer any use as a police dog, and I am seriously thinking of putting forward a recommendation that he be put down.
>
> There is little likelihood of us having a dog suitable for posting to Southern Division in under six months. I am sure you are well aware of the position, and I see no need to elaborate further.[16]

A dearth of working dogs would always plague the Dog Section. Thomas had his hands full.

Chapter 6

Dreams, Nightmares and Other Business

Theophilus Thomas often sat at a desk handling business. He had his dreams, which included writing a book. In the first typed chapter, he presented the history of the Dog Section from the time he, Bridgeman, Alexis, and Piggott arrived in Trinidad and posed on the ship's deck with their dogs, and wrote about the experiences of working alongside dogs as they tracked criminals. But Thomas failed to capture that excitement in the natural way it appeared in the official files. Ironically, the dogs' files had the suspense and energy of an action novel, and the book he struggled to write read like dull official files.

Thomas abandoned the idea of writing a book. The first chapter remained in Bruno's file. In between dog reports, Thomas wrote his thoughts about the future of the Dog Section and highlighted his abandoned dreams and his struggles, which often seemed insurmountable.

Puppies from Princess, one of his beloved Dobermans, proved to be bittersweet. "Trained in obedience and kept for breeding purposes, Princess, a Doberman Pinscher, four years one month and four days, black with tan markings on the face, chest, and legs, gave birth to three litters of pups. She is a very good mother and is in perfect condition. Their breed, however, will no longer be used in our Police Force."[1]

The decision could have resulted from observation and some of the latest information available internationally, which showed Doberman Pinschers had "good tracking tendencies … but an unpredictable temper … hard to control when aggravated, and could not be

Chapter 6. Dreams, Nightmares and Other Business

taught to grab specifically a man's arm instead of just any part of his body...."[2]

Writing off Dobermans as police dogs must have been a difficult decision for Thomas, who was described by Khairool Khan and Hector "Pee Wee" Lewis as generally "stubborn and implacable."[3] Thomas was not liked by everyone, but Michael Roban, the section's future inspector, said Thomas stood up for him when Roban was accused of insubordination early in his career for calling a senior officer, Sgt. Macmillan, by his nickname, Mac. Thomas refused to transfer Roban, which was the easiest and most common way of sweeping problems under the rug in the police force. Roban said, "When officers asked for my transfer, Thomas yelled, 'No! He is a good worker. He will have to conform.'"[4]

The decision to keep Roban would affect the canine section four decades down the road in an unexpected way. Thomas was a tough taskmaster who demanded much from his dogs and officers. He was a private person; officers who worked with him had little information to offer about him. "Thomas was a robust-looking fellow with a heavy voice," said former dog handler Clayton Chandler. "I was twenty-four when I came for an interview to become a canine officer. I saw the horses and fell in love with them. When I told Thomas, he said, 'Do you want to be a canine officer or a mounted officer? I'll give you a few minutes to go outside and think about that.'"[5]

Chandler chose the Dog Section and became a canine officer on July 17, 1982. He remembers Thomas talking to canine officers about the importance of family, and the piece of advice he gave all canine officers. "Thomas always said, 'Make your bed before you leave home in the morning. It gives you discipline.'" Even Thomas's simplest advice served as a reminder of his prescience. Decades later, in 2012, Charles Duhigg's book *The Power of Habit* would point out studies that show that "making your bed every morning is correlated with better productivity and a greater sense of well-being."[6]

At home, Thomas was called "Tom." His niece, Debbie Thomas, said he instilled a love for dogs—especially Dobermans—in his family.[7] At work, no one in the canine section could recall when he retired from the police force, or that Thomas, born on September

22, 1923, had died on December 19, 1998. None of the officers interviewed attended his funeral. Back in the late 50s, Thomas sat at his desk and penned a report on Jett, the only locally procured dog who came close to his required standard for a police dog. "It is not my intention sir, to condemn our local dogs. I know that there are some good dogs here, but their owners rightly demand good prices for them and are very careful about prospective buyers," Thomas wrote to his superiors.

There's always a dog that surprises everyone, and for a time, Jett, the black Alsatian born on March 19, 1956, headed the list. He showed promise from his first case, the Jestine West murder. Jett's initial success must have been bittersweet for Thomas, because it marked a period that defined Bruno's decline. Loyal to Bruno to the end, Thomas defended Bruno's failure in the same case while he acknowledged Jett's success in one of Bruno's reports.

Thomas wrote in Bruno's file on November 7, 1959, that he and Bruno had arrived on the scene to catch the murderer of Jestina West.

> Owing to the lapse of time, rain in the district after the crime was committed and before our arrival, and the area gone over thoroughly by residents. it was impossible to start the dog on a trail, however, he was used to assist a search party with no results. This accused was captured at Blanchisseuse by a police party with the assistance of dog Jett, and a handler who relieved dog Bruno and myself on 9 November, 1959.[8]

The previous day, November 8, 1959, Handler 5007, PC Charles, filed a report on Jett's success in that case.

> At 10:30 p.m. on Saturday 7 Nov 1959 one Jestina West was shot to death at her home at Blanchisseuse by one [X] who afterwards took refuge in the forest armed with a shotgun and three cartridges. Jett assisted in an extensive search in the forest and eventually carried us on a recent trail of the accused and followed the trail. A shot was heard ahead of us. We hastened on to find that the accused was intercepted by another party searching an area ahead of us. The dog was definitely on the correct trail. This was the dog's first case and I find that he worked extensively well all considered because he had but very little from which to work. However during the search when he came up on a recent trail he showed signs of great confidence and determination.[9]

Jett's file is sketchy, but his major cases are recorded in short reports.

Chapter 6. Dreams, Nightmares and Other Business

15, February, 1963

[X] of McClean Street, Curepe committed two offences on 15th February 1962, malicious damages to six drinking glasses and was in possession of a weapon. Warrants were obtained for his arrest. Whilst on patrol the wanted man was seen and held by Cpl. Chandler but he pulled away and ran. The dog (Jett) was immediately released. He gained ground on the fleet-footed prisoner and arrested him about 125 yards away around a corner.

The chase was one of the best the dog ever made. Had it not been for him, the prisoner would have surely escaped.[10]

The ever-inquisitive Thomas copied information about working dogs from newspaper articles and often submitted them to his superiors. The articles pop up in Bruno's dog files or administrative files like parenthetical thoughts.

T Thomas Sgt 4138
SPO Dog Section
Dogs as Policemen

Macy's department store began to use dogs for after-hour police work in 1952. Before that, store detectives had caught as many as nine prowlers in one month—and they had no way of knowing how many burglars hid overnight in the store, scooped up merchandise and escaped by mingling with legitimate shoppers the next morning.

Even armed people will surrender to a dog.[11]

Thomas envisioned a day when police dogs would travel by helicopter to work in remote areas of the country. He would have been fascinated to learn of future dog cognition studies done in universities. Even in his day, Thomas knew police dogs possessed an extraordinary sense of smell. One can only imagine how he would have reacted to Alexandra Horowitz's study, which showed that "explosives-detection dogs smell as little as a picogram—a trillionth of a gram—of TNT or other explosives." Putting that in perspective, Horowitz would write in *Being a Dog* "that if a human walked in a kitchen and smelled one cinnamon roll, the dog entering the kitchen would smell the equivalent of one trillion cinnamon rolls."[12]

There was so much to learn about working dogs' sense of smell, and much of it would come decades into the future.

In December 1963, Thomas filed administrative reports that said the Dog Section had performed 680 night patrols, 88 day patrols, and 59 calls to assist in serious crimes. Fourteen actual arrests were made after "heated chases" by dogs. The annual cost of upkeeping the Dog Section totaled $3,000 for all eight dogs.

> Difficulties are being experienced to acquire suitable dogs locally. Because of this, promising young dogs are taken on probation for one month when, if they fail to display the required qualities, they are rejected. A recruited dog must be between the ages of six to fifteen months to be eligible for training.
>
> Handlers are recruited from regular members of our Force and must have at least two years' service, must be a lover of animals, of good character, physically fit, show interest in his work generally and display unlimited patience. Both dog and handler are trained for at least six months before being considered fully trained, dependable workers to be posted to Divisions.
>
> The division requires at least 16 dogs and handlers to deal with the increase of crimes and hooliganism in the territory.
>
> There is an immediate need for a suitable well laid out training centre. This includes a kennel block to accommodate at least eight dogs, with kitchen, store room and office, an adjoining field for obedience training, suitably fenced and in a nonresidential area and close to areas (that) provide facilities for tracking and searching and training. There will also be the need for construction of a dormitory to accommodate at least eight handlers.
>
> Three dogs arrived from England on Sunday the 8th November 1964 by boat for the police Dog Section. Alsatians, two males, one female, arrived in good condition except for Queenie Dog # 30, born in April, 1964 who had an itch and was being treated.[13]

Thomas documented information about the dogs taken on six-week trial periods at a price of $125.

Amidst all his duties came one of Thomas's biggest nightmares. The bad news about a canine officer Thomas had been particularly close to could not have been unexpected. Though this canine officer had started off with glowing reviews from Thomas—especially since his dog seemed to be particularly challenging—Thomas soon received reports of the officer's dog biting pedestrians. This officer had always demonstrated good control of his dog, but suddenly he seemed to show no remorse or embarrassment over his dog's aggressive actions in public. Other canine officers on duty with the recalcitrant officer wrote reports suggesting that he encouraged his dog to be overly aggressive to harmless civilians.

Chapter 6. Dreams, Nightmares and Other Business

Initially, Thomas appeared to ignore the complaints. An occasional stern reprimand is recorded, but nothing to indicate alarm bells. But eventually, the canine officer became the cause of the Dog Section's first scandal, and Thomas wrote the dreaded letter to his superiors. "[X] arrested on [November 18, 1964] on a criminal charge involving dishonesty and was interdicted from Duty on 19-11-64. In view of the length of time which may elapse before the determination of the case and coupled with the fact that he will be considered unsuitable as a Dog Handler thereafter, I recommend an officer from Western Division be transferred for training as a Dog Handler as of 7-12-64." Thomas never mentioned the officer again.

On November 22, 1963, the day Lee Harvey Oswald assassinated U.S. President John F. Kennedy, Thomas fretted over the dogs' food:

Carcasses of animals that have been obtained for the feeding of police dogs are stored at the Electric Ice Company at a charge of 1¾ cents per pound per month. This is the cheapest rate available. The average expenditure involved in storage at this price is approximately $8 per month while the average weight of meat kept in storage at any one time is approximately 450 pounds. I am recommending that consideration be given to the storing of this meat in the refrigerated chamber of the police canteen at headquarters. In this way a saving in annual expenditure to the amount of $100 is likely to be achieved. Cod liver oil cost to maintain a police dog will be about 80 cents a day.[14]

Letters spanning 1965 and 1966 reveal Thomas's concern for Jett, who had done an admirable job as a police canine and won a place in Thomas's heart. On April 19, 1965, Thomas wrote to Assistant Police Commissioner Claud Anthony May, who would serve as police commissioner for one year in 1973.

Jett, nine years old is becoming lame in his left leg, after a long history of lameness in the hind legs from chronic arthritis of the hip joints. Because of his advancing age, [it is] recommended that he be humanely destroyed.

Jett will be ten on 29-3-66 and was enlisted to our strength when he was purchased fully trained for $120 on 29-9-59. His service in the police force has been a creditable one. I recommend he be stricken from the record because of his slowness of movement and his show of fatigue after a short period of exercise or patrol. I had him examined by the Government officer Dr. De Gannes on the 5-1-66.

Jett was trained by me and lived with a family and me before he became a police dog. I respectfully apply that when he is struck off from our strength he be given to me or to Mr. Hamid so he will spend the rest of his days comfortably. I will do my best to make him comfortable. Jett lived with me at my house from the age of eight months when he was given to me by Mr. Sonny Hamid of Valsayn. I trained him and won several prizes with him at dog shows before he became a police dog. Both my family and Mr. Hamid's will be happy to have him return to us.[15]

Jett remained in his police kennel for over 15 months. A letter dated July 22, 1966, from the Ministry of Home Affairs granted Thomas's wish with one line: "I recommend that sympathetic consideration be given to Sgt. Thomas's application." On July 29, 1966, the canine police delivered Jett to Thomas. The dog settled into his happy ending.

Chapter 7

Sheba and Sheba

It was easy to become lost in the dogs' files. Each police dog had its distinct personality and unexpected escapades, and yet their stories fit together like a jigsaw puzzle presenting a picture of how crime evolved in Trinidad and Tobago. Often, I thought about the missing files. Was it possible to have a reasonably complete picture of the dogs' history with pieces of the puzzle missing? How would the story be different if a particular dog's files had never been found?

Two police dogs sharing the name of Sheba settled the conundrum for me: some pieces of the puzzle will end up missing; some will reveal unexpected connections. You can only work with what you have.

Born on December 6, 1962, and originally named Esta, the first Sheba had been renamed when she entered the Police Service. Dog #27, a black-and-tan Alsatian with tan legs, had been bought from the Caribbean Kennel Club. Her kennel card also shows that her father had been Jett; her mother, Debra; and her lineage could be traced to Germany.[1]

By all accounts, Sheba had a hard life. Her file shows she had been mated with the Texaco oil company's police dog Jasper on November 7, 1964, and had nine pups—six of which were male. The following year, on June 6, 1965, she mated with police dog Howard, and subsequently with Sterling and Benno. On July 8, 1965, Thomas wrote that five of Sheba's six male pups (one died) were fully grown and capable of undergoing training from July 9, 1965, when they would be six months old.[2]

The pups, Dog #32, Bruno II; Dog #33, Remo; Dog #34, Count; Dog #35, Danko; and Dog #35, Darak, had scanty files.

Police Dogs of Trinidad and Tobago

In between having puppies, Sheba worked. On January 6, 1968, she tracked a man who had broken into a house in St. Augustine and chased the culprit as he tried to escape on a bicycle. When he dropped the bicycle, Sheba cornered the man, who was sentenced for unlawful possession of a bicycle.[3] She received a commendation in her file for good work.

At 2 p.m. on Monday, December 23, 1968, she left the St. Joseph police station with PC Narace to investigate the larceny of fowls valued at $50, taken from Winston Chang in Arima.

> The dog took up a scent at the scene of the crime and tracked for about 350 yards to the home of one of the culprits where a bag that held the fowls was found. Sheba discovered the bag full of feathers and then stumbled on some men assembling to gamble. Too frightened to run, they remained in place and were arrested. The dog tracked exceedingly well although it was disturbed when two men were arrested for gambling.[4]

Just four days later, at 7:20 a.m., she traveled to Curepe to find a man who had threatened to hang himself after wounding his wife in a quarrel. In her file, Sheba's handler wrote, "On my arrival I saw the accused standing in the road and reacting in a delirious manner. I came out of the vehicle with the dog, held him and handed him over to investigators."[5] The man was charged with wounding with intent and attempted suicide.

Sheba's biggest case turned out to be a whopping find. On March 11, 1969, at 5:30 p.m. Sheba and her handler, PC Narace, went on patrol along the St. Joseph railway line. They both noticed a suspicious man holding two bags. When the man ran, Narace let Sheba loose and she cornered him fifty yards away.

> His bags contained a quantity of radios, jewellery, watches, alcoholic drinks, gents' and ladies' clothing, sweaters, shop goods, soaps and pots. Some items, (including a stove) were hidden in a nearby carriage. [X], who had eight reports [charges] of housebreaking and larceny, was apprehended.
> Were it not for the keenness of observation of the handler and the dog's alertness, these offenses would not be detected as the culprit never left traces when he broke into houses.[6]

The Tunapuna Magistrates' Court sentenced X to two years of hard labor on March 18, 1969.

Chapter 7. Sheba and Sheba

In seven years and six months, Sheba, trained by Thomas, had served under three handlers: Thomas; PC Narace, who retired on December 4, 1969; and PC Blake, who transferred from the Dog Section in February 1970 after prolonged sick leave. On June 8, 1970, Thomas wrote to his senior officers:

> Sheba, now seven years and six months old, is unsuitable for police duties. She had developed stiffness in her hindquarters and became too slow to work effectively. Sheba had given birth to four good litters of pups, from which the Dog Section was provided with the majority of its now actively working police dogs. Her deteriorating physical condition has also deemed her useless as a brood bitch. Sheba is the type of dog, if treated kindly, will adjust satisfactorily in a home as a good companion, guard and watch dog. I therefore respectfully suggest that she be struck off the strength of the Dog Section and be sold at public auction, please.[7]

A handwritten note in Sheba's file from Thomas said, "Sheba was auctioned off by Mr. Marquez at 2:10 p.m. on September 1, 1970. Mr. Leon Gregoire of Eastern Enterprises at 67 Eastern Main Road, Laventille purchased her for $100."

It seems Sheba's final work would be that of a guard dog. Always a meticulous record-keeper, Thomas wrote to the superintendent, "I will like to have, please Sir, [Sheba's] file returned to me for filing at the kennels." His request assured Sheba's place in canine history. And so ended Sheba's service to the police. She provided puppies to keep the struggling Dog Section running; apprehended chicken thieves, gamblers, and an angry man who injured his wife and attempted suicide. No one could have expected more from a dog who worked until she could barely walk.

In the early 70s, the Canine Section had another Sheba, purchased by Matthews when he traveled to England to participate in a training course. This Sheba first appears in two letters Matthews wrote to Thomas, which would confirm Thomas's suspicions about foreign breeders.[8] Matthews' handwritten letters, on small pieces of paper held together by a rusty paperclip, informed Thomas of his training and the unexpected obstacles in contacting an English dog breeder Thomas had sourced. Matthews' first letter, buoyant in the beginning, soon hinted at trouble finding honest dog breeders. On September 25, 1973, Matthews wrote from London to tell Thomas that most of the dogs used for narcotics and explosive detection in England were Labradors. "There is none available at the present time due to the fact that what we were supposed to get was given to three Egyptians undergoing training in narcotics," he said.

On October 29, 1973, Matthews wrote another letter, saying he had trouble sending home pictures of dogs he considered buying. "Now, sad news: Mr. Peters' camera has gone bad again. The same problem as before. I got it repaired and again it went bad. The problem of the shutters sticking. I have so far spoilt two rolls of films. The pictures of the dogs I promised all have spoilt. I may purchase a camera if funds so permit."[9]

Matthews also raised suspicions about a dog breeder Thomas had been in contact with. The letters sparked one of Thomas's usual long reports to senior officers. "...Sgt Matthews has indicated that he has grave doubts about the dog breeder because of reports he received concerning him from people in the dog world there, he has therefore, embarked on doing his own scouting for the three dogs for us."[10]

Halfway through the long letter, Thomas relayed his fears to senior officers. "It is obvious from facts contained in the letters, that good working dogs are terribly scarce in the United Kingdom."

"Although I have confidence in Sgt Matthews' judgment of a good dog, he cannot be too careful when dealing with dog people who can be very shrewd with the intent on making a sale." Thomas now decided to put more trust in a German dog breeder, who assured he could provide high-quality dogs, which Thomas believed "are, in fact, superior working quality to these obtainable in the United Kingdom." Crawford Williams, a police dog trainer after Matthews, said he traveled to Germany, Czechoslovakia, and Hungary to procure police dogs after Matthews' trip.[11]

Through Matthews, the second Sheba made her journey to Trinidad. A letter from the Mounted Branch and Dog Section dated March 14, 1974, said Sheba had had 11 puppies on March 10, 1974. Two were stillborn. In the end, the two Shebas shed light on the desperate measures employed to procure dogs. The first Sheba demonstrated the hopeful, albeit haphazard and recycled decision to raise

Chapter 7. Sheba and Sheba

puppies to bolster the working-dog ranks. Correspondence concerning the second Sheba exposed the fears and suspicions about obtaining suitable working dogs in the European market.

The conundrum always led to a few dogs bearing the brunt of canine duties or stepping up to fill the gaps as other dogs retired. Take, for instance, Carlo (next chapter), who bridged the Shebas' reigns.

CHAPTER 8

CARLO

ON MARCH 2, 2009, HECTOR "PEE WEE" LEWIS leaned back in his office chair like a detective in a 1950s pulp fiction story. He reached inside the desk drawer in his cramped office, nestled among the boutiques of Town Centre Mall on lower Frederick Street a block from Independence Square in Port of Spain, and pulled out two black-and-white photos of police dogs and their canine officers, dressed in ceremonial white jackets for an Independence Day parade in the 1960s. Lewis and his dog Kim are in the pictures.

In 1997, the retired police officer hung out his shingle for his business called "Confidential Investigation," specializing in insurance investigations. He recalled being a carefree country boy from D'Abadie, about 14 miles east of Port of Spain, who enjoyed taking his dog to the river. Then he joined the police service. He recalled his first day on the job: "We were on the train to Couva, the head of the Central Division, to get our assignments. I remember passing through Caroni and saying, 'I hope I don't get sent there.'"[1]

Lewis got stationed at the Caroni police station, on the same compound as the Caroni Canine Section. Dog #5, Ralph, soon caught his eye.

> Ralph was one of a couple of good dogs in the Dog Section. As soon as he heard a gun click, he'd attack. I took Ralph out of his kennel on Alexis's days off, and I got to like him. I told Alexis I wanted to join the section, and he told Bridgeman. At this time, Thomas was stationed at St. Joseph with his black Labrador, Ben, the first Labrador in the police service. McDonald Charles had Princess, a Doberman.[2]

In 1961, when Lewis moved across to the Dog Section, Bridgeman assigned him Dog #22, a one-year-old biscuit-colored German Shepherd with black markings named Carlo, not to be confused with

Chapter 8. Carlo

Carlos, one of the original four dogs. "Carlo had a defective eye, with a growth of hair on one pupil. It didn't cover the whole eye, and it didn't affect him. He tracked well. He wasn't too big. I used to hug him, lift him up, and walk with him."[3]

But Carlo and Lewis's relationship had a rocky start. "I got frustrated with Carlo during his training. He had trouble paying attention. The pressures often proved too much for him. When the trainer fell sick for two weeks, I spent time with my dog away from people. When he looked fed up, I stopped training him, and he made a vast improvement."[4]

Carlo caught a thief who stole $27 worth of peppers. Lewis placed a note in Carlo's file: "The dog did surprisingly well, considering his training. Attack work had just started a matter of days ago." When Lewis received a report about someone threatening to shoot a boy, the canine officer and Carlo headed to Cunupia. When they approached the man in question, he tried to run away. "I threatened to let loose the dog and he froze. I searched him and found a loaded homemade shotgun in his waist. The accused was charged with possession of an offensive weapon and unlicensed firearm."[5]

On August 6, 1962, Lewis got a call to search for a police officer lost in the forest. He headed to the North Post Station in Diego Martin, a rugged area so picturesque with its rain forest mountains and ocean view that famous Trinidadian artist Michel Jean Cazabon captured it in a lithograph in 1851.[6] "I gave the dog a scent of a shoe belonging to Constable Peyton Jones; we travelled for about three miles through the forest and with the assistance of the station cleaner, we located the officer."[7]

Carlo's file swelled with reports of exciting tracks that Lewis recalled many years later in his office. Because Carlo looked so menacing, he often accompanied police officers serving warrants. He was also a favorite choice to accompany police searching cane fields for nefarious characters. Lewis said:

> No one wanted to run when they saw Carlo. For much of 1962 and 1963, we were stationed in Besson Street, Port of Spain. There were gang wars that started with the steelband clashes like Applejackers against Lawbreakers and the Renegades from Observatory Street. Carlo liked his

work—chasing and holding fellows running through the yards. They were shooting and chopping one another, and I apprehended a lot of fellows with my dog.[8]

The capital had other action too. In May 1963, Lewis, Carlo, and other police officers trailed a woman suspected of carrying food for an escaped prisoner. They traveled along a dangerous route from the East Dry River[9] connecting Gonzales and Belmont to Sea Lots near the port of Port of Spain and saw the woman enter a van parked in an open piece of land. Lewis released Carlo. "Carlo ran towards the van where I saw the prisoner sitting in the company of the woman. The prisoner attempted to run out of the van, but on seeing the dog by the door he remained quiet until the arrest was effected," Lewis wrote in Carlo's file.[10]

That same year, Carlo worked what Lewis described as "a nice robbery" in Santa Cruz at the Stollmeyer cocoa estate. On his way to Santa Cruz, Lewis passed Stollmeyer castle, designed after part of Balmoral castle in Scotland. As the last building of the Magnificent Seven overlooking the Queen's Park Savannah, Stollmeyer Castle stands at the entrance to Maraval. Further down, at a fork in the road leading to Maracas Beach, Lewis turned right heading to the Santa Cruz valley where Spanish and Patois-speaking estate owners had become rich from cocoa, sugarcane and coffee plantations in the 19th century. Conrad Frederick Stollmeyer, a German immigrant had bought land here in 1883 and made a fortune from cocoa.[11] Lewis recalled the Stollmeyer cocoa estate robbery:

> The guy brought some washcloths to the house on a hill where the workers received their wages every Friday. He asked to sell the washcloths. When he got inside, he whipped a gun from a washcloth and stole the money from the paymaster handing it out. Police said they wanted a dog and Carlo and I came from Besson Street. Carlo tracked the suspect through the bush. The guy took a car, then jumped on a boat and headed for Tobago. The mistake he made is telling his brother he just made a hit. The same man got charged for murder in 1961 or 1962, when he killed the owner of Honeycomb Fried Chicken on Duncan and Prince Street.[12]

Then Carlo and Lewis got transferred to San Fernando.

> [Israel Dennis] Figaro and I were stationed there. One day, I said I'm going on patrol. Carlo and I went out and we saw the *Guardian* newspaper

Chapter 8. Carlo

manager, Norman Philip. He liked police and police dogs. Norman said, "Come, we goin' by my girlfriend. I want her to see the dog." Carlo and I got in the car. Some of the fellows from the police station saw me and thought I was leaving the patrol to go and lime with Norman. As we were driving, I saw a known criminal, Blue Boy, walking on the pavement. I told Norman, "Drive ahead a little," and we put on the siren. Norman had a siren and a police light he put on top of his car.

I trusted Carlo and didn't put a lead on him. I opened the door and let Carlo go. Carlo took off. Blue Boy ran into that nasty Siparia River, and Carlo followed. They were both going around each other in the water. I just watched. When my dog was on a hot trail, his ears would stand up and his tail started going. I always said, "When my dog takes judgment, he gets his reward," so I let Carlo rip up the guy's shirt a little. After he caught Blue Boy, we put Carlo—all nasty—in Norman's car. Norman didn't mind.[13]

Lewis and Carlo had been sent to San Fernando to find a suspect wanted for shooting a policeman. Lewis said:

This guy terrorized the area. They had sent McDonald Charles with Jett and me with Carlo to assist in capturing this guy. We spent two or three months tracking that suspect.

One evening Charles and I were on duty. Someone came to the police station and said a man stabbed up a woman in Cocoyea Village. I took up my revolver and dog but didn't have a chance to put on my uniform. One policeman and I put the dog in the police officer's car.

When we got to the spot, we saw a crowd. They said, "Look, the man ran off."

We got one of his slippers left behind when he ran away. As I gave Carlo a smell, he took off, ran through the cane fields and up and down hills. I followed him the best I could through the cane. I climbed to the top of a hill and saw the man and dog fighting and rolling in the muddy field. People ran behind me. The man, covered in mud, fought with the dog and Carlo bit the man on his head.

I apprehended him. When I brought him back out to the scene, people said, "This is a notorious criminal who killed the police officer in San Fernando." That arrest closed off a lot of tension in San Fernando.[14]

After that case, Charles got transferred back to Port of Spain, and Figaro came south with Panther to work with Lewis. "Figaro and I had a good working relationship," said Lewis. "We started training with our own ideas about scent identification. We used clothing with some success, but nothing we could put on the market." Still, Lewis

Police Dogs of Trinidad and Tobago

and Carlo were in a groove and their reputation grew by leaps and bounds. The pair solved a murder.

> Someone killed a woman and dropped his hat at the scene. The dog picked up the scent. Villafana got the call the next morning. We went on the scene, and the dog went to a cap. The dog tracked for about a quarter-mile and went in the back of the Neal and Massy compound in Morvant. When the dog reached a house, a girl came out and said, "That is [X's] hat." [X] denied the hat belonged to him. The senior state counsel at the time wanted the dog to come to court for evidence, but I didn't take Carlo to court.[15]

Lewis never could have guessed Carlo's next assignment: guarding the country's voting machines. When the ruling political party, the People's National Movement (PNM), decided to import voting machines, some people feared rigged elections. Army officer Raffique Shah, a key participant in the 1970 mutiny, wrote decades later, "In Trinidad and Tobago, there have been allegations that the PNM, from as far back as 1961, was involved in gerrymandering, and in wholesale fraud by use of the voting machines [between 1961 and 71]. Well before the 1966 election Dr. Rudranath Capildeo, leader of the opposition Democratic Labour Party [DLP], called for '1,000 men to come forward and smash 1,000 machines.'"[16]

Every night from 9 p.m. to 6 a.m. Lewis and Carlo headed for work at Golden Grove Prison.

Lewis recalled:

> We were in a building in the prison guarding these machines because reports said people wanted to blow up the machines. I couldn't believe a good dog like Carlo could be wasted guarding a machine.
>
> Eventually, I got fed up. I had a good relationship with a veterinarian, and I got him to write a report that the dogs on duty suffered from ticks because of the cows in the fields around the prison.
>
> It came down to a choice, according to the report, between the cows or the dogs. I sent it directly to the senior superintendent and the commissioner of police.
>
> One evening, I got ready to go to work at 5 p.m. Someone said, "Pee Wee, I see a memo from the commissioner saying he suspended the dogs' assignment with the voting machine with immediate effect."
>
> I told him, "Hold that news for a while."
>
> I sat down, groomed my dog, put on my holster, and listened as the news came over the wireless.

Chapter 8. Carlo

That same night Carlo and I helped solve the case of a house break-in at Valsayn. Carlo got some stolen things hidden in the bushes.[17]

Next, Carlo apprehended a mango thief. Even chasing mango thieves beat guarding voting machines. Carlo soon returned to tracking dangerous criminals. On February 23, 1965, George Stewart made a report about a man stabbing a woman at Forest Avenue, Cocoyea Village. Lewis took off with Carlo.

On reaching the scene I was shown a side of shoes which was left by the man who had stabbed the woman. I gave the dog a scent of the shoes which he trailed for about ¼ mile into a dasheen patch and there the dog held down the man and they struggled until I got to them and effected the arrest. Arrested [X] sentenced to four years and 18 months hard labour on repetitive charges at San Fernando Assizes on June 16, 1965.

The news of his capture was a great relief to the Force generally. He is a notorious character whose activities are a constant bother to the police. The dog did a very good job tracking. The man was an escaped prisoner who allegedly had shot two policemen.[18]

Carlo appeared to be unstoppable Then one day, Figaro took Carlo out of the kennel. He turned in circles and ran wild. Figaro rushed him to the vet. The dog died at 4:30 a.m. on August 5, 1965. (See Chapter 9 for cause of Carlo's death).

When Kim developed hip problems and retired, he went home with Lewis and eventually died of old age.[19] "Kim had caught a fellow wanted for several robberies in San Fernando," said Lewis.

Lewis's stint in the Dog Section stretched from 1961 to 1973.

I never knew why I was transferred out of the section. People said they'd talk on my behalf to bring me back, and I said, "No, I joined the police service—not the Dog Section. I enjoyed the time I spent in the Dog Section." People criticized me when I first decided to be a dog handler. They said, "That is where police go to hide." I had offers from other departments in the police service. I chose the dogs, and I never felt I made a bad choice going there. I considered myself to be an expert crime fighter and dog handler. The dogs often didn't get credit for the crimes they solved, but we the handlers had great satisfaction.

Lewis paused, folded his hands on the desk, and said, "It was good while it lasted."[20]

Chapter 9

Panther

On July 9, 1962, Sgt. Hamilton Bridgeman received an unexpected phone call.

Hector Lewis recalled,

> We were asked to come to some bigshot's house in Diego Martin. There, the lady gave us a black Labrador named Punch. It was a very sad separation between owner and dog. The couple had to return to Australia, and she was heartbroken. She gave the dog her slipper to take away with him. The man, Captain Webster, wouldn't come out of the house. He couldn't bear to see us take the dog away.
>
> We took Punch back to the station, and some of the police officers made fun of him. Cpl. Bailey teased the dog and said, "Where you get that common dog?"
>
> I had the dog on a lead. The dog got vexed and tried to attack Bailey. I said, "This dog has some potential, and I renamed him Panther." Bridgeman asked me if I wanted the dog and I said, "Let's give him to Figaro."[1]

Dog #24, Panther, born on January 9, 1962, and enlisted in the police service on March 1, 1963, came to the service as a puppy, but grew into a formidable police dog, outshining many dogs bred for the purpose. "That dog could leap, and he'd go straight for the cheek," said Lewis.[2] Bridgeman did the customary sell to his superiors, who had to grant permission to enlist donated dogs.

> Sir, I have to inform you that on Monday, 9/7/62, Captain Webster of No 4 Mary Avenue, Diego Martin rang me stating that he has a black Labrador dog age ten months old and that he is willing to give the dog to the police or get a good home for it as he was leaving the colony. As a result, I collected same dog and brought it to the kennels. It is a good-looking animal. We are presently short by one dog. If he takes the training, he will be a good contribution, please.[3]
>
> Sgt Bridgeman

Chapter 9. Panther

"If Panther did not take to training, the Mounted Branch and Dog Section had agreed with Captain Webster that they would find a good home for the dog," said Lewis.[4]

Bridgeman took Panther, referred to in canine police files also as "Panta" or "Panter," to the St. Joseph police station for Thomas to see. Bridgeman noted Panther's potential as a police dog, and Thomas relayed this information up the chain of command on July 19, 1962. "He is good at obedience, tracking, and chasing, and has the necessary characteristics for a good police dog. It is with pride that I recommend him to be enlisted officially to our strength, having found him to be ready for duty."[5]

Three months later, Bridgeman wrote to Thomas with an update. "Sir, I have to report that the black Labrador given the name Panter has shown great progress. He is now working satisfactorily at the Besson Street Police Station. May he be taken on and allotted #24, please?"[6] Agile and smart, Panther thrived as a police dog. Figaro kept a running record of his exploits.

January 10, 1963
At 3 am, I joined a search party with dog Panther to capture some wanted men believed to be hiding in a house in the Southern side of the Beetham Highway. On arrival at the appointed place, we met an open shack. In it were the three men sleeping. We woke them up and took them to the Besson Street Police Station. They made no attempt to escape. He was taken on a number of missions to find gunmen and even one on May 13, 1964 to find two lunatics charged with murder and one charged with stealing a bull. They had escaped St. Ann's Mental hospital.

He helped to apprehend [X] found breaking into a factory in Port of Spain. He searched for a peeping Tom.

[Another suspect he tracked] had been evading the police for a considerable length of time. Every time he is spotted, he always runs away from the police who cannot catch up with him as such he is considered a fleet-footed young man. The dog was called to assist on 27 April 1965. On arrival in a cocoa field in the Tamana district, three men were seen plucking cocoa. I held the dog and crept up on the men. They were shocked when the dog and I suddenly appeared before them. No man moved. The defendant was then arrested.[7]

While he supervised the dogs' work, Thomas recognized the dogs' need for recreation. He wrote to the superintendent requesting an outing.

Police Dogs of Trinidad and Tobago

I respectfully apply for permission and transportation to take our police dogs and their handlers to the Las Quavas [Las Cuevas] beach for a bath on Wednesday, February 6, 1963. It has been the practice of taking the dogs for a swim in the sea at least once per month, but owing to emergency duties for which they were required in recent months, this was discontinued. In view of the fact that the situation at the Besson Street district is practically normal, it is my opinion, Sir, that the dogs be given this very much-needed exercise before the Carnival period.

With the hope of having your approval, it is my respectful submission that one of the riot vans be made available for this purpose.[8]

Thomas noted in his correspondence file, "Necessary arrangements made." He also inserted a note about Princess's puppies. "Re: Pups at depot station. All eight pups are in one kennel and they fight. A veterinary surgeon had to be called in. We are trying to get rid of the pups."[9] The pups weren't working out, but Panther exceeded all expectations. He intimidated suspects and tracked them well. Then, out of the blue, Thomas received a disturbing phone call. He rushed to the Mon Repos station in South only to learn he had lost another dog. The next day, Lewis filed a report.

August 7, 1965
From 5854 PC Lewis
Sir, I have to report for your information that on Friday, August 6, 1965 at 9 am I left the station on a tracking exercise with Const Figaro with Dog Panther. I laid a track and after about 30 minutes Const Figaro and Dog Panther found me. We sat down in the bushes for a while and then passed around the Pleasantville area. We returned to the station at 12:45 p.m. and the dog was groomed and put in its kennels by Const Figaro. At that time the dog appeared to be in good health.

About fifteen minutes later, Const Figaro called me and showed me how the Dog was panting very fast and not standing up. Const Figaro contacted Dr de Gannes who arrived shortly afterward and administered an injection to the dog....[10]

Panther died. Thomas wrote, "On my return to Port of Spain, the Government chemist was closed to business for the weekend. I however managed to lodge the perishable exhibit [Panther's body] in the deep freeze at the General Hospital until today when I will take [the body] to the chemist as instructed along with the items of food for analysis."[11]

Chapter 9. Panther

Figaro, Thomas and Dr. De Gannes attended Panther's necropsy performed by Dr. Kanhai.

The lab's findings noted a lack of blood clotting, heavy hemorrhaging throughout the body, and marked congestion of the internal organs. Thomas's report gave the dog's cause of death as distemper—a contagious, often fatal viral disease that affects the respiratory, gastrointestinal, and central nervous systems. (Panther's veterinary report appears in Appendix B.)

Carlo and Panther died two days apart and are buried next to each other at the Mon Repos police station. DeGannes believed both dogs died of poisoning or heat stroke. Dr. Kanhai's necropsy report was not found in Thomas's files.

In a letter to Acting Supt. I. McPhillip on August 20, 1965, Thomas said, "The loss of these two dogs [Panther and Carlo] is most unfortunate." Jonas Dawes, the senior superintendent of the Southern Division, agreed. "We are without a dog now. I am not even getting a single replacement?" he asked in a handwritten note to the police commissioner on August 17, 1965.[12]

Behind the scenes, the Dog Section depended on some dog to leap into action and mitigate the sadness left by the loss of Carlo and Panther. Hope now fell to a litter of puppies that had begun training in January 1965. Winston Matthews, who would become one of the Dog Section's trainers, remembered the "A" puppies well.

Chapter 10

Adolph, ANZAC, and Bullet

WINSTON MATTHEWS ACHIEVED ENVIABLE SUCCESS as a police dog handler and trainer in the 1960s—without ever liking dogs. "I'm still not a dog lover, but I liked the success I got from dogs. A dog is never deceitful. He doesn't report sick. If you have no food in the house, he might look for some food in a dustbin, and probably bring it back to share with you. A dog will die with you. If you spell 'dog' backward, you get 'God.'"

Matthews grew up in the countryside, with several brothers who served as role models. One brother, a joiner, left his job to join the Police Service, a shocking choice in those days.

"In those days, most Trinidadians didn't want to join the police. A foolish myth circulated that if you become a police officer, you'd have to swear you'd lock up your mother. So many Barbadians and Grenadians were brought to Trinidad to serve as police officers," was Matthews' explanation.[1]

The first police force in Trinidad dates back to 1797 when Sir Thomas Picton served as governor. He was recalled to England in 1801 after torturing 14-year-old Luisa Calderon into confessing to a crime then hanging her by a rope from a building. After he was court-martialed he got sent to the Battle of Waterloo and died there. Picton's recruits came from the wealthy French planters he protected. They wore short black pants, thick wool socks, cork hats and carried batons. Detectives in that newly created unit in 1802 wore plain clothes. From 1876, police headquarters was located on St. Vincent Street, Port of Spain. Police commissioner Col. A.V. Mavrogordato introduced the Star of David as the insignia in 1931. No one

Chapter 10. Adolph, ANZAC, and Bullet

knows exactly why, but he had served in the military forces in Jerusalem in 1922. In 1955, 12 women joined the police service to deal with prostitutes, children and sexual assault matters. Calypsoes mocked them. Spoiler sang, "Ah want a policewoman to hold me tight...." Sylvester "Zandolee" Anthony sang "Iron Man," a smutty calypso about a woman police officer arresting him. In February 2023, Erla Harewood-Christopher became the first woman police commissioner.[2]

When Matthews passed the school-leaving certificate at 18, he followed his brother and, at 19, became a police constable. On August 30, 1962, Matthews witnessed the lowering of the British Union Jack and the raising of the Trinidad and Tobago flag. The ceremony at midnight signaled the country's independence on August 31. Matthews said,

> I was among the first independent police officers. Before independence, we had a paramilitary police force, similar to the army, and there was something called "dumb insolence." If you looked at an officer funny, you were put under charge—no tribunal. A drill instructor attached to each division kept police officers in shape. Once a month they had riot drills—just in case there was a disturbance in the country.[3]

While serving his probationary period as a police officer, Matthews was transferred to the launch section, which patrolled the seas. "I was restless and not getting enough out of the job. I wanted a challenge."

After he passed probation, Matthew joined the Dog Section. "We moved like squatters in the Mounted Branch. We had a little area. Thomas was in charge and he had twelve handlers. Thomas handled Sheba; Alexis had his second dog, Ralph. Hicks had the only cross-breed dog, a German Shepherd/collie combination. She looked like a mongrel; she was very vicious and she worked at Besson Street police station. That rough environment suited her," Matthews said. (No one recalled the dog's name.)

Matthews trained directly under Thomas. "After seeing what Thomas could do with a dog, I thought if I had a successful working dog, I'd be a force to be reckoned with. I came from the country; I didn't know town [Port of Spain].... I was devoted to my dog."

On January 9, 1965, a litter of puppies known as the A-series—

Police Dogs of Trinidad and Tobago

Adolph, Andy, Ajax, Adonis, and ANZAC—made their debut working in the Dog Section. "Andy was the best of the lot," said Matthews. [Andy's file couldn't be located]. "[But] Adolph showed promise. I was determined to turn Adolph into a great dog."[4]

Matthews and Adolph, along with Lewis (who had Carlo and then Kim), headed south to work in Siparia, a small town that attracts pilgrims every Easter to see a 2½ foot statue made from dark African cedar wood and called Divina Pastora by Christians or Siparee Mai by Hindus. Capuchin monks fleeing Venezuela in the 18th century brought the statue that belongs to the Catholic Church.[5]

"I learned a lot from Lewis. He was a good dog trainer," said Matthews. "Not everyone had the mindset to learn, but we did. Two things prevent learning: ignorance and suspicion—and there was plenty of that to go around. The army's approach and attitude were good—better than the police in those days." Matthews and Lewis challenged each other to invent new methods of tracking and perfect the methods they were taught. Adolph and Andy didn't quite reach Matthews' standards for police dogs. Matthews blamed the training.

> The dogs struggled because we were asking children to do men's work. We tried to teach the dogs aggression at too early of an age—six months. This is why we had great failures. Many dogs probably would have made it. We didn't realize that dogs weren't mature enough to do this work until they reached about one and a half years old. They didn't have the concentration or the ability to understand. Many of them showed great fear while training.[6]

Still, Adolph and ANZAC had some remarkable stories. During the 60s, the Dog Section covered every corner of Trinidad, with two dog handlers and two dogs assigned to several stations: St. Joseph, Belmont, Diego Martin, Sangre Grande, Mon Repos, and Freeport. The dogs mainly tracked fleeing suspects. Some were involved in drugs, but the police didn't yet have drug-detection dogs. "Drug-related crime always existed," said Matthews. "Before Randolph Burroughs' era as commissioner [1978–1987], the Chinese had opium; Indians grew marijuana and sold it. People of African descent bought marijuana and sold it over, but it wasn't until Burroughs came in as police chief and Dole Chadee established his drug

Chapter 10. Adolph, ANZAC, and Bullet

kingdom that drug-related crimes became so prevalent."[7] Chadee's reign ended when he and eight of his cronies were convicted on September 3, 1996, of murdering Deo, Rookmin, Hamilton and Monica Baboolal of Piparo on January 10, 1994. That day loomed far in the future.

Throughout canine police history, officers most often pinpointed tracking exercises in the forest as their most dangerous and memorable challenges. Matthews was no exception.

In 1967, a murder occurred in the fishing area of La Lune near a remote, highly forested part of Moruga [southern Trinidad]. Two brothers had been fighting in the street and an old lady tried to stop the fight. One of the boys got upset and stormed off to get his father's gun locked up in a gun box. He returned, shot, and killed the old lady; then disappeared into the bush. Adolph and I went to track him.

I was scared. Imagine, this old lady didn't do him anything, and he had just shot her.

I figured by the time I got there in the hot sun, the scent would have disappeared. No one knew which direction the guy had gone.

But the police were so relieved to see a dog and handler, and I was not one to give up. They brought the guy's shoes and clothes. I let Adolph sniff them and told the officers, "Stay twenty feet behind Adolph."

Adolph walked around the edge of the forest and then went in. Eventually, I saw one footprint. I looked back, and I didn't see any police behind me.

About three miles into the forest, Adolph began wagging his tail. I slackened the leash, let him go, and dropped to the ground.

I looked up and saw Adolph going for a gun. I saw some spent cartridges in the balisier.[8] I went after Adolph and saw him spinning around. The dog went down through the balisier after the suspect. He had shot himself under the chin; he was still alive, groaning.

No one was around. I had no way to get him out, and suddenly I realized I didn't know how we had got to that point in the forest.

Luckily, while on guard duty at the prime minister's grounds, I taught my dog to backtrack when I got bored. I'd drop my wallet and have him go back for it. I had learned a lot about backtracking from Thomas. Adolph took me straight out of the forest. When we got out, I hugged up that dog.[9]

Not long after that ordeal, Matthews and Adolph were sent to Point Fortin. "Shell Trinidad Ltd. was closing down and there was a lot of crime," said Matthews. "We patrolled with estate police and

Police Dogs of Trinidad and Tobago

also assisted Caroni Ltd., [the state-owned company that ran centralized sugarcane production,] with a dog patrol attempting to prevent or capture people involved in malicious cane fires."[10] Adolph even had his day in court when a thief denied that he owned a cap being held in an exhibit against him. "Adolph went to court, sniffed the guy, and went for the cap," said Matthews.[11]

Somehow Adolph became injured: he dislocated the cartilage in his sternum. The wound oozed and an x-ray determined the damage. Matthew suspected the injury had occurred on one of Adolph's many searches in the forest, where he went through heavily wooded areas.[12] Meanwhile, Adolph's brother ANZAC, Dog #37, tackled copper-wire thieves in South Trinidad with his original handler, PC Mohammed. On February 17, 1966, the black-and-tan ANZAC, only 13 months old, tackled his first case, tracking Kid Black Hat, who had several outstanding warrants.[13]

In all ANZAC's reports, Mohammed would write the dog's name in the same way as the acronym for the Australian and New Zealand Army Corps (ANZAC) formed in World War I. The ANZAC Corps had demonstrated legendary bravery along the narrow strait of the Dardanelles in the Gallipoli campaign, where the Ottoman Empire defeated the French, British and Russian allies aided by ANZAC. Barely more than a puppy, ANZAC the dog recorded victories in the war against crime in Trinidad.

On April 19, 1966, ANZAC and Mohammed departed on ANZAC's second case. They responded to a call from the Arouca police after three men in a car stopped Krishna Balroop, a waiter at the Bel Air Hotel, while he was walking home from work. The men told the waiter they had a message from his mother. "They persuaded him to get into the car and drove to a lonely trace where they beat him, tied his hands, shot at him and drove off."[14] ANZAC found one of the thieves' shoes. Police with ANZAC in tow pursued tips and stopped motor car HE 94 with the culprits. It was a huge arrest. One of the three men charged with shooting with intent had been infamous for killing his father and canine officer Piggott. (Canine police say the young man escaped a death sentence and got out of prison because he had been a minor when he killed his father and Piggott.)[15]

Chapter 10. Adolph, ANZAC, and Bullet

ANZAC headed to South Trinidad on March 25, 1967, to pursue a suspect who had escaped from custody after being arrested in San Fernando for larceny of wooden stumps. ANZAC apprehended the escaped prisoner in a public bathroom.[16] On December 7, 1967, he assisted the Four Roads police in apprehending another suspect, from Crystal Stream, wanted for malicious wounding. The suspect had several outstanding warrants and a history of running away whenever he saw the police. ANZAC looked on as the police arrested him.

> As he was about to be handcuffed, [the suspect] pulled his hand away and made a dash to run. The dog was released with the command, "Stop him!" The dog jumped on the man and held his right hand. He kicked the dog. ANZAC released him and then jumped on [X], biting him on the left forearm. I was able to arrest him and handed him over to PC Charles and the other police.[17]

Police took the suspect to the Port of Spain General Hospital.

ANZAC continued to rack up cases. In 1968, he assisted Shell Trinidad in dealing with copper-wire thieves. "Shell Trinidad Ltd. has a great amount of copper wire for the purpose of conveying electricity to the oil wells used for pumping oil. On 20 November, 1968, [ANZAC] followed the scent of a thief into the bushes and came across a roll of copper wire, but the ground was saturated with crude oil overflowing and ANZAC lost the scent of the culprit."[18] But ANZAC's track led the police close to an area where they later found and arrested a man who was convicted in La Brea Magistrates' Court and sentenced to nine months in prison.

On Christmas Day 1969, while most people celebrated with baked ham, black cake, (fruitcake) and ginger beer, Matthews sat at his desk and wrote a report about ANZAC's brother Adolph.

> The accused, a sailor from the Norway Shipping Company broke the glass case of George F Huggins and went into the store. He was held at the company for damages of $750. Dog Adolph was taken to the scene of St. James Street, San Fernando in George F Huggins Store. He took up a trail and cornered the culprit in an underground room in the store. The dog worked very good. Accused charged with malicious damages.[19]

On January 4, 1969, Adolph tracked a dangerous suspect from La Lune Village, Moruga.

> The suspect shot a woman to death at the said district and ran into the high woods. The dog after getting a sniff of the suspect's boots took up a trail and tracked for about three-quarters of a mile where he brought me to the suspect who apparently shot himself with a shotgun which was discovered by the body together with four rounds of ammunition.[20]

On January 19, 1969, Matthews wrote that he left the Mon Repos police station for Princes Town to investigate a crime that had happened on January 18.

> [X] of Princes Town was sleeping in his house with his family when he was awakened by a man pulling his door. As he approached the door, the man stabbed him with a dagger and ran. Police dog Adolph was taken to the scene of the crime where he took up a trail and tracked through the cane fields then on the road where he cornered the culprit in his house. He tracked very good for a long distance. The culprit was caught on his bed. Charge was wounding.[21]

Adolph kept his stride into the new year, but died on October 11, 1970. No cause was recorded.

ANZAC changed handlers (no reason is recorded), teaming up with PC Sifontis, who had transferred to the Police Dog Section on August 1, 1968. Sifontis and ANZAC worked together from February 20, 1970, and had four solid years of adventures.[22]

Near the end of the A's era, Matthews worked with Bullet. The case he recalls most vividly and joyfully (with a description that matches the official police report) came on January 24, 1969, at 8:20 p.m., when Mary Wong of Techier Village reported to the Point Fortin police, in the Southwestern Division, that she had been robbed at Frisco Junction. The thief grabbed her purse, which held $16. With no police vehicle available, Matthews put Bullet in his car and took him to the scene of the crime. They arrived at 9 p.m.

> The man who stole the purse went through the swamp and ran into the forest. I took the dog by the bushes that Mary Wong pointed out. He picked up a scent and started on a trail. Bullet jumped in the water and swam. I kept seeing him looking at something. The purse floated on top of a water lily.
>
> I didn't get the fellow, but Bullet got the purse and the money. I showed the purse to Mary Wong. The girl started to cry and hug up the dog. She

Chapter 10. Adolph, ANZAC, and Bullet

kept saying, "Oh puppy, oh puppy!" Bullet didn't take to people, but he let the girl hug him.[23]

Then Matthews was transferred to Belmont. "I tried to find people wanted for crimes. I went up and down the East Dry River, but that is a concrete jungle," he said.[24] Occasionally, Bullet got assignments out of town.

> At 2 p.m. in the heat one afternoon, I got a call to bring Bullet to Carlsen field to track a man who kept robbing people. We went to a marshy area. I couldn't follow Bullet so I took him off the line. The dog headed for the river and started to swim. I tried to call him. I kept seeing the dog looking at something. The man went under the water and Bullet kept picking up the scent when he came up for air. Every time he tried to make a dash for the bank, Bullet grabbed him—and Bullet was big, about ninety-eight pounds.
> I called out to the man, "Come!" The guy said, "No, the dog is going to kill me." I called off Bullet, and he just sat down next to the guy. I said, "I want the cutlass, the mask, and the money." He had hidden the money in the bush and thrown the cutlass in the river.
> The guy got five years.[25]

Matthews' fondness for Bullet grew as the dog met every challenge beyond Matthews' expectations. On November 6, 1970, Bhadase Mahabir, a Special Reserve Police Constable at the Freeport police station, filed a report for the Dog Section.

> On Friday October 3, 1970, I was on station sentry and at 9:15 am I booked No 6161 Constable Matthews with Police Dog Bullet on exercise. Constable Matthews with his dog Bullet left the station and went east along the Freeport Mission Road. At 10 am Const Matthews with his dog Bullet returned to the station area saying that the dog was not breathing properly and he put it to sit on the eastern veranda of the station and placed a fan close to the dog.[26]

Matthew's report stated:

> Left station at 9:15 a.m. Whilst walking south along the proposed Express Highway after covering about ¾ of a mile I observed that the dog started to stagger and was breathing very abnormally. As a result, I took him to the nearest tree which was shady, and rested him. When he appeared to be breathing normally, I started my journey back to the station. As I got about one hundred and fifty yards from the station the dog collapsed.
> I tried to get some water down his throat from a nearby standpipe and

in the process, he bit one of my fingers on my right hand. I lifted him up and took him to the station and rested him on the eastern verandah at the station where it was quite breezy. In addition to that, I placed a fan very close to him. I called the St. Joseph Govt farm to contact a doctor, but none was there. I called the clinic at San Fernando there was none there either. I called the Dog Section and was told that no one was at the Section at that time.

The dog eventually died.

That said that morning the dog was apparently in good health. The previous day I took him on the same form of exercise and he showed no sign of ill health. I took the dog to the Depot Kennels the said day on instruction from Inspector Thomas where a post-mortem examination was performed by Dr Moe in the presence of me which revealed that his heart was not functioning properly, which the Doctor says was the cause of death.[27]

Bullet died of a heat-stroke-related heart attack.[28] Seven months later, on May 4, 1971, Juno, Dog #38, another successful dog, spent the day tracking through tall grass, bamboo and grapefruit. "The day was very hot," Figaro wrote in Juno's file. At 3:40 p.m., Juno died of heat exhaustion.[29]

Early in 1973, Sifontis noticed ANZAC passing blood when he urinated. He took the dog to Dr. Amy A Hosein, the government veterinarian. She removed a tumorous growth on ANZAC's penis in April and diagnosed a venereal granuloma. Nearly a year later, Sifontis brought ANZAC back to the vet.[30] The vet's official report said, "I found on examination that the granuloma had re-occurred and was now more extensive. I feel that surgery at this time is not indicated due to the age of the dog and the nature of the tumour involved. I, therefore, recommend that police dog 'ANZAC' be relieved of his duties as a police dog at this time."

ANZAC suffered greatly from a severe skin rash and swelling of the cancerous section. He retired to the Depot Barracks where he had been born. The veterinarian euthanized him on March 12, 1974.[31] In the face of constant disappointments, ANZAC, Adolph and the A-team puppies had offered some semblance of security and a feeling that the Dog Section might just successfully raise police dogs.

Chapter 11

Trigger

Saturday evening at the Queen's Park Savannah, Port of Spain, and all appeared calm on November 4, 1972. PC Noel James and police dog Trigger walked across the street from the Belmont police station to the 260 acres of grass where boys flew kites and played cricket. Couples walked the perimeter of the sprawling field, 2.2 miles long. At about 6:20 p.m., in the fading light, James strained to make sense of the scene unfolding in front of him. A young man with no pants and no shoes bolted out of the blue and ran in his direction.[1]

> The young man reported to me that he was just attacked by another man, near the public convenience [toilet]. The attacker offered the young man money and when he refused to take it, the man held something to the young man's neck, made him remove his pants, and tried to have sexual interference [sic] with him. The young man, fifteen years old, was collecting bottles in the Savannah to sell. He gave his name and reported that eventually he escaped after bawling [shouting] when he saw someone approaching. He fled the scene leaving his pants and shoes behind. I took him back to the area, where he pointed out a man to me. This man was some distance away. I called out to him, and he began running.
>
> I released Dog Trigger who chased and held the man. I observed that he was fighting and kicking off the dog. As a result, he received several bites on his feet and hands. I eventually held the man. I secured the dog and took the man to the Belmont Police station where I performed the charge against him, indecent assault on a male person. He was later taken to the General Hospital, attended to, and discharged. I recovered the victim's pants and shoes. Police dog Trigger as usual worked well in chasing and capturing the fleeing culprit.[2]

The aging Trigger, a spry German Shepherd with a black-and-tan coat, still relished physically challenging duties. He was born on March 26, 1964. His first handler, PC Feracho, had written in his original file that Trigger reached merely 20 inches in height. At the time of his first posting from the Depot Kennels on April 1, 1966, to the Southern Division, Trigger would have been two years old.[3] He came to be a police dog, as many had, quite by accident.

Lystra D. Lewis, the owner of 17-month-old Trigger, had offered him—the little brother of police dog Butch—to the police commissioner on September 29, 1965. The brothers came from an agreement for the service of an Alsatian bitch to be mated with police dog Bobby for a pup. The police had chosen Butch over Trigger as the pick of the litter. Lewis wrote,

> Trigger has grown to be a fine dog, but is very determined and somewhat aggressive. To top it all, he is too strong and sometimes difficult for me to manage, nevertheless, I love him very much. Sgt Thomas knows the dog and thinks that he will make a good police dog. He further expressed his desire to have him in the police force. I am therefore offering him to the police for $100 and the next young male pup.[4]

Theophilus Thomas recommended Trigger without hesitation. On December 2, 1965, he enlisted Trigger, Dog #40, in the police service.[5] He followed Juno, #38, enlisted on September 21, and Ringo, Dog #39, enlisted on September 22. (Winston Matthews recalled that "Ringo did good work in St. Lucia).["6]

Although Trigger entered the police service midway through the 60s, he would make his mark mostly in the 70s. His fearlessness, despite his small size, and his love of a good chase, made him a success. Trigger's exploits with PC Feracho were satisfactory, but hardly extraordinary. But when Feracho transferred to "ordinary duty" on January 10, 1968, Trigger was assigned to James. He thrived under James's care, working in the Northern, Western, and Eastern divisions of the police service. Bandits couldn't outwit him in the forests; miscreants couldn't outsmart or outrun Trigger in town.[7] James and Trigger seemed to have a knack for being in the right place at the right time.

> At 2 am Wednesday, 24th February 1971, Neal Neptune of Carson [Carlsen] Field, Chaguanas was sitting on a bench at Woodford Square, Port of Spain when [X] of East Dry River came up enquiring the time, then snatched the watch off Neal's hand and ran away with it.

Chapter 11. Trigger

Police Dog Trigger as usual is a very active Dog and it was no surprise that he chased and held the fleeing man and stood over him till I got there. The culprit was charged with larceny of a wristwatch and received six months' hard labour. Trigger has not lost any of his speed or ability when coming to his function as a police dog.[8]

Trigger was seven years old.

The following year—the year of his Savannah case with the teenager—proved even more notable. On March 14, 1972, Trigger pursued a man who had stolen a gun in Sangre Grande, the main town in northeastern Trinidad. The suspect fled about a mile into the dense, Manzanilla forest bordering the beach in eastern Trinidad. James wrote that "On arrival in the forest, we discovered another culprit who was cultivating marijuana. He was arrested and charged with this offense."[9]

Trigger didn't always have the opportunity to give chase. His snarl was menacing enough to stop most thieves in their tracks. When James cried, "I have a police dog with me!" most suspects opted to rely on their lying excuses rather than face Trigger.[10] The next month, Trigger came to the rescue of a drunk man lying in the road in Brooklyn Settlement in Sangre Grande. He had been robbed of $35. "The dog was taken on the scene of the incident and given a command to chase after a fleeing man who ran into the bushes. He held the man some distance away ... [X] was charged for larceny, convicted and fined $75 or two months' hard labour in prison."[11]

Trigger then came to the aid of a farmer in Sangre Grande.

> Rampersad Bolai had some cows grazing in some bushes ... on the morning of June 14, 1972. On his return, he called the cows at about 12:30 p.m. and discovered one of the cows dead. The cow was cut across its belly with a cutlass.
>
> The dog was taken to the scene of the crime and tracked through the bushes [and] headed to the dwelling house of [X], where he found one pair of rubber boots, clothing, also a cutlass with bloodstains. Police Dog Trigger is a very efficient tracker and he did very well to track through the bushes and find the house of the accused where the bloody items were being kept.[12]

James and Trigger never seemed to rest. James's assignments, a combination of patrols and tracking exercises, challenged Trigger.

Police Dogs of Trinidad and Tobago

Their quick response time to assignments indicates that once James was on duty, Trigger was always by James's side and not in his kennel. The dog's file often shows that James and Trigger responded to reports and left the station within one to five minutes. Clearly, both officer and dog were always ready for action.[13]

On July 5, 1972, the owner of a business place in Sangre Grande locked his shop at 8 p.m. and went home. James and Trigger, who were on patrol duty at about 3:20 a.m. the next morning, saw a man riding a bicycle away from the shop with a bag in his hand. Further investigations revealed the business had been broken into, and the man had house-breaking implements in his possession.[14]

> I shouted at the man to stop. He kept on riding. I then shouted, "I have a Police Dog with me" and the man immediately jumped off his cycle and waited for my arrival. Meanwhile, Dog Trigger kept barking at the man whom I had told to stop. [The suspect] was convicted of shop breaking with intent and possession of four breaking implements. He was sentenced to eight months hard labour in Sangre Grande Court.[15]

The following year James and Trigger apprehended a suspicious-looking man riding a lady's bike straight towards James, now a corporal, and PC Quammie at 4:45 a.m. on January 24, 1973.[16]

> The two officers on special duty patrolling along the Eastern Main Road in St. Joseph with Police Dog Trigger, observed the cyclist slow down and behave suspiciously.
> I called out to him, and he suddenly jumped off the cycle and began running in the opposite direction. I shouted to him to stop or have the Police Dog come after him, and after a few more paces, the accused stopped. As a result, the dog was not released. I noticed the man's bulging pockets and on searching him I found a pair of motor vehicle mirrors. The mirrors, the cyclist said, belonged to him. Then he changed his story and said a friend gave them to him, but he couldn't remember the name or address of the friend. [The suspect] was convicted of unlawful possession of the mirrors and a bicycle. He was fined $50 or two months' hard labour.[17]

But Trigger's biggest case arguably occurred near the end of that first year James and Trigger became a team and a force to be reckoned with. They were on duty at the Belmont Police Station when a man ran inside at 6:50 p.m. and reported an incident involving

Chapter 11. Trigger

his girlfriend. A minute later, at 6:51, James and Trigger dashed out of the station, crossed the street and entered the Savannah at 6:55 p.m.[18]

> On Tuesday, November 26, 1968, the female victim [Y] was walking through the Queen's Park Savannah with a male friend named [Z] at about 6:40 p.m. The accused whose name is [X] of Laventille chased [Z] away then dragged the victim further into the Savannah, took off all her clothing and raped her. She also received several blows to her face, which was swollen and bleeding.
> Police Dog Trigger was taken to the scene and after searching for some distance came upon the culprit actually in the act of raping the woman. I called out to him and he ran. Dog Trigger chased and held the man. He fought the dog and was bitten in several places. The dog did a very good piece of work in chasing and detaining the accused and as a result of his brisk action, the accused was held.[19]

James's pride in his dog's work shows in the official Police Service Dog Report, where, in the upper right-hand corner, he wrote in large, red capital letters, ARREST in the case of the Savannah rape. No other report in Trigger's files features such a big and bold entry. His other arrests are noted in small, cursive writing.

The cause of all dogs' deaths is recorded in their files, along with veterinary reports of illnesses—especially those leading up to their deaths—but Trigger's death is recorded only between the customary diagonal red lines on the front of his brown file. There, in red ink, James wrote: "DOG DIED 15/9/73." The donated dog, beloved, but too aggressive and rambunctious for his original owner to handle, performed heroic work, then simply disappeared from the police files. There are no records of Trigger slowing down or facing a painful decline; no records of sickness or an agonizing death. His file contains only memorable exploits, untainted by any sad ending.

CHAPTER 12

SHEP

TRINIDAD PULSED WITH EXCITEMENT and change in the 1970s. The land of calypso had a new music, soca—the soul of calypso—a fusion of Garfield "Lord Shorty" Blackman's blend of East Indian and African rhythms, Cecil "Maestro" Hume's upbeat tempo and Winston "Shadow" Bailey's bold basslines. In 1978, the country danced to Lord Shorty's soca "Money is no Problem," a sentiment tossed around since Prime Minister Eric Williams declared it during the 1976 election campaign. Oil money flowed, particularly after the Arab oil embargo in 1973, when the Middle East protested the U.S. support of Israel in the Arab-Israeli war.

On the surface all looked well, but Trinidad and Tobago was no carefree paradise. Calypsonians like Llewellyn "Short Pants" MacIntosh, sang about *bobol* (corruption) in the government. Even if the government didn't speak about it, the people sensed it. "Bobol as such is local knowledge with a long transhistorical back story and social context," wrote anthropologist Dylan Kerrigan.[1]

Just slightly smaller than the state of Delaware, Trinidad, the most southerly island in the West Indies, capitalized on its strategic placement seven miles off the coast of Venezuela to become an increasingly well-known transshipment hub for illegal drugs and guns. The rise in drug-related crimes surfaced in the police dogs' files. A turning point came for the canine police when drug-detection dogs arrived in the 1970s to meet the growing illegal drug problem in the country. The need for drug-detection dogs usurped the need for single-purpose tracker dogs to catch suspects gambling or fleeing from crimes. Drug dealers always seemed to be one step ahead of the police. Sound tips and frequent searches often failed to turn up

Chapter 12. Shep

narcotics where police knew they were being hidden.² But that was about to change.

Dog #79, Shep, described by the late Leonard Dyer as "a black-and-gold massive German Shepherd and marijuana expert,"³ had been purchased by Matthews in the UK on January 18, 1974, and shipped to Trinidad as the Dog Section's first official narcotics-detection dog.⁴

At 18 months old, Shep joined the Depot Kennels to train with PC Marcellus Grant. Shep's bulging police file is filled with drug busts—all marijuana.

On August 17, 1974, Shep began a search at a home in the coastal village of Mayaro. When Grant took him to a garage, Shep ran up to a stack of wood and started scratching and barking. The police removed the wood and discovered a parcel containing marijuana. Grant's elation shows in Shep's official police file.

> Being a young dog in this field and also his first experience in searching premises, I am of the opinion that the dog did a remarkable job. Although he is still in the process of being trained in the field, I am happy with the way my dog carried on the search. Had it not been for the dog we might have never looked in the area of removing the stack of wood to search.⁵

The following year, Shep made history again with a find so significant that two of Grant's senior officers registered handwritten notes on the back of the officer's handwritten report and two additional high-ranking officers wrote letters noting the dog's work.

> On April 23, 1975 a party of policemen from the Narcotics Squad and myself with Shep executed a search warrant at the premises of Dole Chadee, Pascall Road, Piparo. During the search, I saw Dole Chadee surprisingly make a dash to some bushes to the back of the house with something in his hand and disappeared. I took the dog in the bushes and we made a search. The dog found a plastic container and, on opening it, found ten pounds of cured marijuana. The dog worked exceedingly well and there is no doubt as to his ability in this field.⁶

Chadee and two relatives were arrested for possession of marijuana. The Dog Section had recorded its first arrest of Chadee, who would become one of Trinidad and Tobago's most notorious drug dealers in the 1980s. Sgt. Matthews penned his praise first on the back of

Police Dogs of Trinidad and Tobago

Shep's report and sent it to Thomas, now an assistant superintendent of police (ASP): "Sir, Forwarded please for your information. I associate myself fully with the comments made by Shep's handler, in that this dog always shows a keen interest in searching for drugs while on practices. I believe that [with] frequent uses of the dog on such searches by the Narcotic Squad and other outstations, this dog can be an asset to the service."[7] Thomas sent his comments on Shep in a report to Superintendent Yearwood of the Mounted Branch.[8] Yearwood replied, "I have started a record of the work of this dog and handler for references as may be required. This is a good piece of work about which I have already congratulated the handler with encouragement to continue in that trend."[9]

Shep found marijuana hidden under a sheet of galvanized iron in a backyard; in bushes and in an old shed. He foiled attempts to hide marijuana in clay blocks. He discovered marijuana at the back of a house on a cocoa plantation in the remote eastern village of Biche. He trekked through the mud in Biche and sniffed out marijuana hidden in a fallen fig tree.[10]

On March 19, 1977, Grant and Shep left the Depot Kennels at 5:25 a.m. for inquiries with the Narcotics Squad. They arrived and searched the home of a suspect in San Juan, a town east of the capital where industry continued to grow around the family-owned, Solo beverage company founded by Joseph Charles (born Serjad Makmadeen) in 1949. The police exercise proved another milestone for Shep.

> Shep was taken off the leash and he began to sniff about the yard in a workable manner until he reached near a fig tree in that yard. There he began to scratch at a recently dug hole and took out about 2 pounds of cured marijuana hidden there. This was the first time Shep had found marijuana buried and much praise must go to him for such a satisfactory piece of work.[11]

Shep's file does not record the dog finding any drug other than marijuana.

The last entry in his file shows that Shep was euthanized on April 1, 1980.[12] In the 70s. Shep had ushered in the era of the drug-detection dogs, but the canine police had a new challenge now: the Black Power movement.

Chapter 13

Black Power, Daemon and Rex

The Caribbean islands shared many concerns about racial inequality voiced up north in Canada and the U.S. by Civil Rights leaders—including Trinidad-born Stokely Carmichael (Kwame Ture). Prime Minister Eric Williams banned Carmichael from visiting Trinidad,[1] but it couldn't stanch the flow of the Black Power movement to the country. By 1968, the Black Power movement from up north had hit Trinidad and Tobago, creating a wave of attacks from the National United Freedom Fighters (NUFF) and spirited protests from university students, trade unionists, and the newly formed black conscious political party National Joint Action Committee (NJAC) with Geddes Granger, now Makandal Daaga, as its leader. Daaga had taken his name from one of the Africans involved in the St. Joseph, Trinidad, mutiny against the British in 1837.[2]

The socioeconomic remnants of colonialism still prevailed in Trinidad and Tobago, seven years after Williams (then the country's premier) had delivered his "Massa [Master's] Day Done" speech on March 22, 1961, at the "University of Woodford Square," a park in central Port of Spain across from the Red House, where Parliament convened. Working people gathered there regularly to hear politicians and trade unionists speak, and Williams, with his trademark cigarette tucked in the corner of his mouth, and balisier-embroidered tie around his neck, could work up a crowd in those pre-independence days.[3]

Now Williams couldn't contain the outrage that poured onto Trinidad's streets. People saw him as the problem—not the solution. Political independence did not address prejudice in the workplace and Williams, once the nation's trusted leader, faced growing rage. Many jobs—most visibly in banks—appeared color-coded, with non-white Trinidadians finding it difficult, if not impossible, to advance. Future Nobel laureate in literature V.S. Naipaul exposed that prejudice in "The Baker's Story,"[4] a humorous fictional account of a black bakery owner who saves his failing business only when he puts the expected Chinese employee at the front counter.

Traditional Trinidadian humor uses *picong* (satire) in speech and double entendre in calypso as a form of rebellion that masks anger and resentment. But prejudice had become intolerable.

Raffique Shah, a former army officer and a leader of the Trinidad and Tobago regiment's 1970 mutiny, said,

> April 21, 1970 proved to be one of the most extraordinary days in the history of this country. It was not as if the close-to-calamitous events that would shake the foundations of the new democratic state were wholly unexpected. Following almost two months of daily meetings and mass demonstrations staged by disparate groups that came together under the banner of the National Joint Action Committee (NJAC), Prime Minister Dr Eric Williams had advised the Governor General Sir Solomon Hochoy to declare a State of Emergency.[5]

The mutiny happened to coincide with the Black Power Movement, though its causes were internal and had to do with leadership. In any case, Williams had much to deal with.

As Shah said,

> Before the Seventies turned into the Eighties, Trinidad and Tobago experienced a mutiny in the army, guerrilla warfare in the hills, unprecedented labor unrest. The [NUFF] movement didn't have a chance. By the time the dust settled, everyone knew the names of National United Freedom Fighters (NUFF) leaders Guy Harewood, Brian Jeffers, John Beddoe, Rudy John and Beverly Jones, killed in a battle in Caura at seventeen.[6]

Like all social and political revolutions, NUFF had supporters and enemies. To many, the young, socially conscious Marxist protesters were heroes fighting to rid the country of the racist remnants of colonialism. Politicians deemed them guerrillas. The police clashed with them in the forests.

By the end of 1971, police dogs tracked members of NUFF,

Chapter 13. Black Power, Daemon and Rex

emboldened enough to raid the Texaco Estate Police Station in South Trinidad. In the 1960s, the canine police had unknowingly prepared for tracking them in the forest. Khan, Lewis and Matthews, often bored with long shift work, challenged their dogs and each other by laying tracking for their dogs to follow. The dogs practiced on canine police officers by following their scent. The officers practiced item searches too, with wallets, clothes, and hats. In the 60s, rural crime suspects often fled to the forest; now the canine police searched for NUFF members there.[7]

"Canine police played an important [but] almost invisible role in tracking guerrillas," said Khan.[8]

Trinidad and Tobago used police dogs quite differently during the Black Power Movement.

"I can't ever recall police dogs being used here for crowd control," said Shah.[9] Snapshots of protests in the U.S. show snarling dogs attacking protesters, while police dogs in Trinidad and Tobago were rarely seen or heard about—except for a high-profile case in St. Vincent. Mainly, the police Dog Section searched for members of NUFF.

In 1972, armed members of the movement attacked an estate police outpost, robbing the deep-south Forest Reserve of arms and ammunition. They robbed banks and engaged police and the army in scuffles in the forests.[10] Work during the Black Power Movement ranked among some of the most dangerous assignments that canine officers and police dogs ever faced. Khan recalled, "Once we were in the forest looking for members of NUFF, and I told the Texaco guy with us, 'Put your dog on a lead.' He didn't do that. The dog ran through the swamp. We saw the dog come back. A mapepire [poisonous snake] came in the dog's path and bit him. The dog went straight up in the air and that was it. He lost his dog."[11]

Behind the scenes, Thomas wrote numerous letters to kennels in the U.S., UK, and Germany.[12] The Dog Section, stretched to the limits with its routine police work, needed even more dogs to deal with the Black Power Movement. Thomas filed a formal letter from the section's superintendent to the Deputy Commissioner of Operations to the new Minister of National Security, Overand Padmore, which documented the dilapidated state of his section.[13] Both the Mounted and Dog sections faced serious understaffing: the Mounted Branch fell short of one assistant superintendent, one sergeant, three corporals, and sixteen constables, while the Dog Section fell short of one corporal and six constables. Yearwood's letter read:

> These shortages are according to the sanctioned strength, and this shortage of staff is keenly felt; functioning as we do under a shift system. Parts of the stable buildings and kennels need painting and repairs mounted because of the constant use of water to clean stables and kennels. Bad conditions worsened because the Works Department did not respond to requests.[14]

Once again Thomas pleaded for a dormitory for dog handlers and mounted men quartered at the Police Training College. The branch headquarters had no wireless sets. Yearwood asked for floodlighting and fencing. Constant problems with transport thwarted the Dog Section's efforts. Both sections shared one jitney and a truck. Officers in the Dog Section complained that the Mounted Section took precedence over them, but mounted officers struggled with a shortage of supplies, including saddlery and horses. Superintendent Yearwood pointed out that Thomas, now an inspector, had written the Commissioner of Police two years ago, in 1971, of the pressing need to have the kennels re-sited. The letter said, "The original kennels were designed to accommodate four dogs and handlers when the section was formed in 1952. Since then the strength has been greatly increased but the area in use is not conducive for the effecting of commensurate extensions required."[15]

On August 9, 1973, seven handlers with young dogs qualified for active duty. Two decades into the development of the Dog Section, the division had now registered its 70th dog. Thomas listed the new handlers and their dogs:

1. Constable Kunu with Dog #62 Carlos
2. Constable Joseph with Dog #64 Andy
3. Constable John with Dog #66 Devil
4. Constable Forbes with Dog #68 Dipper
5. Constable Dsarath with Dog #67 Danny
6. Constable Singh with Dog #69 Duchess
7. Constable Daniel with Dog #70 Duke[16]

Chapter 13. Black Power, Daemon and Rex

On Monday, September 24, 1973, police #6161 Sgt. Matthews left on a British Overseas Airways Corporation (BOAC) flight for the United Kingdom for a training course with the Metropolitan Police in advanced methods of police-dog training, with special emphasis on training dogs for narcotics and explosives work. Matthews had been entrusted with bringing back working dogs as well.[17]

The 70s would be the defining era for Khairool Khan.

Daemon and Rex

The two dogs could not have been more different. Rex, the little black-and-tan German Shepherd, rarely seen in public, was a stark contrast to Daemon, a large, imposing German Shepherd,[18] who got nationwide attention. Both dogs worked with Khan, who was transferred to the Dog Section on July 20, 1970. Rex and Khan passed out of canine training together.

"No dog handler wanted to go near Rex. His aggression made everyone fear him. Rex only weighed 60 to 65 pounds. I bought him eggs, meat, and pasta, but he wouldn't put on size." Rex, considered "small and unattractive," remained in his kennel for events like police displays, where Khan always played the bad guy, with a padded sleeve for dogs to bite.[19] But Khan and Rex's first post at the Mon Repos station earned the pair respect when they teamed up with station police for raids and some of the most exhilarating tracking exercises recorded in canine-unit history. "Rough terrain suited Rex," said Khan.[20]

No one but Khan remembers Rex, but Daemon became an unforgettable dog that evoked smiles, excitement, and tears from Matthews and Khan. Daemon, Dog #51, looked the part of a champion police dog. Born on December 13, 1967, donated to the Dog Section when he was fourteen months old, Daemon was an "attractive, large, compact, well-built, very aggressive dog. He responded to hand signals—not just verbal commands," said Khan.[21]

Inspector Thomas wrote Daemon's first report to the superintendent.

Police Dogs of Trinidad and Tobago

I have to report for your information that on the evening of the 5 Feb 1969 one Mr. Richard Wallace, an Englishman, of Santa Flora, brought to the Depot Kennel his fourteen-month-old Alsatian dog of sable color and answers to the name of "Daemon" stating that he has to leave the Territory shortly and want the Police Dog Section to have the dog as a gift.

He further stated that if for any reason the dog cannot be used for Police work, he prefers that the dog be gently put to sleep than be sent off to a home where he might not be properly cared for because of the dog's aggressive tendencies to strangers. From appearance and attitude, the dog seems to be the suitable type.

I have not yet put him to a test, but it is my opinion that he can be trained to be useful to the Police Service. In view of this Sir, I herewith submit the dog's pedigree and inoculation certification and respectfully ask that approval be obtained for his acceptance Please. Veterinary report attached. This dog is already accustomed to the name of Daemon. And I suggest that he is enlisted as such. With the Number 51.[22]

The Canine Section paired Daemon with PC Septimus Paul, who had been transferred to the Dog Section on April 1, 1968. "Daemon was devoted to Paul, and he didn't want anyone else to touch him," said Khan.[23] Paul filed a report about an incident on June 10, when he left the St. Joseph police station for a routine patrol on St. Joseph Hill and Mt. Lambert. At 1:30 a.m., they encountered a suspicious character coming out of a vacant house and walking toward the police.

Paul wrote:

He was dressed in black wearing a cap on his head and had a handbag in his hands. The man then saw us and realising we were policemen turned and ran back into the yard. We gave chase calling on him to stop, but he continued running into the bushes at the back of the house. I then released the dog with the command to "get him." The dog responded promptly to my command and gave chase after the man, who ran out of the bushes with the dog behind him. The dog then detained the man by circling him and he took out a piece of iron from the bag he was carrying and began swinging it wildly at the dog in an attempt to hit it and was bitten on his right hand and buttocks.[24]

In the bag, police found a bunch of keys, a box of matches, a pair of socks and a white shirt in addition to the piece of iron. When they asked about the items, the suspect said, "I was only walking with them for so [sic]." The 26-year-old man was charged with being in possession of housebreaking implements at night and convicted.

Chapter 13. Black Power, Daemon and Rex

Daemon's work became more dangerous. On September 27, 1969, Paul answered a call from the Cunupia police station in central Trinidad at 3 a.m. and headed for Las Lomas, a small, agricultural village near the Piarco airport. Paul's report said:

> At Las Lomas, a paymaster and his son were accosted by two men, one armed with a shotgun. The paymaster was gun butted and his son was shot in the legs. The paymaster later died at the hospital. They were robbed of about $600 in cash. The dog was given a sniff of the bushes through which the men ran and immediately picked up a trail. He tracked through cocoa, forest, river and canefields until we reached a garden. He acted very excited, running to and fro. Daemon continued the track to about a quarter-mile from the victim's home, where it was lost due to a heavy downpour. The suspect was later arrested at his house, identified in an ID parade, and charged with murder. The case was set for a hearing on November 12, 1969.[25]

Paul noted in Daemon's files that his dog particularly seemed to enjoy tracking in the dark of night. He also possessed keen awareness, spotting fleeing suspects that the police didn't see. Thomas's reports show that Daemon routinely made the Police Commissioner's official reports, entrusted in confidence to members of the Police Service and not for publication in the press.[26] In June 1972, Khan, based at Mon Repos Police station in the region of San Fernando, was relaxing at home for the weekend when he and Paul were called out to work with the San Fernando CID. Khan said:

> Someone with a bag tried to distract the police. He fired some shots. We arrived and began to search. The police started to shoot wildly, the suspect got shot in the knee, and a bullet grazed his forehead. He fell by someone's house. The suspect had a sawed-off shotgun and his cartridges between his fingers. He was lying quietly and pretending to be dead. As soon as the police officer stood over him, I heard, "Click, click," but the gun didn't go off. Rex and Daemon led the police to a NUFF camp. I surveyed the situation.
> I said, "Make sure the men have the four corners around the camp covered." The guerrillas started to shoot from on top of the hill. I dived inside a picka [thorny] patch and held my dog because he had been trained to attack when he heard gunshots. The guerrillas dispersed when they heard shots and met somewhere about a mile from the camp.[27]

Paul filed an official report on June 6, 1972.

Police Dogs of Trinidad and Tobago

Sir, I have to report for your information that on Monday 5th June 1972 PC Khan and I with our dogs Rex and Daemon respectively, were members of a search party, which was combing the Fyzabad Forest for the men who were wanted in connection with the robbery of arms and ammunition from the Fyzabad Estate Police Station.

We were shown the area where the men were first seen. I gave Daemon a sniff of the area and he eventually picked up a trail which I began tracking. PC Khan followed closely behind with dog Rex and a party of policemen tracked up the dirt trace through a pitch track. They headed into the thick forest. Here and there heavy army-type boot prints could be seen in the ground.

Tracking about two miles at a brisk trot, I realised that the dog was tiring. I then called Khan with his dog Rex to see if he could continue the track. Rex immediately picked up the trail and we continued on the track behind Rex. At this time there were eight men besides the dog handlers.

After tracking for a further mile or so through the thick forest, Rex brought us to an area where we found diary pages from the Fyzabad Estate Police scattered on the ground and just beyond this we came to a camp, apparently used to hide out. We searched it and found several items including some ammunition, subversive literature and the Estate Police Station Diary. The robbers then ambushed us and by opening gunfire on us we returned fire but no one was injured. On the following day the search was continued and one man was arrested.

The success of the search is a tribute to both dogs, and their tracking ability when it is considered that the sun was very hot and the thick forest and the terrain very difficult to negotiate. Also, both dogs working jointly together successfully is very commendable since this is rarely seen in the police service. The finding of the hut played an important point in the decision to continue the search, which resulted in a man being arrested the following day. Sir, these two dogs should be highly commended for the part they played in the exercise.[28]

In 1973, Rex developed a slight ear problem after a forest track. "He always scratched his ears," said Khan. "In those days the vets were kind of afraid of the dogs. They didn't take any chances. The vet gave Rex an anesthetic as a precautionary method to treat his ears, and he gave Rex too much. I was holding Rex. He died in my arms at the Mon Repos police station."[29]

In 1973, Paul traveled to the U.S. and never returned to Trinidad. "Paul had been the only one in his family left in Trinidad," said Khan. As luck would have it, Khan and Daemon paired up. They had

Chapter 13. Black Power, Daemon and Rex

hardly had time to start working together when an exciting assignment came their way. On May 16, 1973, Daemon's file shows a temporary transfer from the Southern Division to the island of St. Vincent. It would be the Dog Section's most baffling case.

Chapter 14

Murder in St. Vincent

Cpl. Khairool Khan had worked with Daemon for less than two months before Winston Matthews, now the sergeant in the Dog Section, got a call about a murder investigation in St. Vincent. Matthews chose Khan and Daemon, along with PC George Douglas and his dog Viking, for the assignment. He accompanied the canine officers to supervise them.[1] Khan had no passport and had to procure a temporary one to travel. The officers and dogs flew on a Liat propeller plane, and the dogs traveled in portable kennels. Their orders were to track down the persons who had assassinated St. Vincent's acting attorney general.[2] "We heard the attorney general in St. Vincent was a friend of Trinidad and Tobago's Attorney General, Karl Hudson-Phillips," said Matthews. (Hudson-Phillips said they weren't friends, but he did know of the incident and had offered Trinidad and Tobago's assistance—including the use of police dogs—to solve the case when the government of St. Vincent and the Grenadines approached him.)[3]

Matthews and Khan learned that 50-year-old Cecil Eric Rawle, a magistrate, and acting attorney general, had been assassinated on May 11, 1973. Rawle identified Patrick Junior "Spirit" Cottle and Lorraine "Blackie" Laidlow as suspects on his deathbed. The *Dominica Star* reported the details in its May 18 edition.

> Shot down by assassins at 7.30 last Friday night, Hon Cecil Eric Rawle, son of the pioneer federalist (CA Rawle) and acting AG of St. Vincent, died soon afterward in [the] hospital. He named one of his attackers while dying, and an exhaustive manhunt was set in motion. Mr. Rawle was buried with state honours; notables of the region flew in to attend. This outrage has horrified the public throughout the islands.

The propeller plane carrying the canine officers and dogs landed on a road that doubled as the airport's runway and checked into

Chapter 14. Murder in St. Vincent

the Heron Hotel at Bridgehouse in Kingstown. Daemon and Viking stayed in the police headquarters' jail cells. The officers and dogs began to work. Daemon settled in with no problems, but the canine officers felt uneasy.[4] "We drove through mountainous areas to get one of the criminals' clothing," said Matthews.

(The dogs had been trained to track suspects by sniffing some belonging like clothes or a wallet.)

"The senior St. Vincent police officer did not appear happy with our presence. We had trouble getting information from the police, so we began to lime [hang] around and get information. People were very willing to talk." Khan agreed with Matthews. Meanwhile, Daemon kept finding one of the suspects' trails.

Matthews recalled:

> One time, Daemon picked up a track leading to a cave, but the entrance came from the sea, and we were on a height. We couldn't get there. I wanted a launch [a motorboat]. The police wanted to give me a pirogue. I said, "No way." I put the St. Vincent police to watch in case the suspect came out of the cave—and they let the suspect run past them. Clearly, the senior police didn't want these guys caught. Every time Daemon found a trail, and the police could have caught him, they didn't act on it.[5]

"This looked like a political thing," said Khan. Both officers suspected the police were somehow involved with the murderers. Matthews said he asked and eventually begged for the team to return home, but orders came from Trinidad for them to stay. Then came a tip, on May 22, 1973.[6] Matthews remembered:

> Inspector Bascombe of the St. Vincent police said he got information that Spirit, the main suspect, was hiding in Bottom Town—a shanty-town in Kingstown. The police had identified two shacks, and we went to search. Douglas went inside one house with Viking. I sent the dog inside to search that house. I went to assist Douglas because I was the more experienced man. I left Khan, Daemon, and the inspector outside of the other house. The St. Vincent inspector disappeared from in front of the house.[7] I was then about to enter the first house and Daemon was off-leash. As my foot hit the step of the house, I heard a commotion inside the next house and then a "rat-a-tat-tat"—about seven shots from an automatic gun. I saw Inspector Bascombe coming from the house. I didn't see Daemon. I said to myself, "Don't tell me that dog is dead." The inspector had walked

around to the back and entered the shack. I ran back to Khan in the front when I heard him yelling at Bascombe.[8]

Khan recalled:

Bascombe said he saw a shadow, thought he saw Spirit, and shot the dog by mistake. I said, "When you shoot a man, you aim at his chest—not down to the level of a dog." Then he changed his story and said he thought the dog was going to attack him.

I yelled, "The dog wasn't tracking you."

I broke down and cried. I was so mad at the time, I had my hand on my firearm.[9]

"I restrained Khan. He had his gun, and I was afraid of what he might do," said Matthews. Then all attention turned to Daemon, who lay dead in the house. "We called Trinidad, got someone to dig a hole, and buried Daemon at Arnos Vale Airport, in an area that hadn't been used regularly, at the end of the runway, near the sea. We all cried at the burial," said Matthews. They cried through their interviews, too. "I thought about that dog all the way back to Trinidad," said Khan.

When they returned home from St. Vincent, Matthews and Khan both submitted reports to Acting Superintendent Thomas.[10] Only Thomas's report, submitted to the acting commissioner of police, was in Daemon's file:

The attached reports of No. 6161 Sgt Matthews and No. 7073 Const Khan are herewith forwarded for your information, please. From the facts contained in the report, it is my opinion that the inspector's action was senseless and without initiative as expected of a senior Police officer. If as he claimed, he saw movements in the room, the best he could have done was to challenge who or whatever it was, before using his rifle. This in itself was a show of nervousness and lack of confidence in himself.

It is further my opinion that he should not have ignored Sgt Matthews' direction that the dogs be left outside of the building to give chase if the culprits attempted to flee through a back door or window. This is the method adopted on such searches. Normally the dogs are only used inside buildings if the search is for exhibits.

The loss of Dog Daemon is gravely felt in the Dog Section, he being one of our very good working dogs. Replacing him will be difficult, particularly at this time when we are experiencing great difficulty to acquire suitable Dogs.[11]

Chapter 14. Murder in St. Vincent

News of Daemon's death spread from St. Vincent to Trinidad and Tobago. The following year, Vincentian calypsonian Quentyn Toby, the Mighty Toiler, became calypso monarch and road march king of St. Vincent with "The Puppy," about Daemon's demise.

"That St. Vincent exercise turned out to be quite costly. Daemon and Brutus, handled by Hendren Brown, were the two best dogs we had at the time," said Khan. Few of Brutus's exercises are recorded. His official card from the Caribbean Kennel Club lists his father as Benno and his mother as Esta, the dog whose name was changed to Sheba. It said Brutus, born on February 27, 1966, and raised in the police kennels, was jet-black, like his grandfather, Jett.

Brutus and Brown tracked down fleeing gamblers, accompanied police in issuing search warrants and joined stakeouts to catch suspects fleeing from their homes. On January 15, 1974, Brutus and Brown left the Arouca police station and walked to Golden Grove Prison to guard voting machines.[12] Khan claimed, "Somebody passed with his car and bounced the dog. The dog was in plenty of pain and bit Brown innocently as Brown tried to calm him down. He died in Brown's arms at the side of the road. That incident caused the dogs to stop guarding the voting machines for good."[13]

Khan got a Labrador, Toby, the first trained explosives-detection dog in Trinidad and Tobago, acquired after the terrorist bombing of a Cuban flight from Barbados to Jamaica on October 6, 1976. All 73 passengers on the Douglas DC-8 aircraft died in the explosion.[14] "We'd go to a grocery store and hide something for Toby to find. He performed bomb duties in the airport and visited schools from 1981 to 1988. I always left the dog on a high," Khan said.

Khan became a police dog trainer. He always remembered the exercise in St. Vincent that cost Daemon his life.

The St. Vincent courts convicted Cottle and Laidlow for the murder of Cecil Rawle. Unknowingly, the canine officers had become entangled in St. Vincent's Black Power struggle.

"They [Cottle and Laidlow] were members of a radical political organization which was branded as a 'Black-Power Rasta' type," Dr. Kenneth John wrote in a newspaper column a decade after the murder.[15]

Police Dogs of Trinidad and Tobago

In that celebrated case, the cards were heavily stacked against the accused. The Prosecution had in its armory a dying declaration; in which the deceased had identified his assassins, which was probably enough to swing the case the Crown's way. The courts placed Cottle [22 at the time of the assassination] and Laidlow on death row for the attorney general's murder, but Her Majesty's Privy Council subsequently quashed that decision on a legal technicality.[16]

Cottle and Laidlow had committed a robbery on the same day they killed the acting AG. Somehow the prosecutors had made the mistake of bundling the murder charges with the robbery charge, which was illegal. The Privy Council ruling (Appendix C) explains the technicality that freed the two assassins. Junior "Spirit" Cottle confirmed the newspaper reports of the assassination.[17]

Rawle was gunned down at his home in Fort Charlotte. We were all armed when we went to the house. We knocked on the door. When Rawle saw us, he screamed. In the process, he was assassinated. He got shot seven times. It's true. Rawle did give a dying declaration, and he identified me and two others. He did see my face, and he knew me. He was familiar with the Black Power Movement we were involved in.[18]

Cottle denied that he and his accomplices had police support when they hid from police after the assassination.

We were always in conflict with the police. I was before Rawle in court several times and the last time he prosecuted me before the assassination, he had sent me away for six months. So he knew me.

We were very critical towards the judiciary, and the role Rawle was playing. No police officer in those days was on our side. The police were afraid of us and wanted us dead. Saying we got help from the police is a joke—a blatant lie.

There was also a rumor that the opposition paid me to kill the attorney general. The opposition had nothing to do with it. Rawle's death came strictly out of the Black Power Movement.

We were accusing all of the political parties of being traitors.[19]

Cottle believes any tips the canine officers got from the public were meant to steer the officers in the wrong direction.

The people were on our side. They supported the Black Power Movement, hid, and fed us. They just weren't as militant as us. We were young, adventurous, and revolutionary, and saw colonialism as our enemy. We came out of a community of crime and violence.

Chapter 14. Murder in St. Vincent

People coming from that background who become revolutionaries are more fearless and violent. The people who weren't from our community of poverty weren't willing to overthrow the government violently, as we wanted to do. The government passed us off as criminals. They didn't want the Trinidad police or anyone in St. Vincent to feel they weren't in control of the situation with the Black Power movement.[20]

Cottle claimed he never saw the police dogs sent to St. Vincent.

The same night the dog was shot, we were supposed to go to the mountains in the interior. We hid at the edge of town, I think in an abandoned attic in an old schoolyard at Bishop's College in Kingstown, less than half a mile away from where the dog was killed.

We had revolutionary literature—Fidel Castro, Che Guevera, Joshua Nkomo—guns and ammunition, camouflage clothes, and foodstuffs hidden in Bottom Town and were trying to get them around the time the dog was shot. The plan was to head for the mountains.

When we eventually got someone to get the bags out, the police intercepted the vehicle, confiscated everything, and kept it quiet. They passed it off as a theft and didn't want people to know these items were for the Black Power Movement.

Cottle said St. Vincent was buzzing with news of Daemon's death.

The rumor was that Bascombe thought it was me. I don't believe he purposely set out to kill the dog. I believe Bascombe panicked and shot the dog.

In those days, before the Black Power Movement, men were fighting police with bottles, stones, razors, and cutlasses, and now this was an era where young men were picking up guns. Bascombe was a very militarized police officer, but the police were not accustomed to what they were now facing.[21]

Cottle said there's no doubt in his mind that the Trinidad government knew it was sending canine police officers to deal with a Black Power matter.

No one in either government saw this as an ordinary criminal case. They had to see it as a political case. The Black Power movements were all connected in the Caribbean. We had communication with NUFF and NJAC. We all knew each other. The Trinidad government knew about us. There was a network of all the movements in the area. We had ties to [future president] Cheddi Jagan in Guyana. There was a revolutionary atmosphere everywhere.

Governments got more nervous when the Black Power Movement went into a Marxist/Leninist movement. That was something they could use to instill fear in people.[22]

When told Cottle's side of the story, Khan said, "We never knew we were dealing with the Black Power Movement in St. Vincent. The civilians didn't say that. Matthews was the senior person, and he didn't know."[23] That well-guarded secret cost Daemon his life.

Chapter 15

Dyer Memories

In the 1980s, the Dog Section slipped into the doldrums. Money to buy dogs proved so scarce the canine police accepted donated Rottweilers. Protecting the President's and Prime Minister's residence became the Dog Section's main role from 1980 to 1987, and Rottweilers were as good as any other dog for that purpose.[1] Dog files held nothing more than the dogs' enlistment dates, veterinary reports, and the dogs' date of death. Canine officers wrote pithy paragraph-long reports about the dogs' exercises in station diaries.

Dyer experienced the transition from the exciting 70s to the quiet 80s. In a 1992 interview, when he pleaded for air-conditioned vehicles, Dyer reminisced about his first dog, Shane, acquired in 1976.[2]

> Shane, a very aggressive dog, had an aggressive handler before I got him. Cpl. Morris, another aggressive person, trained him. But Shane made me a real handler. He used to attack me; I forced him to stop. A dog like Shane will fight. He'll dominate. We couldn't let him out with other dogs because he would attack them; you couldn't stand in front of the kennel to let him out or he'd attack you.
>
> Shane was arrogant. When he came out of the kennel, he'd have to throw his tail and rub against me—just to show that he would have his say. He passed all the kennels to rile up all the dogs.[3]

Dyer gazed off into the distance.

> Maybe Shane wasn't so bad. I'd like to think he started off with the wrong handler. Well, I couldn't let him out of my sight on exercises. If he attacked, he didn't want to stop. I knew if I left him alone with a bandit for five minutes, the bandit would be dead.
>
> But I overly loved him. Once we formed a union, he became a loving, loyal dog to me. If I went upstairs to sleep, he'd be with me. The other officers would say, "Don't go up there, Shane's there."

Police Dogs of Trinidad and Tobago

> We really couldn't send him out much, but I took him on patrols. One day we were on patrol in Freeport, and we got a message about a guy delivering drugs who ran from the police. Shane wasn't a drug dog, but when he saw the man running, he knew what to do. Shane took off. I called for him to stop. He didn't stop. Shane took down the man. Eventually, I got Shane to listen, but no one could ever come up to him but me.[4]

Dyer wondered what would happen to Shane when he went on vacation.

> The day I returned to work, I called Shane's name on the way to his kennel and didn't hear a sound. I saw him lying in his kennel beating his tail against the ground. His foot was swollen. We rushed him to the vet. He had been stung by something in the night, and died in the vet's office in 1979.
>
> Then, from 1979 to 1986, I had Lady, an 18-month-old German Shepherd from England—a real lady: easy to manage, well trained in obedience and aggression. I considered her to be my masterpiece. Lady did guard work. She never did nose work.
>
> All the dogs were pooled and located in Caroni. Lady was trained to attack, but who would she attack? [Dominican Prime Minister] Eugenia Charles?[5]

When Dyer became a trainer, he handed Lady over to Donna Mae Tom, one of the first two women officers in the canine section.[6]

The 80s had its action-packed moments with controversial, publicity-hungry Commissioner of Police Randolph Burroughs, and his Flying Squad, a much-feared covert operations unit. On February 25, 1982, canine officer PC Samuel filed a report about himself and Rover accompanying the Flying Squad on a mission to free a six-year-old boy reportedly held by kidnappers in a house in Gasparee, an island less than .50 square mile in size located 7½ miles west of Port of Spain in the "Dragon's Mouth" between Trinidad and Venezuela. Samuel, Rover, Burroughs, and the Flying Squad stormed Gasparee from a pirogue.

"On arrival, we encircled a house on the island but unfortunately, the kidnappers were not there. We then returned to small boats on one of the police launches. On this exercise, dog Rover did not go into action, but he was alert and comfortable at all times, especially on his voyage at Sea," Samuel wrote.[7] Rover died suddenly on September 21, 1984.[8]

Chapter 15. Dyer Memories

Cpl. Clayton Chandler did tracking exercises with Wesley from 1980 to 1984. "In 1986 I had a dog named Ike, who was one of the early dogs trained to find narcotics," said Chandler.[9] Suddenly, everything changed.

"In 1987," said Dyer, "drugs on airplanes became a serious problem, and the US threatened to seize our planes. Ironically, the drug problem became the police dogs' salvation. That year, we took dogs back from guard work and reintroduced narcotic dogs. ... Lady went to the airport as a deterrent, but she never found anything."

In 1988, the U.S. government sent Dyer and PC Peter George on a narcotics detection course in West Yorkshire, England to learn more about marijuana and cocaine detection. Dyer returned with Sam, and George got an English Springer Spaniel named Whiskey.[10] "Sam became the first dog to find drugs in the airport on a British West Indies Airways [BWIA] flight bound for Canada. I couldn't believe it when Sam started scratching on a suitcase. There were three suitcases filled with marijuana wrapped in sheets. No masking agent. Two Canadian men were arrested and convicted," said Dyer.[11]

Sam's find became legendary. "One day I went to St. Helena for doubles [a popular street food made with curried chickpeas, tamarind and cucumber sauce between two pieces of a soft bread resembling pancakes]. The doubles vendor described Sam's find to people standing around him eating. The man dramatized the story. He said, 'I heard the dog dragged the suitcase all over the airport.'"[12]

In 1989, Bonnie arrived and became a star narcotics detection dog. Her handler, Mahabir, migrated to Canada in 1993; Dyer retired, battled blindness, and died before his dream of air-conditioned vehicles to transport the dogs came to pass.[13] He never knew how his interview in 1992 had piqued my curiosity about the police dogs' history.

With 300 pages of transcribed dog files to sift through, I took a two-year break to work on my library science certificate. Sometime in 2014, I phoned Helen Cox-Modeste, a new superintendent of the Mounted and Canine Branch, and said, "I'm ready to continue my work with the dogs' history." "I'm not interested in that," she said. Click.... The phone sounded like a heart monitor that had just flatlined.

CHAPTER 16

INSIDE THE CARONI KENNELS

THE WORKING DOGS IN THE CARONI kennels whirled in circles as they impatiently waited for their police partners who work a shift system of 24 hours on and 48 hours off work. Cpl. Premnath Maharaj paused by Maverick, a retired German Shepherd/Malinois mix with a long, graying face. Retired dogs often wait more than two years for the official government papers that allow them to go home with their handlers.

"That's a million-dollar dog,"[1] said Maharaj. Maverick, a lanky brown dog resembled the cartoon character Wile E. Coyote, but looks can be deceiving. "Dogs accrue value from their drug finds," said Maharaj. As a tactical dog, Maverick also tracked criminals before he retired.[2]

Maharaj led the way to a row of kennels from where a few police dogs have a view of the grass and the blinking lights of the pedestrian crossing by Vishnu Boys' Hindu College. The dogs hear the school bell ring in the morning and afternoon and the din of students' voices at lunch and recess. They take in a panoramic view of the Old Southern Main Road that meanders through Caroni.

When the sugarcane burns, everywhere smells like simmering brown sugar. It's strange that a place in central that smells so sweet was once called the wild, wild west, but many people had stories about badjohns (hooligans) and shootouts when I first came to Trinidad in 1984 and settled in this area.

April 2015 marked the month I returned to the Caroni kennels. It didn't seem possible after that phone call to Cox-Modeste. But one day, while visiting Prison Commissioner Sterling Stewart, my book

Chapter 16. Inside the Caroni Kennels

Retired tactical police dog Maverick (photograph by Miquel Galofré, March 16, 2016).

about the police dogs' history crossed my mind. I told him I'd like to get back to the project and asked, "Can you get me a hearing with the police commissioner?"

Stewart called acting Police Commissioner Stephen Williams and handed me the phone to plead my case. "I have no problem with that. Call Supt. Patsy Joseph of the Mounted and Canine Branch and tell her to contact me," said Williams. Joseph was excited about having the dogs' history written, and so I was back.

The officer who had helped me with the files was gone and now I relied on Maharaj. Sitting on his working dog Beny's wooden bed and doling out hearty pats on the back, Maharaj said, "Beny is a crazy dog. Very possessive."[3] He pointed to the scars on his arm where Beny had bitten him on several occasions. Beny, always eager to work, never wanted to return to the kennels. Maharaj slipped out of Beny's kennel and opened another creaking metal gate. Bouncy trotted out,

Police Dogs of Trinidad and Tobago

Cpl. Premnath Maharaj and explosives detection dog Beny at the Caroni kennels (photograph by Miquel Galofré, March 16, 2016).

stood before me and bounced up and down like one of those toys with springs. Taking care of a working dog is a full-time job, and Maharaj had two retired dogs to care for, Bouncy the straw-colored Labrador Retriever and Buddy, a Golden Retriever with a demanding bark.

I volunteered to help by coming every weekend to play with the retired dogs. One Sunday afternoon in August of 2017, I was at the kennels with Buddy and Bouncy when Maharaj returned from an exercise, opened the back door of the police vehicle, and unlatched the portable plastic kennel with Beny inside. Beny lunged and latched onto Maharaj's arm. Maharaj choked the dog, trying to wrench his arm free. This bite inflicted the deepest, longest wound yet. Maharaj secured Beny in his kennel and showed me his arm.[4]

"But I love Beny. If you see this dog work," said Maharaj. Beny panted. His glassy eyes turned yellow—like a wolf's.[5] No one understood Beny's problem, but Maharaj, who had joined the Canine Section with no real love for dogs, wouldn't give up on him.

Chapter 16. Inside the Caroni Kennels

On January 4, 1999, two years after joining the police service, Maharaj volunteered to work as a police officer in Tobago. When he couldn't get transferred back to Trinidad, he joined the Canine Section, thinking it would be his ticket home. Instead, he received orders to remain in Tobago and become a founding member of the Tobago Canine Police Section (see Chapter 25). Before that, officers from Trinidad rotated duties in Tobago. Maharaj teamed up with the narcotic dog Biest, a German Shepherd from the Czech Republic, to work the Tobago airport and the port.

"This was not the best time for the police dog handlers," said Maharaj. "Due to the depleted stock of dogs, they decided to mate my dog, Biest. She had four pups in her first litter and five puppies in a second litter that they planned to integrate into the service."[6] After Biest's second litter in 2005, Anthony Piegaro arrived from the U.S. to set up an explosive-detection unit in the Canine Section. Maharaj and Jason Donawa signed on as the first police officers in his training class. Donawa handled Charlie; Maharaj worked

PC Sherwin Cedeno and explosives detection dog Jed at the Caroni kennels (photograph by Miquel Galofré, March 16, 2016).

with Woody, the slobbery Labrador who worked the dustbin explosive case in St. James and Port of Spain[7] (see Chapter 19). But Woody developed arthritis in both shoulders and limped into retirement. He languished in the kennels for more than a year after he stopped working.

"Seeing me and not going out to work stressed out Woody. His hair dropped out. He withered away. On vacation, I received a call: 'Woody passed away in his kennel.' When I returned to work, I had Buddy, then Bouncy, and now Beny, said Maharaj." After Maharaj left for the hospital, I sat on the grass with Buddy and Bouncy. PC Sherwin Cedeno, with a gun strapped on his thigh, rolled on the ground with Jed, his English Springer Spaniel. Eddie returned from an exercise and scoped the scene for a dogfight. PC Saadiq Hosein reined him in. Cezar loped across the grass to investigate me as Cpl. Akil Bernard prepared for an exercise.

Soon, canine officers would recall an ambush, canine controversies, criminal apprehensions, drug busts, explosive-detection exercises, a jailbreak, and kidnappings.

Chapter 17

Jango and Strike

A FEW WEEKS BEFORE HIS RETIREMENT, PC Kenny Winn sat in the kitchen of the Caroni Canine Section and remembered becoming a canine police officer in 2003 and getting six-month-old Gino, one of Biest's puppies. "I expected a working dog, but they only had puppies available because the police service had no intention of bringing in working dogs at the time,"[1] said Winn.

The police canine section's state of flux only mirrored the country's political and economic state. Everything seemed up in the air around the time Winn arrived in the Canine Section. In 2001, although there had been a general election the previous year, Prime Minister Basdeo Panday asked President Arthur N.R. Robinson to dissolve the legislature for another election. The ruling United National Congress (UNC) had lost its slim majority in Parliament after four of the party's members defected. The election in December 2001 resulted in a tie between the UNC and the PNM. The President declared Patrick Manning of the PNM, the previous opposition leader, prime minister. But without a parliamentary majority, Manning could not even get a Speaker of the House of Representatives elected. So for almost a year, the country went without a sitting parliament, until Manning called another general election in October 2002, and this time secured a majority.[2]

A significant economic decision with historical implications happened the following year, when the state-owned sugar company Caroni (1975) Ltd. was shut down, after losing money for over 28 years.[3] Many workers forced out of jobs traced their ancestry to indentured sugar workers who were brought from India, between

1845 and 1917, to replace enslaved workers of African descent after slavery was abolished in the 1830s.

Slavery under Spanish colonialism from the 16th century, followed by British colonialism in 1797, and then indentureship, had created the country's racial mix, with 37.6 percent of East Indian descent, 36.3 percent of African descent, 24.4 percent identifying as mixed-race and less than 2 percent of the population of European, Chinese, Arab and "Amerindian" (First Peoples) descent.[4]

While the Canine Section struggled with a dwindling number of police dogs and tried to compensate by raising its own puppies, people became increasingly angry about crime in the country. On October 24, 2004, 10,000 people in Port of Spain participated in a "Death March" to protest the government's inability to control crime.[5]

The new millennium had begun with a 25.39 percent increase in serious crime. In 2004, there had been a 12.96 percent increase in crime over the year and there would be a 47.73 percent increase the following year in 2005.[6] Besides making a visible point of the population's concern and anger over crime, the Death March brought no overall change to the crime situation.

While the country coped with a state of flux, Winn placed his hope in Gino. He knew it would take about 1½ years to see whether his puppy would make the grade. Meanwhile, Winn scrubbed kennels and served as a sentry. Then an unforeseen opportunity came his way. In 2004, PC Ryan Bissessar relinquished his narcotic dog Jango, after deciding to leave the Canine Section to work with the new Special Anti-Crime Unit (SAUTT). Jango needed a new handler. Inspector Roban asked Winn if he could handle Jango, the Belgian Malinois bought in West Germany by canine police trainer Crawford Williams. Jango had a reputation for being one of the most aggressive dogs in the Canine Section.[7] Winn said,

> Jango was one of the best dogs we had. He was ferocious and crazy. Other officers had been offered Jango, but they refused because they knew he had bitten Bissessar and tore up his pants.
>
> I decided to win Jango over. Every morning, I went to his kennel with salt biscuits to bribe him.
>
> He allowed me to get inside the kennel and play with him. He was only about 26 inches from his chest to the ground—not a big fella, but the

Chapter 17. Jango and Strike

manner in which he walked; the way he put out his chest, he acted ten feet tall. Just the posture felt intimidating—and his eyes....[8]

After six weeks of bonding with Jango in Caroni, Winn headed to Chaguaramas to train with Lenford Blades. For the next three years, 2004–2007, Winn worked with Jango.

"At that time the canine operated with low esteem. There was no real belief in what the dogs could do. (Most of the dogs were getting too old to work.) We went out on a couple of tracks with no real success. We did a lot of patrols." Then, in 2004 the U.S.-based dog trainer Anthony Piegaro arrived, first with bomb-detection dogs; then the drug-detection dogs. Suddenly Chaguaramas bustled with excitement.[9] Winn remembered,

> The police built kennels. Canine went into first gear to revitalize, with an unbelievable transformation.
>
> I still had Jango, and when I worked as the sentry in Caroni taking down information from Chaguaramas, I could see a total turnaround taking place.
>
> Before Piegaro, I would say we had about seven good dogs with a success rate of five per cent. Now, every time dogs went out, they succeeded.
>
> The first two officers trained by Piegaro were Maharaj and (Jason) Donawa—the bomb men. Then came John Phillips, Rawle Ryan, Neil Perez, and Reynold Bahadoor. They were the elite.
>
> I wanted to be a part of that, to make Trinidad and Tobago a better place.
>
> Sitting in my gallery, sipping an alcoholic drink, licking my wounds, knowing they were on the third set of trainees, I prayed to train with Piegaro, but no one called me. It was 2007 and I thought, why is everyone getting a chance but me? About 10:30 a.m. one day, Inspector Roban called and said, "You're on the training team. Try to reach down to Chaguaramas by midday."[10]

Winn rushed to Chaguaramas, knowing he had to give up Jango.

> That first day of training felt like a spiritual, magical time. Our team had about sixteen of us who were supposed to do training with this white man.
>
> I had to run in circles around the men because I missed the morning session, through no fault of mine. I was over thirty-five years old and training with younger officers, but I wanted this so much. On the last day, only three of the original sixteen men in training were left.[11]

Police Dogs of Trinidad and Tobago

Winn survived training, and Piegaro paired him with Strike, a large, aggressive, strong-minded Belgian Malinois tactical and narcotics dog. "You couldn't watch him in his eyes. He wanted to growl at me. That is my luck. I get all the aggressive dogs."[12] Training with Strike began and the two teamed up from 2007 to 2012.

> I can't remember the date, but one night, just after 8 p.m., we were in Chaguaramas, and I listened on the wireless that an alleged murder suspect escaped from the Arouca police station when the police let the suspect bathe. Reports came in that the suspect escaped to some house in Trincity.
>
> I got a call to investigate. PC Enoch Romeo, Maverick, Strike, and I are going down there with sirens blazing. Maverick is with Romeo. He's too big to fit in any kennel, so he sits in the back seat with his paw on Romeo's shoulder, and if you see how excited Maverick gets on when he spots another police car.
>
> The search began. Strike meandered his way through the compound littered with about fifty old cars. About fifteen minutes later, Strike went to a vehicle and pushed his nose inside.
>
> I saw an old sugar bag on the back seat. An officer opened the vehicle, raised the sugar bag, and found the man right there in a vehicle in the police compound waiting for things to calm down.
>
> I gave Strike plenty love.[13]

On another day, Winn and Strike were about to finish work at 7 a.m. when a call came in from the Organised Crime and Narcotics Bureau (OCNB) that a helicopter and boat had come ashore in Toco, on Trinidad's northeast corner. The helicopter had packages on board. A police search turned up nothing. Winn and Strike arrived and searched around the shore; then Winn decided to head into the interior.

> I observed a little track you could hardly see. We continued walking for about a quarter-mile, going over a river, and up a mountain. The dog indicated on a parcel with marijuana.
>
> I know now I'm in the vicinity. I'm not seeing anyone, and the dog has found about ten kilos of marijuana. The dog pulled to a vine-covered shed with books and 157 kilograms of drugs—a whole boatload of drugs piled up.
>
> Strike had his biggest find. Me and this dog were very close by this time.[14]

Chapter 17. Jango and Strike

Strike continued to have his grumpy days. Winn shrugged. "Everyone has his bad days."

One typical day in 2012, Winn and Strike went on a police exercise at Bamboo Settlement, found narcotics, and returned to the station.

> I had another exercise to go on later, and I felt sick, so I asked an officer if he could feed my dog. That's normal. Upstairs in the dorm, I felt weak. I dropped asleep and had these dreams or visions. Everything me and this dog went through—every find, every nice time—flashed back to me. I wanted to rest, because Strike and I had to go out at 3 a.m., but I kept waking up.
>
> About midnight, I walked downstairs to the charge room and went to the kitchen.
>
> I didn't want to check on the dog because he needed his rest. At 2:30 a.m., I got the vehicle started and went for Strike. I didn't see him or hear him.
>
> It hit me: "Kenny, something wrong, boy." I reached the kennel and saw saliva all over. That was the end of Strike. The necropsy said he had a twisted stomach and bloat.
>
> I found him on a Saturday morning. We wrapped him up and put him in the deep freeze in the kitchen.
>
> Strike was only six years old.
>
> My father died on September 30. My mother died on December 22 and then my dog died in March. I was in a mess.[15]

Winn didn't try to hide his tears when canine officers entered the kitchen. After a long, thoughtful pause he said, "I never regret coming into Canine. We're not perfect here. We have our ups and downs, but I'm glad I had the opportunity to be here. It might not mean a lot to people, but it means a lot to me."

On December 7, 2016, Winn went on pre-retirement leave, leaving behind his dog, Tess.

"She found narcotics and firearms, but it's not the same. You try to get back a dog like Strike—that special one—but it never happens again."

"They're like people. They have their own personalities, their own spirit that entwines and coincides with yours. It's like that one dog is part of you—like a finger or foot. I love my dog Tess, but this dog is not Strike, Kenny Winn's dog."

Chapter 18

A Line in the Sand

ANTHONY PIEGARO'S PRESENCE POLARIZED the Canine Section like nothing else in its history. He had been on a training mission in Panama in 2004 when the U.S. Embassy invited him to Trinidad to deliver five explosive-detection dogs to the Trinidad and Tobago Police Service and Customs.[1]

The world had become ever more vigilant about terrorism after Al Qaeda jihadists flew two planes into the World Trade Center in New York City and another plane into the Pentagon in Washington, D.C., on September 11, 2001, killing about 3,000 people. The next year, on the other side of the world, Jemaah Islamiya, a terrorist group active in Southeast Asia, planted three bombs in the Kuta Beach Nightclub area in the tranquil tourist resort of Bali in Indonesia, on October 12, 2002, and killed 202 people. Nowhere was too small or too remote for terrorist attacks.

Piegaro had no shortage of work—especially when it came to canine narcotics and explosive training. The Exxon oil company and Sealand Services had used his expertise for port protection. He had been working with U.S. embassies in Central and South America.[2] Piegaro faced other, unexpected challenges in Trinidad, particularly clashes with Canine Inspector Michael Roban. Piegaro worked from the canine section in Chaguaramas, where the U.S. once had a naval base during World War II. Officers remembered those tense and exhilarating times. "When I came into [Caroni] canine to work with my dog Max, we found it difficult to make an impression because John Phillips, Rawle Ryan, Neil Perez and Reynold Bahadoor, training under Piegaro, set the trend with their dogs in Chaguaramas," said Canine Police Inspector Raphael Mohammed. "In Caroni, we were in

Chapter 18. A Line in the Sand

the shadows of these guys. We were always compared to them. At the time we had four or five great dogs, and many dogs we had to retire."[3]

Piegaro thought he was only making a quick trip to Trinidad. "The embassy had information about a bomb threat. I thought I'd come, give canine police and Customs the dogs, and be on my way. I told a trainer in the canine police, 'Bring me some explosives tomorrow. I'll show you what to do, and then point me to Tobago.' I was told the canine police had no explosives for training."[4]

Piegaro said he called the Prime Minister's office and got what he needed. "At the training exercise the following day, I realized the officers didn't know how to handle explosives. So it went from me turning over five dogs to me doing a training course. I couldn't just leave the dogs. They didn't know what to do with them. We were then looking at fourteen weeks of training," said Piegaro.[5]

Two weeks into training came a series of incidents that put Piegaro on the front page of local newspapers. The dustbin bombings and a series of homemade bombs exploding in St. James in the west and Port of Spain propelled canine officers Premnath Maharaj and Jason Donawa from novice bomb-detection trainees in Piegaro's course to bomb-squad elite on the streets. Those explosions raised the specter of terrorism in Trinidad for the first time since the Jamaat al Muslimeen's attempted coup, led by Yasin Abu Bakr in 1990. The first bomb, planted in a dustbin near Independence Square and at the corner of Queen and Frederick Streets, Port of Spain, detonated on July 11, 2005—just four days after a coordinated suicide-bombing spree had wreaked havoc in London: 52 innocent people were killed in the 7/7 subway and bus attack in London[6]; 14 were reported injured by the blast in Port of Spain.[7]

On July 12, 2005, Trinidad and Tobago caught its first glance of Piegaro, dressed in a white polo shirt, white track shoes, and high-waisted, loose-fitting jeans. He made the front page of the *Trinidad Newsday*, misidentified as a "British bomb expert." He looked pensive and official despite his casual dress.[8] In *Trinidad and Tobago Newsday* on June 15, 2007, reporter Nalinee Seelal said 16 of Piegaro's dogs had been in the country since 2005 and had uncovered $4 million in narcotics.

Police Dogs of Trinidad and Tobago

The tension between Piegaro and Roban mounted. Really, the problem was how to deal with a civilian operating in the police service. From the time he arrived in Trinidad, Piegaro's penchant for bypassing Roban to get what he wanted escalated the problem. Meanwhile, Piegaro identified other needs in the Dog Section, now referred to as the Canine Section.[9] "There were murders and missing bodies, so I brought in Red, the Golden Retriever cadaver dog," he said.

Amid all the controversy and conflict with Roban, Piegaro said he found joy and fulfillment in the officers he trained. "They were solid police officers. I put them in exhausting situations so they knew not to be afraid, because when you have a dog that depends on your stability, you have to learn how to stay calm and have trust in your dog—especially when you're tracking in the bush." Piegaro took great pride in seeing his trainees develop. His controversial training included working with a brick. He said:

> "You get a brick, a choker, and lead [leash]. You name your brick and go everywhere with it. I want you to learn what it's like to have something next to your side. If you don't hold the brick right, it's going to bang you in the side," said Piegaro. "You're also learning dogs' commands. The brick showed me you want to be there, and I'm going to put you through everything your dog is going through."[10]

Piegaro's second class began with 15 officers, some from the Customs division. Ten officers survived Hell Week, which started on a rainy day. Piegaro walked into the pouring rain, and the officers didn't follow. Piegaro said he told them, "If you trust me, and you work hard you will see results like you never saw before."[11] He continued making demands. "When Prime Minister Manning came for the first graduating class [of officers trained in bomb detection], I said on that day, 'I am not putting these dogs in the back of trucks. The dogs have to be in air-conditioned vehicles.'"

Two months later, Piegaro said, the air-conditioned vehicles arrived. (Some canine officers recalled air-conditioned vehicles since 2000.) Maharaj said, "Before Piegaro arrived, we had some vehicles with air-conditioning for the officers, and fans for the canine compartments, but that hadn't worked, because the fans always got clogged with dog hair."[12]

Chapter 18. A Line in the Sand

Grateful for the direction in which the Canine Section was now moving, canine officers training in Piegaro's drug detection program offered unconditional allegiance. "Anthony Piegaro spoke his mind. He had to change the mindset of officers in the Canine—including me—and only then is when we became so successful," said Lenford Blades, a top trainer in the Canine Section who worked with Piegaro. "We were moving like the 70s before Piegaro came. He changed the way we respond to dogs, and we were very successful."[13]

Emboldened by government support and inspired by the serene surroundings of spacious Chaguaramas, Piegaro dared to dream big.

"I told myself, 'I am going to turn this place into the Canine Academy to serve as a training center for the entire English-speaking Caribbean'—and damn if I didn't get close to it. I think of that program in Trinidad as one of the best training programs I ever got involved in. The golden goose was right there in Trinidad—and they slaughtered it," said Piegaro.[14] "A dog handler is a different kind of person—an approachable and affable person. Some guys come and do a little training, and feel they are above everybody,"[15] said Inspector Roban.

In the beginning, he was optimistic about Piegaro's arrival. "Most of the dogs we had when Piegaro came were brought in 2000. They were getting old, and we needed new dogs."[16] Roban didn't dispute the excellent quality of the first set of dogs that arrived under Piegaro. "We got our money's worth out of the bomb dogs. As for other dogs, we got Bahadoor's dog Jack and Winn's dog Strike, and after that, it went downhill."

Canine officers training with Piegaro, noted how he cut through bureaucratic red tape, and were impressed with his dogs. Roban acknowledged them. "They were good officers. Ryan was always quiet, and never complained; Maharaj was a hard worker, always smiling; Cedeno always smiled. They were young."

But Roban felt the men were too eager to follow Piegaro blindly at the expense of the Canine Section's unity. Roban said,

"The officers who say Piegaro brought in superior dogs don't know their history. We had good dogs before Piegaro. It's all there in the files. I wouldn't say the dogs Piegaro brought were better than the ones we got in the past."

Police Dogs of Trinidad and Tobago

All the narcotics dogs we got from the Royal Air Force in 1989 were good. In the 90s we had Bonnie and Lucky, a black mixed-breed Labrador; a German Shepherd/border collie mixed dog named Ben, and Pariagsingh's dog Kiki—all good narcotics dogs.[17]

"Kiki was my first dog and as good as any of our dogs," said Cpl. Shane Chase, one of the Canine Section's police dog trainers.[18] Roban insisted the difference in the Canine Section before and after Piegaro's arrival never came down to the dogs. "His dog-training skills made the difference. The level of training Piegaro provided for the dogs increased their working span,"[19] said Roban. He said that no one in the police service stood up to Piegaro. "He was an influential kind of guy. He always had a problem with me because only I stood up to him. I became an obstacle to him. Piegaro was an excellent trainer. It would be dishonest to say otherwise. But you had to keep checks and balances on him."[20]

Jason Donawa found himself in the middle of the Roban/Piegaro tug-of-war, though he didn't entertain many of the issues that arose, such as Piegaro's penchant for cursing police officers he trained. "I came from the army, so I was accustomed to the cussing. That's just noise to us. The cussing prepares you for what you meet when you go out there in life as a police officer,"[21] said Donawa.

Roban considered Donawa Piegaro's staunchest supporter, but Piegaro remembered Donawa as the officer who ultimately jumped ship. "I didn't sell out," said Donawa. "I work for the police."

While the feud fired up, Donawa became the center of a strange controversy over his explosive-detection dog Charlie, who died suddenly from a twisted intestine. Charlie had a 21-gun salute, a formal burial ceremony in Chaguaramas and media coverage. In Caroni, a dog's funeral felt out of place; in Chaguaramas, Charlie's funeral served as further proof of Piegaro's respect for his officers and the dogs. In the Piegaro/Roban war, even a dog's funeral caused division.

In the end, Donawa said the Piegaro era ushered in the era of dogs with a high drive [desire for work]. Donawa said,

> It was evident. Currently the dogs we're getting have an even higher work drive than the ones Piegaro brought in. The dogs now would be like Piegaro's dogs on ecstasy. The first four Piegaro-chosen dogs that made an

Chapter 18. A Line in the Sand

impact in the underworld were Atos, Rex, Nissan and Jack. Then Romeo had Maverick and Winn had Strike on the tactical side. Sunny, the yellow Labrador, a passive [non-tactical] drug dog, [not trained to chase and capture suspects] was quite successful. Buddy, Nitro and Red, the cadaver dog, were the Golden Retrievers.[22]

In the battle between Piegaro and Roban, the Canine Section emerged as the clear winner despite the two men's differences. Piegaro returned to the U.S. in 2013 to run his company, CSI International in Palm Beach, Florida, and Roban retired in 2014. In 2023, Piegaro had one police dog training programme in the Dominican Republic, and his company ran a helicopter rescue service.

CHAPTER 19

THE PIEGARO TEAM

"EVERYBODY HAS AN OPINION about Mr. Piegaro. I opened up my mind and kept politics out of it," said Cpl. Premnath Maharaj. "Mr. Piegaro turned the Canine Section around. He even changed our uniforms for going out to work, from those denim jumpers we also wore to clean kennels, or those heavy navy-blue sweaters we sweated in on duty, to the polo jerseys with his company's logo, CSI International, printed on them. Then we worked in polo shirts with the police badge on the front and 'Police Canine' written on the back."[1]

In July 2005, Maharaj and his dog Woody, along with Donawa and his dog Charlie, became the newly formed Trinidad and Tobago Police Service bomb detection unit under Piegaro. Maharaj had just received Dog #250, Woody, a yellow Labrador with a noticeable droopy chin, when the dustbin bomber struck in Port of Spain, on the corner of Queen and Frederick Streets.

> Woody and I were training in Chaguaramas on July 11, 2005 when the call came, "Bombing in town! All you have to respond. That means the dogs." You're hearing the excitement all around. We ran to the kennels. Got our dogs. Sirens all the way to town.
>
> We reached Port of Spain. Crowd. People. Panic. Ambulance. Everything moved so fast. Craziness.
>
> On the corner of Queen and Frederick Street, I saw blood close to a dustbin. Boy, my belly turned. I started to get weak right there where the lady sells watches. They had just removed a woman who got her leg damaged in the explosion.
>
> We had to search for secondary devices. It was chaos. Our trainers, Blades and Piegaro, were there.
>
> I still did not realize what I had got myself into by working in this newly developed explosives detection unit. On the day of the bombing, I saw the excitement and the pace of the work, the anxiety on people's faces.
>
> Then, as Woody and I made our way to the scene of the bombing, I

Chapter 19. The Piegaro Team

turned and saw the relief on people's faces when they realized the dogs had reached. They felt safer. The police were clearing the area; getting people to move back. I felt ready to put my life in Woody's hands. I felt that confident in him.[2]

The dogs switched into work mode, combing the cordoned-off area of Frederick Street where someone had placed an explosive device in a bin.[3]

After the initial report, we got information that someone left a bag on Henry Street and ran. So from Queen and Frederick Street we ran across to Henry Street and saw the bag hanging from a tree.
Mr. Piegaro touched me on my shoulder and said, "We have a bag to search here. You up for it?"
I said, "Yes."
He said, "You sure? If you're not up to it, I will take your dog and search it."
I said, "I will take my dog."[4]

Woody, the slobbery dog who loved air-conditioning and soft surfaces—the dog that Maharaj noted "lifted his paws whenever they hit a hard surface and walked like a sissy," approached the bag swaying in the tree—then walked away. Woody had not signaled that there were any more explosive devices in the area.

On September 10, another explosive device went off, this time in a pile of rubble on George Street, a residential area with government housing in Port of Spain.[5] "Rain fell heavily that day. I don't know if that deterred pedestrians from walking along the street in that open area, because if they had been walking by, there could have been real damage," said Maharaj.

On October 14, 2005, came another explosion, between two telephone booths near Smokey and Bunty's, a popular pub in St. James, where patrons spilled onto the Western Main Road, along with blaring calypso.[6] "Someone had placed an explosive device outside there. It went off and damaged three vehicles that evening. Panic again," said Maharaj.

Maharaj and Donawa came with Woody and Charlie, a big mastiff and Labrador mix, described by Maharaj as a "fat dog with a big head and plenty of spit.... We never made any headway finding the person responsible for those explosions," said Maharaj. It had been a baptism by fire. "During that period, we had about nine bomb threats a week. While people ran away from trouble, Donawa and I ran towards it, counting our blessings and praying hard before we went into danger. We learned how to work bomb dogs, and have trust in our dogs. I still have great respect for Mr. Piegaro."

PC Rawle Ryan remembers the rain "falling in buckets" in Chaguaramas on the day officers reported for Piegaro's training program as the second group of canine officers and the first tactical/narcotic officers trained by the foreigner. Piegaro quickly whittled down 24 recruits to four: Bahadoor, Perez, Phillips, and Ryan. It had been a rough road to get to this point in their careers, and this new direction felt exciting. Before Piegaro's arrival, Ryan recalls an eight-month stint doing patrols on Tobago beaches with his dog.[7]

> I'd call the Task Force; they put me in a pick-up and dropped me for four hours with my dog and revolver; then I'd call them to pick me up. I gave the dog water at a standpipe. Hot sun; hot asphalt.
>
> We only did patrols—no narcotic work. There were two of us—me and an officer named Serrette, nicknamed after the English comedian, Benny Hill because of his sense of humor.[8]

More patrols awaited Ryan on his return to Trinidad, where he and his dog Alan worked the Botanical Gardens across from the Savannah in Port of Spain. There had been a spate of robberies in the gardens.[9] In 2002, Prime Minister Patrick Manning's government had put a new crime-fighting policy in place. *Newsday* reporter Nalinee Seelal wrote:

> Appropriately named "Operation Anaconda," for the squeeze that it will put on escalating crime in this country, the long awaited National Crime Plan rolled into action early yesterday morning [on February 21, 2002] as a convoy of more than fifty vehicles with three hundred policemen and soldiers left St. James Barracks and throughout the day carried out raids, stopped motor vehicles, searched and frisked people and made their presence felt in areas along the East-West Corridor.[10]

She pointed out that the "squeeze" mainly inconvenienced law-abiding citizens—especially commuters coming from the east on their way to work in Port of Spain. While Operation Anaconda

Chapter 19. The Piegaro Team

was in full force a masked gunman in the west robbed the Chaguaramas branch of the Republic Bank at the seaside hotel Crew's Inn where there are docks with yachts around the peninsula. He escaped with $25,000. His accomplice shot a 79-year-old yachtie and tried to steal his dinghy. The two struggled in the water. The gunman and his accomplice fled.[11]

Roadblocks and raids targeted poor areas like Laventille and Morvant on the outskirts of Port of Spain. No dramatic change came for canine officers during these crime-stopping initiatives.

Then, in 2004, senior officers told Ryan he had been picked, with six other officers, to go to Chaguaramas to work with a foreign instructor.[12] "They said he might have a new method of training. I had no idea of the massive impact this would have on canine police," said Ryan. When Piegaro finally matched dogs and officers, the bespectacled Ryan, who looks like a cross between a scholar and a bodybuilder, got Rex, a German Shepherd/Belgian Malinois tactical dog. Ryan said:

> I didn't want Rex. I found he looked too intimidating.
> He was a handsome dog, mostly tan and very strong—the most muscular dog I had ever seen—like he had come from the gym where he pumped iron. That dog was so strong that after working with him for a few days, my skin peeled off my hands. My hands were a bloody mess.[13]

Piegaro's work day started at 6 a.m. Officers washed down kennels and practiced three disciplines with their dogs—obedience, tracking, and a property search with keys, bank cards, plastic, and metal—until Piegaro arrived at 8 a.m.[14]

> We cut denim jumpers and put them out for the dogs to find. One day, Rex found a big piece of denim and swallowed it. I panicked. I said to myself, "Mr. Piegaro is going to kill me."
> Mr. Piegaro arrived in Chaguaramas just as I decided to call him. I told him what happened. Calmly, he said, "Give him some water with hydrogen peroxide."
> He told me how to mix it, and the dog vomited up the denim.[15]

Rex's size and demeanor intimidated everyone except Ryan.

> While working on rotation in Tobago, I left Rex in the kennels in the police station and went to Store Bay to buy breakfast. When I returned, I

found the door to the station locked. Everyone had climbed on top of the desks. Mr. Rex [had] got out of the kennel and came looking for me. He went upstairs and all around the office.[16]

Rex could be both shocking and embarrassing. Ryan remembered,

> Rex did some crazy things. Once we searched in the Plannings [government housing] in Port of Spain, and he went under a dog kennel." I smiled and said, "Yes, we got drugs"—and he came out with four kittens in his mouth. Dead. Rex killed them. The people carried on, [yelled at the officer] and I felt awful. I love all animals. I moved down the road quickly to look for drugs. Rex specialized in finding cocaine. They used to call him "the piper" [cocaine-sniffing] dog.[17]

Under Piegaro, canine officers swiftly built a reputation. Ryan recalled:

> When we started going out with Piegaro's dogs, a rumor circulated that drug lords put a hit on the dogs.
> Drug dealers lost their work and their lives. They had taken drugs on consignment and couldn't pay back the money because we kept finding the drugs.
> We had a feeling of job satisfaction. Police officers felt glad to see us. Every day when we hit the scene we found cocaine, marijuana, and firearms—even though the dogs weren't trained to find firearms.
> We closed down major drug blocks in Port of Spain. We would do four, five, or six operations in one day. Our success was over ninety-nine per cent. I can't even begin to calculate Rex's worth, and Nissan and Atos found even more drugs than him.[18]

Rex and Ryan worked together from 2005 to 2011. When Ryan took a vacation, Rex went to Cpl. Gray in Tobago from 2011 to 2013. Near the end of his life, Rex returned to Caroni. Ryan said:

> The last time I saw him, I could tell he recognized me. Tears came to my eyes when I saw how old he got.
> When Rex died, I cried my heart out. I felt burnt out. I knew I had to take a break. The leave I went on did a lot of good. I saw another world out there, and when I came back to work, I felt ready to go out there again.
> Those dogs Piegaro brought changed us. We were no longer just "dog men"—a term police officers once used to belittle us. We became canine handlers. We made a difference.
> I don't know where we would have been without Piegaro. His standards were high, and we knew it.[19]

Chapter 19. The Piegaro Team

Cpl. John Phillips remembers being transferred to the canine police section in 2000.

> Canine was quiet when I came to work here. I worked a dog named Chico from 2000 to 2003. When they told me, "That dog is yours. Take him out," I watched this grizzly bear inside the kennel. "Rah," he growled.
> An officer, Clayton Chandler, sitting on a metal chair and smoking a cigarette, said, "Hey, breds [brethren], if you don't take out that dog, I'm going to take it." So I had Chico; Bissessar had Jango. If either Chico or Jango got loose, they would go looking for each other. Once they fought for about twenty minutes. Someone cleaned the kennels and didn't close my kennel. Bissessar turned around and saw Chico watching him, ready for a fight.[20]

On August 31, 2003, Phillips worked the Independence Day parade, handed over his dog, and went straight to the airport to go on vacation with his family. By the time he returned nearly a year later in 2004, many handlers had left. He thought about going to SAUTT [the Special Anti-Crime Unit of Trinidad and Tobago], but when a corporal asked, "If you leave, who will be left here?" Phillips decided to stay.[21] It turned out to be a life-changing decision.

> We had some guys training some pups of Maharaj's dog Biest, and I didn't have a dog for about a year. Then Piegaro came. I respected him. They were saying those of us who went to Chaguaramas to train with him were the "white boys," the "Piegaro clan"—but we had autonomy down there. Piegaro was a professional and a businessman.
> On the first day when we went down to Chaguaramas, we all wore jumpers and garden boots for normal training. This Caucasian man came out in a white polo T-shirt, light blue jeans, and white sneakers. Stood up there. Arms crossed, shades, feet apart. He called out to our local trainer, "Blades, let those guys fall in." We lined up.
> Rain fell, so we got up and ran out of the rain.
> When we looked back, this white man with this American accent was standing in the rain saying, "Goddamn, this is some good weather."
> We now had an international instructor introducing something we weren't accustomed to, and I welcomed the challenge, physically and mentally.
> Before training, we couldn't eat anything big because we'd feel to throw up in that training with food in our bellies. We had to do the hurdles and agility work that the dogs were expected to do.[22]

Police Dogs of Trinidad and Tobago

At the end of the intense training the officers called Hell Week, Phillips got canine Nissan.

> Nissan was a normal-looking German Shepherd, but an extraordinary dog. With him, I became the first handler to get over a kilo of marijuana.
>
> Romeo, with Maverick, and I with Nissan are the only two canine officers who ever found heroin. They hid it in a PlayStation 3 and were about to ship it out, in 2006 or 2007.
>
> We were finding drugs every single day. Perez with Atos and I with Nissan were on one team; Ryan with Rex and Bahadoor with Jack were on another team. We found so many drugs in Port of Spain that after a while it made no sense to have drugs in the areas we were searching.[23]

Like the other officers who trained with Piegaro, PC Neil Perez considered the American trainer a "great teacher and motivator" with high expectations and high standards.

> They called me Mr. Piegaro's blue-eyed boy because he and I were close.
>
> I have a lot of memories of working with Mr. Piegaro. One day we were teaching the dogs to track, and he was real hard on me. I was a bit angry, but didn't express it.
>
> When I walked past him at the end of the day, he said, "Don't worry about it. Tomorrow we will fix that."
>
> That was motivating to me. I realized it wasn't anything personal. He was just trying to get me to go the extra mile.
>
> When we completed training and went on our first operation, we searched for four hours. When we came back, Mr. Piegaro said, "What do you have?"
>
> We said, "Nothing," and he said, "Ok. Go back out, and don't come back until you find something."[24]

Perez and Philips returned to where they had searched, and found marijuana. Working with Atos, "a well-tempered, loyal, and loving" German Shepherd, Perez said he and the other canine officers learned to confront fear in unexpected places for a canine officer trained in narcotic searches.

> When they were constructing the new Customs building on Wrightson Road in Port of Spain, the scaffolding collapsed. [John] Phillips and I went up there with our dogs, and we were supposed to go inside the building they were constructing. We didn't know if it was safe.
>
> Piegaro came and said, "You have to go in and search."
>
> He went in himself. We did a field search, where you teach the dogs to

Chapter 19. The Piegaro Team

find a human scent, to see if anyone was trapped in the building. We felt like heroes on that day for going inside that building.[25]

Meanwhile, Atos's drug finds were off the charts.

In one exercise in the mountains of Maraval, we found so many drugs I was coming down that mountain with a crocus bag [burlap bag] full of drugs on my back and a bucket of drugs in each hand. Atos started to pull me. I unclipped him, he ran about 25 meters and found another crocus bag full of marijuana.

The guys on the exercise said, "Pull that dog away, because we can't carry any more drugs."

I was amazed, because I was carrying all of that marijuana on me, and Atos still smelled more drugs to find.[26]

Every exercise brought new challenges.

We went to the port for a ship with drugs on it. Piegaro was there. He said, "We're going to board the ship, but we have to board from another ship," and then he told everyone, "Perez volunteered to go first."

I was shocked, because I didn't volunteer. There was a rope ladder for me to climb onto the boat, and I was studying how it was swinging.

Piegaro said, "Just don't look down. I will throw your dog up to you."

I had to pull my dog up with a harness and a rope. I felt like a hero again.

If Mr. Piegaro's training wasn't so successful, the canine section wouldn't be where it is today.[27]

"Anthony Piegaro used to call me 'One Shot, One Kill,'" said Cpl. Reynold Bahadoor. He earned the epithet on an assignment with his dog, Jack, in the Las Lomas countryside of central Trinidad near Piarco airport.

Some men had robbed a bar in the area and escaped. The report said they had a shotgun and another firearm, and that they had run into a forested area. We arrived on the scene, and Jack led the track. Some distance deep inside the bush, we reached the top of a hill. I heard some noise like people walking towards us. I motioned the police to be quiet and stand their ground.

Two men came up to the top of the hill. One of them had a shotgun in his hands; the other had a knapsack on his back. As I yelled, "Police! Stop!" he raised his shotgun, and as soon as he raised it, I fired off one shot.

It appeared they both turned and ran back down the hill.

I let go of Jack and said, "Get him, boy."

Police Dogs of Trinidad and Tobago

> A short distance down the hill, I heard Jack biting one of the guys. The guy was breathing loud when I got to him. I saw he received one single shot in his forehead. I didn't even know I had hit him.
>
> We found two firearms and a knapsack with weed and cartons of cigarettes. The other guy got away and the one I shot was pronounced dead on arrival at the hospital.[28]

Like other officers who worked under Piegaro, Bahadoor credits Piegaro's arrival with fueling his drive as a canine officer. He remembers:

> We had an operation at Chanka Trace in El Socorro. The police got a tip about seeing a man walking inside the bush by a river and coming out with drugs.
>
> The sun was hot, so some officers went to a bar to get some water. I keep my water on me, so I stayed outside as Jack searched.
>
> When he found about twelve kilos of marijuana, I called the police to come and meet me. They came, and we got the drugs.
>
> The next day they killed the barman because they thought he gave the police information. [But] the dogs—not any tip—led us to everything.[29]

Bahadoor said drug dealers couldn't fathom how quickly everything had changed. Police often requested Jack for house searches.

> Three times the police paid a visit to a man's home in Barataria. They knew he had a gun because neighbors reported he threatened them and went back inside the house with the firearm.
>
> I brought Jack to the house. He circled the living room, looked up, climbed on the couch, and tried to climb a wall that didn't reach the roof. I took him down, and he came back to the same spot. He wouldn't move from that spot.
>
> I went outside, got a ladder, climbed up, and found a secret hiding place just on top of the other side of the wall where Jack stood. I pushed my hand down inside the hole in the wood and got a gun, cocaine, marijuana, and ammunition.
>
> I gave the guy some real fatigue [teasing]. I said, "Today is your day, buddy. We brought a dog named Jack."
>
> The police hugged me up and spun me around. They couldn't do that with Jack.[30]

Every successful exercise brought Piegaro's officers closer to him.

"I liked Piegaro," said Bahadoor. "When you did the right thing you got praise. If anyone gives you bad stories about Piegaro, they would be lies."

Chapter 20

Ambush and Kidnappings

When Cpl. Kirt Antoine transferred to the canine section in 2000, he and his black-and-tan German Shepherd, Lynn, settled into a mundane routine, mostly of patrol work around the Botanical Gardens in Port of Spain. But later he grabbed a chance to join Anthony Piegaro's third training group and got paired with Wilson, a skinny, energetic tan-and-brown Belgian Malinois with a black nose.[1]

> In 2009, we went into Diego Martin—North Post Road—a place where you would get drugs every time you go. We walked in the backyard, climbed a wall, went up a hill, and heard a growl. A pit bull ran out and started to bite Wilson. Another officer wanted to shoot the dog. I said, "No, wait," because the dogs were fighting.
>
> The officer shot Wilson by mistake. The bullet went through Wilson's rectum and came out the left leg. The officer and I had a short exchange, because I knew I wasn't shooting my dog.
>
> The pit bull rushed me, and I shot and killed it. We're animal lovers and we don't want to shoot another dog, but I had to do it.
>
> Wilson ran off. When I found him, he watched me, ears down, tail between his legs. He went limping down the hill, finding drugs as he went.[2]

Then came the problem every canine officer dreads: finding a vet in an emergency.

> We couldn't find the government veterinarian. Mt. Hope was closed, so we went to Mucurapo Road [in St. James] and a vet treated Wilson. It was an entry and exit wound. Wilson wouldn't settle or rest. We had to put a portable kennel inside the kennel where he slept. Monday morning we took him to Mt. Hope.
>
> After that, he never walked the same again. He couldn't come out of the vehicle. His big eyes would watch you. He limped. His attitude changed,

and he became a little more conscious of other animals. When he first came, he'd walk up to the baddest dog, smell him, and was like, "If you want to fight, we'll fight."

After the shooting, he became scared of loud noises. Wilson stopped working.[3]

Antoine's next dog, two-year-old Nero, came in April 2014.

Nero, a Belgium Malinois, was a small, vibrant dog. He always had this mischievous way about him. He was a one-man dog. He hated females and bit every one of them in the branch.

Nero was easy to train, very intelligent—skinny, though. You could see all his ribs and spine. We tried double-feeding him and giving him potted meat. Every place we would go, people said, "Where you get that? You don't feed that dog?"

People underestimate him, but he wins everyone's heart in the canine police shows for the public.[4]

In 2015, Antoine had an unusual assignment: tracking an illegal immigrant who had escaped from the immigration detention center in Cumuto. Antoine and Nero went into the forest surrounding the center to catch the man.

We had to extend the parameter and try to do some physical searching where no one had gone previously. For a short while, Nero and I got separated from the other police officers.[5] I was deep into the forest, tracking, with a thirty-foot lead. Nero was ahead of me in the bush, and he seemed to pick up a scent.

The funny thing with tracking in the forest—after ten seconds of walking, you lose track of how far you're separated from everyone.

Suddenly, I felt a blow to the back of my head. I don't know what he hit me with. This Nigerian fellow we were tracking was huge. I'm close to six feet tall, and he was bigger than me.

The Nigerian and I struggled. I felt my leg holster shift, and I knew what he was going for. I got to my gun and pulled off one round. He got shot in the leg. I was hoping another police officer heard the shot.[6]

Cpl. Akil Bernard had just returned to Cumuto from a training session with his new dog Cezar when he and Cpl. Shane Chase got the news Antoine was missing.

Bernard said,

We heard Cpl. Antoine and canine police officer PC Balkissoon, who had accompanied Antoine without a dog, had not come out of the bush on a

Chapter 20. Ambush and Kidnappings

search, and Antoine had been injured. I suggested we go to see how we could assist them. Cpl. Chase and I loaded Cezar up in the crate.

When we arrived at the location, by a farm in Aripo, there were lots of police vehicles, but no one was able to tell us where Antoine was.

We drove up a roadway off the main road, and then walked inside about 1½ to 2 miles. Cezar was on a long lead, and he kept his head low to the ground. He wagged his tail, so I knew he was following a good scent.

About twenty minutes inside, he led us straight to Antoine. The suspect was on the ground too, about four feet away. Antoine was conscious, but in plenty of pain. Balkissoon was standing nearby with Antoine's dog.[7]

It was Cezar's first track with Bernard. "I was studying Antoine, lying injured on the ground, and with all the excitement, I forgot to reward Cezar with his toy. He must have wondered what happened to me," said Bernard.[8]

Police officers took turns carrying Antoine out of the forest; then he was taken to hospital.[9]

"When I got out of the hospital, they asked if I needed counseling, but that's not our culture," said Antoine. "Later, they asked if I could go back to work again. I am an officer who lives my job. I joined the work so young—I was twenty. I grew up in the service. I enjoy what we do; I enjoy busting [having] we little cook and the arguments about whose dog is better. I wanted my dog back. You get attached to your dog."[10]

For the next five years, Nero continued to serve on operations and patrols. Slowly he developed coordination issues. He began to drift while walking and had trouble jumping onto his bed.[11] "It went downhill from there," said Antoine. "He went through a series of tests, but nothing could be pinpointed. Nero went on sick leave in March 2020. One morning in July, I was on my way to work, and they called and told me he died. He was one of the most mischievous dogs we had in the kennels."

In 2022, Antoine would get an unexpected new challenge. His new dog would lead him in a direction he never imagined he would go.

Meeting new challenges comes with the territory for a canine officer. From the inception of the unit in 1952, the geography of Trinidad, with marshland, tropical forest, extended plains, hills,

Police Dogs of Trinidad and Tobago

mountains and densely populated urban areas, required tactical dogs trained to track down suspects hiding or fleeing from the law. In 2001 those dogs' expertise would be put to a new test when kidnapping for ransom became Trinidad's latest crime surge. International news highlighted the contrasts in oil-rich Trinidad, with its carefree Carnival culture and gang-ruled slums. NPR radio said:

> Port of Spain, Trinidad, used to be known for Calypso music, steel drums and wild parties during Carnival. Then, when the price of natural gas skyrocketed, it enjoyed all the fruits of a boom town. Shiny glass skyscrapers began to fill downtown, and the economic gap between the island's Indians—who tended to be the merchant class—and blacks widened.[12]

When kidnappings rose from 10 recorded in 2001 to 58 in 2005, the *Los Angeles Times* wrote a story saying Trinidad and Tobago ranked number two in the world for kidnappings.[13] It would get worse. In 2007, kidnapping-for-ransom cases would rise to 155. After 11 kidnappings in 2008, that crime fell to single-digit numbers between 2009 and 2018.

The dramatically declining statistics suggest that SAUTT and the police Anti-Kidnapping Unit, which got some specialized training from the FBI, developed an effective strategy to deal with this crime. SAUTT canine officers were reportedly involved in every kidnapping case,[14] and TTPS canine officers with dogs trained for tracking also assisted. Cpl. Reynold Bahadoor, a TTPS canine officer, remembers answering the call for a kidnap case.

> On the morning of October 28, 2009, Imran Mohammed Khan, his mother and his brother were about to leave their San Juan home for work at their family-owned jewelry store on Queen Street, Port of Spain. Imran opened the gate in the driveway for his brother, who was driving the family's vehicle.
>
> A white Nissan Almera with three occupants pulled up alongside Imran. Two of the occupants jumped out of the car. One grabbed Imran, while the other accosted his mother and snatched her bag while she entered the family's vehicle. They pushed Imran into the Almera and sped off.
>
> Imran's brother took off behind the Almera.[15]

The kidnappers pulled into Grand Bazaar, a large shopping mall off the Uriah Butler Highway heading south, and ditched the victim's

Chapter 20. Ambush and Kidnappings

brother's car, which had been following them. The police, already alerted, spotted the kidnappers' vehicle when it reached Chaguanas in central Trinidad, and chased them. The kidnappers headed south and pulled into a bushy area along a back road in Freeport, near the Water and Sewerage Authority dam. They ran the car off the road. The three assailants grabbed the kidnap victim and headed into the bush. Police reached the vehicle, but didn't know in what direction the kidnappers and their victim had gone. Johnny Abraham, the senior superintendent of the Central Division, called for canine support.[16] Bahadoor said,

> Constable Rasheed Mohammed and I had just taken our dogs Jack and Tango from the kennels to go on routine airport duty when the news of the kidnapping came in.
> We went flying down South, sirens blazing. At 10:30 a.m., we reached the scene, received a police briefing, and were pointed in a direction. We saw tracks around and asked the Chaguanas Task Force for a team to accompany us into the bush.[17]

Jack, the black-and-tan German Shepherd, led the track, with four police officers trailing him into the bush.[18]

> Four men had passed, so it was a strong track. Jack followed their tracks so fast he ran ahead of everyone. After about five minutes, I looked around, and it was me and dog Jack alone.
> On going a fair distance into the bush, we came to a heavily forested area. Dog Jack displayed a highly aggressive demeanor, and I knew the men weren't too far away.
> The forest was so dense, I realized it would have been dangerous for me to go in there by myself. I pulled dog Jack back to me, knelt down, and fired three shots in the air just to see if the kidnappers would fire back. The Special Anti-Crime Unit [SAUTT] helicopters whirred overhead, creating so much noise it proved difficult to call out to other officers. They would not have heard me. Dog Jack was rarin' to go. He has no fear.
> No one fired back. I stood my ground and hoped the other police officers would hear the shots. They did, and they came in my direction in about five minutes.
> I let Jack off the leash, and he bolted deeper inside the forest, followed by me and the police. We heard loud screaming.
> Jack can only bite one person at a time, and he had a guy. Another guy pulled out a gun and started shooting at us. We returned fire. Jack was still on the ground, biting one of the kidnappers.

The kidnap victim was lying flat on the ground with his hands tied behind his back and a bandanna over his eyes.[19]

Chaos ensued. The kidnappers and police exchanged more gunfire, and in the middle of the melee, Bahadoor noticed his dog operating on his own. "Dog Jack grabbed the kidnap victim's pants and was pulling him away from the kidnappers," said Bahadoor. "I can't explain how he knew to do that." When the gunfire stopped, the kidnappers lay dead.[20]

"We had to lift them up and carry them out of the bush. We told the kidnap victim, Imran Mohammed Khan, 'You're all right. We are the police.' He had no idea what was going on. Later, he told us he thought, 'This is it.' He didn't think he would get out alive."[21] Bahadoor noted that Jack had bitten two of the kidnappers. "They were in such fear of Jack they couldn't shoot at first. They were more afraid of the dog than the bullets. Jack bit up their hands."[22]

All good dog stories come to an end. Jack got old and retired. "He couldn't work as he used to," said Bahadoor. "I had got another dog, Zuco, and Jack missed going out there. Sometimes I would carry him with me on assignments, and Jack would still find drugs. I was based in Cumuto at the time, and I carried him for long walks in the forest up there. Jack and Zuco became close friends. When I carried them out on exercises, they would work together and cooperate." Then Jack got sick.

> He had a cyst that never got better. The veterinarian recommended he be put to sleep. I was against it, but in 2015 the seniors said the time had come. I talked to Jack on the way to Mt. Hope Hospital and said, "Buddy, don't worry. I'm with you all the way. You're going for a long sleep."
>
> He was such a strong dog he had to get a second shot to go to sleep. I had to hold him, because he would growl at the veterinarian. I spent a little time afterward with him.

Bahadoor wiped away tears. "Jack was a real faithful dog to me. No one could come near me. That dog loved me."

Five years after Jack's death, other police officers still asked canine officers about Jack.

Chapter 20. Ambush and Kidnappings

"When I go out on exercises, Jack's name comes up the most," said Cpl. Akil Bernard. "Police officers ask, 'What happened to Jack? We haven't seen him for some time.' I think he is the best-known dog in canine."[23]

Chapter 21

Springing into Action

PC Renrick Texeira had a string of bad luck. His German Shepherd Nicolay had developed a kidney problem, and then his dog Yeyo had got so excited after discovering drugs under a bed that he ran outside and fractured his paw jumping off a step. After that, Texeira sat in the Chaguaramas Canine Section with no dog. Then one phone call, in 2011, changed the course of Texeira's career.[1] "Inspector Roban called and said, 'Government is disbanding SAUTT and they're looking for handlers who have no dogs to take their dogs,'" said Texeira.

Texeira envisioned the extraordinary dog he would get from SAUTT, a combined military crime-fighting force assembled in 2003 under Prime Minister Manning and the PNM government. In 2011, after the People's Partnership coalition and Prime Minister Kamla Persad-Bissessar of the UNC came to power, the government disbanded SAUTT, which consisted of the best officers the prisons, the army, the police, and the coast guard had to offer. Texeira rushed to Camp Cumuto, where the SAUTT dogs were located. "I thought I would get a big, tough dog—and they showed me Jackson—this black-and-white fluffy Springer Spaniel with long ears."[2]

In SAUTT, Jackson had established a reputation for his tenacity and consistent finds. Canine police trainer Cpl. Shane Chase recalled exercises with Jackson. "One time, SAUTT packed up to leave a search and a prison officer who was Jackson's handler, came back to the officers saying, 'My dog is showing a lot of interest in a particular area. Something's there. We returned, and Jackson found a buried PVC pipe with guns hidden inside. Jackson would

Chapter 21. Springing into Action

become one of the most amazing dogs to pass through the police service."[3]

At about the same time, PCs Kiff Singh and Sherwin Cedeno, who had just returned from vacation, took their dogs for assessment by Cpl. Chase in Cumuto. (After SAUTT was disbanded, Chase returned to the TTPS Canine Section as a police dog trainer.) Neither of the canine officers' dogs passed their tests, so Chase paired Singh with Penny and Cedeno with Jed.[4]

"It was a good pairing. Jed, a black-and-white Springer Spaniel, was long and thin like Cedeno. Penny, a brown-and-white Springer Spaniel, was shorter and stockier—like me," Singh laughed.[5]

Penny turned out to be a tease. The first time Singh took her into a large open field in Cumuto, she would not listen to his commands to return. For twenty minutes, Penny zig-zagged through the field, playfully glancing behind as Singh lunged to catch her. "She'd come close, spin away; then turn to watch me." Singh lured Penny close to him with a tennis ball—her prized toy—then grabbed her. Training brought even more surprises for Texeira.

> They had big German Shepherds there, and I'm watching Jackson work and thinking, "Big is not everything." On police exercises, officers would see Jackson coming and say, "Ah, we're getting guns and drugs today."
>
> One day, on an assignment in Trincity, we received a brief about a suspect skimming people's credit cards. Police believed he was dealing in heavy drugs. Police found $20,000 in his car.
>
> We went to search the house for drugs. Downstairs, I saw six bags of money in the corner—only blue notes [TT$100 bills]. Jackson indicated on a bag in another corner. No drugs. We went upstairs, and in one of the rooms, Jackson searched and froze. When I looked under the bed, I saw five more bags of money, all with seals. The tally turned out to be about $400,000.
>
> That's when I realized Jackson could find money. I asked the trainers, and they said he was trained to find firearms, narcotics, and money.[6]

(Currency-detection dogs work with law enforcement to detect large sums of money. They are trained to sniff out the ink and the substance—paper, linen, cotton or anything money is made from.)

It didn't take long for Singh to become impressed with his

Police Dogs of Trinidad and Tobago

explosive-detection expert. "The first time in training, we did a field search with an explosive device hidden deep in the bush. I stood on the road. Penny picked up the scent and ran straight to it in about forty seconds. I felt amazed at her speed," said Singh. Cedeno quickly noted Jed's eagerness to please, his drive, and total concentration. He knew Jed was working with a heart condition, an irregular heartbeat. "But that never kept Jed back," said Cedeno.

Jed found a grenade in an abandoned area of St. Augustine, but the highlight of Cedeno and Jed's partnership came with an assignment to the U.S. Vice President's security detail, when Joe Biden visited Trinidad on May 28, 2013. Jed and Penny did security checks of venues where Biden would appear, and route sweeps, checking the road he took from the airport to Port of Spain. The Secret Service awarded medals for the dogs' outstanding service. Cedeno kept his medal in his locker at the Caroni Canine Section.[7] "It inspires me every time I open the locker," he said.

Over the years, Penny had surgery for a growth on her tail, and she developed arthritis in a leg, but she always bounced back.[8] I often saw Cedeno laughing and rolling in the grass with Jed after a police exercise.

> I feel like I'm on top of Mt. Everest when I'm with Jed. It's about the nose, not the dog's size, and Jed has a good nose.
> I'm not intimidated by the big dogs. They're intimidated by Jed.
> He puts most of those young guys [dogs] in the shade. I totally trust Jed, and he totally trusts me. I trust him more than a person. If Jed tells me there's something suspicious and someone said there's nothing there, I'm going with the dog. Jed understands I'm not leaving him, and I know he's not leaving me.[9]

English Springer Spaniels had once been raised in the Caroni kennels. In 1992, Cpl. Ashram Pariagsingh teamed up with three-month-old Condor, a liver-colored, male English Springer Spaniel who grew to be only 15 inches tall—about three inches shorter than the average Springer Spaniel. Condor became a successful drug-detection dog. He found 110 pounds of marijuana in two suitcases with a street value of about (TT)$500,000. He had about six big finds, including one at the Tobago wharf. Condor died in 2000

Chapter 21. Springing into Action

PC Sherwin Cedeno tosses a ball for Jed at the Caroni kennels (photograph by Miquel Galofré, March 16, 2016).

while Pariagsingh was on vacation.[10] The Canine Section has had no Springer Spaniels since Jackson retired, but their boundless energy, endearing personalities, sense of humor, and outstanding performance have ensured a special place for them in the working dogs' history.

CHAPTER 22

DOG DAYS TWO

PASSING CLOUDS GAVE NO RELIEF on July 24, 2015, a hot day in the middle of the rainy season. In the Port of Spain Prison (still sometimes referred to as the Royal Gaol), inmates crammed into overcrowded cells with no fans, toilets, or running water. Those fortunate enough to have visits got a brief reprieve from the dark cells where rats often scampered through.[1]

In the courtyard, under the watchful eyes of prison officers in khaki uniforms, inmates in navy-blue uniforms with short pants mingled with remanded inmates dressed in street clothes. They collected plastic bags of laundry soap, greasy blocks of cheddar cheese, and bottled water bought at the prison canteen by their families and distributed on a folding plastic table at the edge of the courtyard separating the prison cells from the administration building.[2]

Suddenly, three inmates rushed through the courtyard. Two of them, brandishing guns, stormed past the stunned crowd of prisoners and officers, breached the wrought-iron gate of the holding area at the prison's entrance, forced the guards to surrender the keys to the front gate, and burst onto Frederick Street.[3] In the confusion of visiting hours, just thirty minutes past noon, Allan "Scanny" Martin and Hassan Atwell, accused of kidnapping and murder, escaped. Another inmate charged with two separate murders seized an opportunity to join the gunmen as the prison's front gate swung open. Martin and Atwell fired at police officers stationed outside the prison and mortally wounded PC Sherman Maynard.[4]

The escapees jumped into a Nissan Navara pick-up truck, fled past the prison, and swung left, heading onto Charlotte Street. The van crashed near the Port of Spain General Hospital, around the

Chapter 22. Dog Days Two

corner from the prison, and Martin ran for cover into the hospital's guard booth. Police shot him dead. Atwell and the other man disappeared into Port of Spain. Terrified workers fled the capital city.[5]

At the prison, police noticed something dangerous outside the prison walls. On the asphalt street, in a small puddle—odd for that dry day—authorities spotted a purple-labeled Peardrax sweet-drink bottle, two cigarette butts—and a grenade. The chain of command kicked in with alacrity. A police officer on the scene called the police Special Branch bomb unit; the bomb unit contacted the superintendent of the Mounted and Canine Branch, Patsy Joseph, and she gave the order to send two dogs to the prison.[6] Cpl. Premnath Maharaj and PC Sherwin Cedeno were working on an explosive-detection sweep for a political meeting in southern Trinidad when they heard the news. They loaded Bouncy and Jed back into the police car and rushed north, with sirens wailing.[7] "All kinds of things go through your mind when you get a call like this," said Maharaj. "I thought back to 2005 and the dustbin bomber in Port of Spain and St. James. (See Chapter 19.) I thought of the Trinidadians now going to Syria to join ISIS."

The ISIS recruits from Trinidad had not escaped local or international media attention. Muslims make up an estimated 5 percent of the population.[8] Some of them migrated here from India during the period of indentureship; others (mainly Afro-Trinidadians), converted to Islam during the Black Power movement. A story in the U.K. Guardian said that Trinidad and Tobago, with a population of around 1.5 million, had seen more than 100 of its citizens leave to join the Islamic State, while only about 300 recruits had come from larger countries like Canada and the U.S. This meant Trinidad and Tobago had one of the highest ISIS recruitment levels in the western hemisphere.[9] Simon Cottee's article in the U.S.-based *Atlantic* magazine noted that even as ISIS recruits crossing the border illegally from Turkey had dwindled, Trinidadians were crossing the Atlantic and traveling over 6,200 miles to join ISIS. All the foreign media pointed out that the 1990 coup attempt led by Yasin Abu Bakr of the Jamaat al Muslimeen had been the only Muslim coup attempt in the western hemisphere.[10]

Police Dogs of Trinidad and Tobago

The ISIS recruits had nothing to do with what was happening at the Port of Spain Prison, but for a canine officer working in explosives detection, a grenade makes the imagination explode into all kinds of possibilities of what the present—or future—could hold. Police had cordoned off Frederick Street in front of the prison for Bouncy and Jed to work. Maharaj and Cedeno arrived and unclamped their dogs' leashes. Calmly and systematically, the dogs, noses down, worked the street and headed for the grenade. The canine officers watched with confidence and concern. They knew exactly what the dogs would do as they turned the ghost-like street into a working grid. They could feel their dogs breathing, sniffing, searching. One by one, Bouncy and Jed hovered briefly over the grenade, but neither "indicated" on it.[11]

"The dogs did not sit down in the street and stare at the grenade to signal its danger," said Maharaj. "It was a dud," said Cedeno. "There was no doubt in my mind. I had been with Jed when he found live grenades before, in St. Augustine."

Jed and Bouncy deemed Frederick Street safe—but two escaped convicts were still at large. Just two days after the prison break, on July 26, police discovered Atwell's bullet-riddled body crumpled on a street in East Dry River, Port of Spain. It appeared that Atwell had wandered into Calvary Hill, an area claimed by Rasta City, one of Trinidad's most notorious gangs, which has a running feud with a union of gangs with some 600 members from Beetham Gardens that calls itself the Muslims.[12] Atwell had no gun on him when police found his body.[13] Hours later, the third escapee walked into the Barataria police station and surrendered.

Relieved, Cedeno and Maharaj packed up their dogs and returned to Caroni. Maharaj said:

Working in explosives changes a police officer. I don't stress out on simple problems that everyday people are fighting and fussing about.
    I don't have any kids. That could be good, because I tell my wife, Sheryl, "This is my life; this is my job. I'm going to work, and I might not come home."
    In the beginning, she asked, "Are you crazy?"
    Some of us don't fully explain what we do to our wives, or else we might not have wives to come home to.[14]

Chapter 22. Dog Days Two

Cpl. Premnath Maharaj and Bouncy (photograph by Miquel Galofré, May 22, 2016).

Prison investigations never turned up any evidence as to how the escapees obtained guns. Three prison officers were suspended during the investigations and later re-instated.[15] It's possible the getaway car was organized by an illegal cell phone. The role Bouncy and Jed played behind the scenes that day in Port of Spain was never reported in the media.

CHAPTER 23

WHERE THE AIR IS RARE

DANI, A MUDDY-BROWN BELGIAN Malinois with a black face and ears, appeared to be an ordinary dog—just part of the pack of drug-detection and explosive-detection dogs—but he performed a job in the Canine Section that no other dog could do. Dani came from the U.S. as a fully-trained cadaver dog who searches for bodies.[1] He was the only cadaver dog in the country after his partner Jack, who found a body with Sgt. Raphael Mohammed, died in 2014. Between 2015 and July 2018, Cpl. Stephen Swanson and Dani answered 26 calls to search for corpses.[2] "He never officially found a body, but after we left an area, no one ever discovered anyone, so officially, Dani hasn't missed anything. He has drive. He's always hunting, searching. I am moving on faith when the time reaches and that scent is there, he will find a body," said Swanson.

Swanson delivered KFC before joining the police in 1998 and becoming one of six police canine officers chosen to be part of SAUTT's 26-dog canine section. When SAUTT was disbanded, Swanson returned to the Canine Section as a police dog trainer. Together, Swanson and Dani searched for bodies deep in Biche's forests (near Sangre Grande and Rio Claro in the east) and Debe's hills (near Penal and Monkey Town in the south). They covered beaches, swamps, and rugged terrain.[3] Dani's training was a secret, but his work was not.

A cadaver dog is used days after a suspected death, as opposed to a tracker dog, which searches for live human scent. For cadaver dogs, it works like this: "The body bloats and bursts and the dog tracks the body fluids," said Swanson. When on duty, he carries a long metal

Chapter 23. Where the Air Is Rare

Cpl. Stephen Swanson and cadaver dog Dani at the Cumuto police dog training center (photograph by Sureash Cholai, *Trinidad & Tobago Newsday*, July 16, 2018).

probe to poke the ground in areas suspected of holding a makeshift grave. Too much rain or sun impedes a search, "but the wind helps a lot, once the body is above ground," said Swanson.

Cadaver dogs abroad train with donated body parts, but Swanson didn't always have that option. He was reluctant to use dead pigs, which are said to be the next best option to humans for training. "We don't want Dani tracking dead animals." PC Vincent Hinds handled the first cadaver dog brought to Trinidad by Anthony Piegaro in April 2006.[4] There had been 386 murders the year before.[5]

In June 2006, the police received tips about a body buried in the hills of Morvant. Soldiers and officers of the Morvant CID and Task Force swarmed the reported area while Red searched for the body of Nick Augustine, a 39-year-old father of five. On June 28, Augustine had been cooking food for his children. He left the house to buy something from a nearby shop and kidnappers captured him at gunpoint while he was returning home. Police believe he had witnessed the June 22 murder of Kriston Cooper, said to be part of a Morvant gang. Cooper had been shot dead in reprisal for the murder the week before of Selvon Roberts in the area of Morvant known as Never Dirty. At 2:30 in the afternoon, Red led his handler to a shallow grave in a gully at Romaine Lands. Red found Augustine.[6] Red also found human bones in Maraval (a northern suburb of Port of Spain located at the bottom of the Paramin hills and east of the Diego Martin valley), and in Arima (a town in eastern Trinidad).[7]

Red and his handler investigated tips on the Vindra Naipaul-Coolman case, but never found the businesswoman kidnapped from her driveway at Lange Park, Chaguanas on December 19, 2006. (Nine of 12 men charged with her murder were found not guilty nearly a decade later, in May 2016.) Red retired in 2013 and went home to live with his handler.[8]

Handling a cadaver dog might seem to be a macabre and melancholy job, but Hinds begged to differ. "Remember, somebody's family member is missing. The family needs closure."[9] Swanson hoped police would use cadaver dogs more often.

"If the police call us when they find a body, the dog has an

Chapter 23. Where the Air Is Rare

opportunity for training. The more live hits Dani gets [meaning smelling a dead body], the better the dog's training."[10]

On May 23, 2020, Swanson and Dani accompanied police from the Arouca homicide division to help search for a man last seen on February 6. They arrived at about 9 a.m.[11] Supt. Geoffrey Hospedales of the Mounted and Canine Branch noted in his report to the Commissioner of Police, Gary Griffith, on May 29 that "the canine team together with other officers from the Homicide Bureau, Crime Scene Investigation (CSI) Team, Trinidad & Tobago Defence Force Personnel and personnel from the Ministry of Works with an excavator went to a bushy area at Bridge Road Circular Mt. Lambert." The officer in charge pointed out an area. Swanson probed the area with random holes.[12] "Due to the ground being very hard, I used the cracks in the ground to get the probe down to a good depth. I then tasked canine Dani to search the area," wrote Swanson in his official report. Dani sniffed the holes.[13]

> Canine Dani indicated on one of the holes. As a result, he was re-tasked three times to search the area and indicated all three times on the same hole. I informed the officer in charge and the excavator was asked to dig the spot. After a hole of approximately five feet in depth, five feet in width, and five feet in length was cleared and nothing was found, I requested permission from the officer in charge to return to Cumuto K-9 post which he granted.[14]

"The police ordered the excavator to keep digging and about ten feet from the initial hole which Dani had indicated on, human skeletal remains were recovered," Hospedales wrote in his report to the police commissioner.[15]

The body had been found at the top of a slope. "It should be noted that when a body is buried, the blood and other decomposing juices from the body would travel with the water-flow from rainfall and travel in the direction with the slope of the land and settle in a spot. I believe this is what happened in this situation," wrote Swanson.[16]

Dani had finally discovered his first body.

"…[It] is still the skill of the dog and handler which would have resulted in the discovery of these human remains," wrote

Police Dogs of Trinidad and Tobago

Hospedales. "Dani is the only cadaver dog in the Canine Section and continues to perform at a high level through the skill and ability of the handler, who incidentally is also one of the top trainers in the Branch."[17]

Swanson had little time to celebrate Dani's first find. On June 20, 2020, he accompanied a friend to Coffee Street in San Fernando and remained in the car while his friend shopped for groceries. When his friend returned, he discovered Swanson shaking as if he had suffered a seizure. Police at a nearby station rushed Swanson to San Fernando General Hospital, where Swanson died of a heart attack. He was 49.[18] Insp. Jason Donawa became Dani's handler. Dani retired in March 2023 and went to live with Donawa.

CHAPTER 24

A WOMAN'S TOUCH

IN 1982, WOMAN POLICE CONSTABLE (WPC) Donna Mae Tom found no fulfillment in her job, supervising new police recruits.[1]

"They acted like they had more power than me," said Ms. Tom, who joined the police service in 1976. When Tom and Rosamund Alexander-Clifford saw that the Canine Section was hiring women, they transferred together and became the first two women canine police officers. They worked under Matthews, and Tom worked Dyer's dog, Lady, while he went on vacation. "Lady was a gem. She would sit, I would shake my shoulders for her, and she would sit up straight," said Tom.

One day in Port of Spain, Tom let Lady off her leash while talking to her police partner. "I didn't know I was supposed to keep her on a leash," said Tom. "Lady wasn't a drug dog, but she ran around some guy. I walked up to him and said, 'Just give me the drugs. She knows you have them,' and the guy handed me marijuana." When Dyer returned to work, Tom relinquished Lady and took care of police dog Amber's puppies. "Dyer didn't like me too much, but he learned to like me," she said. "It's not just in Canine that men oppose women in the police service. I didn't find it difficult, because I wanted to be there, so it didn't matter. As long as the treatment wasn't overbearing, it didn't bother me. I loved the dogs."

In 1988, Tom was transferred to the Homicide Section, and retired from the police in 2001.

Women dog handlers say that the Canine Section is still perceived as the domain of men.

"Being a woman in a male-dominated environment, you're judged and critiqued. [But] I've worked everywhere in Trinidad,

Police Dogs of Trinidad and Tobago

Donna Mae Tom and Lady in Caroni, 1989 (courtesy Donna Mae Tom).

Chapter 24. A Woman's Touch

walking miles into the forest, miles over mountains, with all the male characters of canine," said Woman Police Constable (WPC) Malissa Narine.[2] She is not bothered by criticism. Narine follows her own instincts when it comes to her relationship with her dog. "My instructors tell me I spoil and mother my dog Adina too much, but I can't help it."

She laughed at the memory of one assignment when Adina barked at something under a bed.

"I thought, 'This is an intense alert.' Police heard Adina and rushed into the room to see her big find. Miss Lady had found a cat and tried to play with it under the bed. That's Adina. She is hard-working, but has a playful nature. She goes into prey drive and likes to chase down cats. Instinct takes over any training."[3]

Malissa Narine and Adina on the training field in Cumuto (photograph by Miquel Galofré, May 22, 2016).

Police Dogs of Trinidad and Tobago

Behind the scenes, many men in the Canine Section claim women don't pull their weight, and aren't suited for the physical demands of being a canine officer, but women canine officers feel they add a different dimension to canine culture.[4] "Women are stronger and more resilient than men. We work well under stress and give balance to an organization. We're good at multitasking, and that makes us perfect police officers," said Narine. "Women bring a humane touch where there is normally a harsh reality. We tend to influence the men to have a softer side. The police can be brutal and authoritative, and I think we sensitize them a bit."

When WPC Jiselle Andrews returned home from the U.S. after finishing a degree in business administration in 2007, she wanted a physically challenging job. She thought the police would be a perfect fit. It turned out to be far more of a challenge than she ever imagined.[5] "The police service is male-dominated, so you must work twice as hard to get to where the males are, but believe me, it's one of the sweetest experiences you'll ever have," said Andrews.[6]

A Labrador named Bear changed the course of Andrews's career. Seven months after police training, Andrews saw Bear, a Labrador Retriever, while she was attending the police driving school at the Caroni police branch. "Canine officers put on a show for us with this big old white dog." That encounter with Bear persuaded Andrews to become a police dog handler. One day Andrews came to work and saw she had an interview with the Canine Section.

> I got smartly dressed in a three-piece suit, and I was the only female in the interview. When I got in the door, the panel had six men. I had my hands on my knees so they wouldn't see my knees shaking. I'm thinking, "How am I supposed to flatter these six men?"
>
> They asked, "How are you at cleaning dog tootoo [feces] because there's a lot of it. Have you ever been bitten by a snake? Have you ever been in the forest?"
>
> I said, "I live six miles from the Pointe-à-Pierre Wild Fowl Trust" [a protected fresh water habitat of lakes and ponds with 40 species of trees and 86 species of birds, located inside the Petrotrin oil fields].[7]
>
> They said, "That's a trust—not a forest."[8]

The questions kept coming. "'You're very active, you play hockey but I never see you,'" said one of the officers.[9] "Whenever you go to the

Chapter 24. A Woman's Touch

Petrotrin Sports Club, Pointe-à-Pierre, my picture is on the wall," I answered.

Weeks later, Andrews went to work, looked in the message book, and read: "WPC Andrews is temporarily assigned to the Mounted and Canine Branch. I danced around and celebrated. Everyone thought I went crazy," said Andrews.

In the Canine Section, Andrews trained with eleven men. "They hated me because I outran them all."

Then came the day all canine officers wait for: the assignment of dogs. "I got the big fluffy one, Skeeto, a spotted, short haired German Pointer, and I thought, 'How sexist,'" said Andrews. Skeeto, a firearm and narcotics dog, found guns, drugs, and the occasional chicken or duck. "I thought, 'Oh my God, nobody knows my trouble. He can't see a chicken or duck and leave it alone.' I got a dog that is 199 per cent energy. But they always say it's good to have a dog with drive."[10]

Skeeto also had an issue with cars. "While other dogs found narcotics in cars, he would get in the front seat, sit there and look at me. I'd go back at night and cry. Still, I kept thinking, 'We're going to get this.' We kept working," said Andrews.

When officers in training got an opportunity to go on their first assignment, Andrews and nine men showed up for an exercise in Valencia.

> All the men searched around the house. I stood there, the only girl, with the fluffy dog, and everyone wanted to play with my dog. I felt so terrible. Sgt. Raphael Mohammed said, "Come, let's go inside."
>
> We began searching. We had been taught to search clockwise, and there went Skeeto, a hundred miles an hour. We came to the position of three o'clock on a couch, and my dog just dropped. He froze at the foot of a La-Z-Boy chair.
>
> Sgt. Mohammed stuck his hand in the chair, and said, "Reward your dog."
>
> I couldn't catch my breath. I gave him his ball. Skeeto was ecstatic.
>
> The guys outside heard me carrying on. The girl with the fluffy dog found cocaine and marijuana.[11]

Soon after her interview, Andrews went on maternity leave, and Skeeto went to work with Cpl. Mapp in Tobago. Men in Canine Section have to face the possibility of losing their assigned dogs when they go on vacations, but women also face that possibility when they go on maternity leave. Finding the right balance between men and women dog handlers continues to be a challenge. For the women, it's all a case of perseverance.

Chapter 25

Tobago Tales

Although it's unofficial, a little stretch of the imagination makes it possible to picture just how far canine Zando's career as a rescue dog could have gone. If nothing else, Zando's story made him one of the most memorable dogs in Tobago canine history. PC Delroy James and Cpl. Deon Mapp both spoke of Zando's heroism during training in Chaguaramas.[1] "One day at the beach some guy flailed around in the water," said James, re-enacting the drowning scene. "Zando jumped in the ocean, swam around to the back of the man, grabbed his collar and pulled him to safety." Mapp nodded in agreement.

Zando's former handler, who was in a Tobago park finishing off a dog-training exercise for two civilians, burst into laughter when asked about Zando's story. "Here's what really happened," said former Tobago canine officer Cpl. Anthony Duke.

> In 2000, we were lucky to get some new dogs. They came from homes, and we didn't know their breed or their capabilities. We went down to the old U.S. army base in Chaguaramas to do a refresher training course with them.
> Afterwards, someone said, "Let we go and bathe [go to the beach]."
> We took our dogs. I had my German Shepherd, Zando. We jumped in the water and enjoyed ourselves. When Zando and I came out, some fellow playing the fool [joking around] in the water began to shout, "I got a cramp!"
> Zando shot a look at the man throwing up his arms. Zando was laughing all the time until now. His face got serious; he turned away from me, jumped in the water, and swam to the fellow. He still wore the lead [leash] he had on in the water.
> Zando swam to the back of the man so the lead would float to the man. The man held the lead. Zando pulled him out and dragged him onto the sand.

Police Dogs of Trinidad and Tobago

Riko demonstrates his tactical training skills at the Mt. Irvine Hotel golf course, Tobago. From left: Sgt. Darren Baptiste, Riko and PC Collis Joseph (photograph by David Reid, May 28, 2023).

Everybody laughed and yelled, "Wayyyy, we never saw that before. You have a search-and rescue dog."[2]

Duke shrugged. "In 2000, we didn't have the facilities to train a rescue dog. We never dived into it and developed it, but he might have become our first search-and-rescue dog."[3] Zando's surprising action that day had taken Duke's mind off how much he longed to return home. Tobago canine officers always miss their island when they must train in Trinidad. Picture-postcard Tobago, just 19 miles northeast of Trinidad, is a far cry from the bigger island's hustle and bustle. Just 25.5 miles long and 7.5 miles wide, Tobago has mountains, a forest reserve and fertile valleys to explore. Its swashbuckling past can be conjured up from names on a map: Black Rock, Bloody Bay, Bon Accord, Cinnamon Hill, Pirates Bay, Scarborough, and Les Couteaux (the French word for knifes or swords).

Long stretches of gentle, tourist-friendly beaches surround the island, and glass-bottomed boats take trips to the coral reefs. The

Chapter 25. Tobago Tales

Argyle waterfall cascades into pristine pools. The Buccoo goat races at Easter are more like Tobago's speed, but the annual Great Race, with sleek, speedy powerboats, starts in Trinidad and ends here. The two islands have differing stories from their colonial past. Christopher Columbus named Trinidad and sighted Tobago on his third voyage in 1498. Like other Caribbean islands, Trinidad and Tobago had populations of "Amerindians" (First Peoples) who had migrated to the islands from central and South America at least 6,000 years before the Spanish arrived.[4]

Trinidad remained sparsely populated and underdeveloped until the king of Spain issued the Cedula of Population inviting immigrants—particularly from French Caribbean islands such as Martinique—to settle there. By the 17th century, Tobago was in constant turmoil, the result of European wars and colonialism. Naval battles, invasions, or peace treaties in those European wars decided the island's fate. The Spanish, British, French, Dutch, and Courlanders (from modern-day Latvia) would all claim Tobago, which changed possession more than 30 times. Merchant ships brought problems too.

Tempers flared on those long voyages across the Caribbean, and resolutions to those matters depended on an admiralty court, often absent because it circulated through the British Caribbean. During one such absence, in 1773, the Scots sailor John Paul fled Tobago after killing a man in a swordfight. He surfaced in North America, where he joined the American revolution of 1776 and became the naval hero John Paul Jones, later hailed as the "father" of the U.S. Navy by President Teddy Roosevelt.[5]

Finally, the British took Trinidad from the Spanish in 1797, and paired Tobago with Trinidad for government purposes in 1889. By then it was difficult to imagine a period when Tobago had been so peaceful and remote that author Daniel Defoe had chosen it as the perfect place for his fictional character Robinson Crusoe to be marooned.[6]

These days, Tobago fights its battles with crime. The task requires personal sacrifices from the island's canine officers—like living in the Caroni police dorms if they have no family or friends in Trinidad to stay with, during months of training. This was the case for Cpl. Darren Baptiste when he left Tobago in 2009. First, Baptiste worked with Buddy, the Golden Retriever explosives-detection dog eventually handled by Maharaj. Lonely for family and Tobago, Baptiste spent extra time exercising Buddy, who always had a weight problem. After he learned he couldn't return to Tobago with an explosive-detection dog because it wasn't felt they were needed there at the time, Baptiste traded Buddy for Bruno, a three-year-old yellow Labrador narcotics-detection dog.[7] "I never saw a Labrador big like Bruno." "He found cocaine at the airport and in an apartment in Crown Point," said Baptiste. When Bruno turned eight, he stopped eating, and Baptiste knew he had to face another dreaded trip to Trinidad.

> Bruno had a wound on his back that I treated, but it wouldn't heal. In October 2014, we traveled to Trinidad to visit the Mt. Hope veterinarian hospital.
> Bruno had cancer. The veterinarian euthanized him the same day.
> I didn't go in when they did it. I didn't want to see it. I walked away with his leash and cried while walking through Mt. Hope hospital.
> I heard a boy who had brought a dog to the hospital say to his mother, "I never saw a big man cry like that."
> They aren't going to understand. When I went back up to Caroni Canine, I was still crying. Sgt. Beepat said, "I understand what you're going through."

Baptiste's wait began for another dog. He returned to Tobago waited for the next trip to Trinidad for training. Eventually, he got Viper, another drug-detection dog. Everything changed for Baptiste when Tobago had its first bomb threat in February 2019 at the Tobago House of Assembly cultural office. Then came a bomb threat on the Spirit, a water taxi, on June 24, 2019.

"Senior officers here stated it was necessary for one of us in the canine section to give up our dog and take an explosive-detection dog. I volunteered. I gave up Viper, got Arco and returned to Tobago," said Baptiste.

Subsequently, PC Enoch Romeo and Riko transferred together to Tobago, giving the island its second explosive detection dog. (When Romeo got called back to Trinidad to train police dogs in 2023, Riko remained with Baptiste, and Arco retired.)[8]

Chapter 25. Tobago Tales

Sgt. Baptiste and Riko at the Mt. Irvine Hotel golf course, Tobago. Riko, a Dutch Shepherd, who previously worked with Enoch Romeo, is the only explosive detection/tactical dog in the TTPS (photograph by David Reid, May 28, 2023).

In 2016, Cpl. Ronnie Caruth, from Scarborough, worked with Cordon.

He's like me: playful, but get me angry, and I will deal with you.

He's my best friend. I can tell him stuff, and he acts like he understands by shaking his head left to right. I know if I tell him secrets, I wouldn't hear them back from anyone. He's very intelligent.

Anyone can boast about his dog, but the proof of his worth is in his finds. Cordon once found drugs in an old tree stump during an exercise in Bethel. All the officers were walking past the drugs, not noticing the tree stump.

Cordon pushed his head into the stump and sat. Without Cordon, a known drug dealer would have gone scot-free.[9]

On another day, Caruth and Cordon searched an area strewn with garbage.

Police Dogs of Trinidad and Tobago

"Cordon went next to an officer's foot and sat down. It looked like nothing was there but garbage, but the police officers were standing right next to the drugs." But the find Caruth remembered best happened on the beach. "A guy selling drugs spotted us from a distance and buried the drugs in the sand. While he was talking to another police officer, Cordon dug up the drugs."

Tobago canine officers say most of the marijuana in Tobago originates in Venezuela or St. Vincent, which is said to have a better grade of "the herb."[10] "To me, the drug problem has just gone from bad to worse," said Caruth. "Drugs will lead to other crimes, and then it's not like there's police or coast guard on every point in Tobago. There are so many beaches. Drug shipments often land in Friendship, near Scarborough. If we had more dogs, we could do a much better job."

Upstairs in the Crown Point police station, the Tobago Canine officer on sentry duty works in a 12-by-14-foot room with a desk, 12 small lockers, and three bunk beds. An electric tea kettle and a microwave rest on one of the bunk beds. There's a refrigerator and two office chairs. From here, all of Tobago's canine operations are dispatched. The dogs' accommodation is also cramped. The small kennels have poor ventilation and no room to expand, and are crammed against a walkway near a side door, so the dogs have little space to move. Officers often take their dogs to the beach to get them out of the kennels.

There seem to be obstacles at every turn. Still, station officers who see working dogs in action occasionally ask to transfer to the canine section. While he worked for the Task Force, PC Kenon Baynes remembers going on a joint exercise with Trinidad canine officers WPC Racine Miller and PC Winn that sold him on becoming a canine officer. "Miller and Winn conducted a search where I had been standing, and her dog indicated on a stone. She rewarded the dog with his toy, moved the stone and found drugs. I had been standing right on top of the drugs and didn't know it. When I saw this, I wanted to join the branch immediately."[11]

Baynes' first dog, Niko, was diagnosed with a heart problem. "I cried from the vet back to Cumuto," said Baynes. "I cry when my dogs

Chapter 25. Tobago Tales

at home die." His second dog, Fando, retired after working on the movie *Green Days by the River*.

The third time turned out to be the charm, because Baynes ended up with the notorious Jackson, PC Texeira's high-energy black-and-white Springer Spaniel. Baynes felt utter shock when he first saw Jackson.

> I got him in September 2016, and I thought, "This short thing is really a police dog?"
>
> [But] it gave me great joy to see him search. His detection rate is very high. I have had several memorable moments working with Jackson.
>
> In Castara, we searched a house and the backyard, then decided to go on the beach. Jackson went to a boat on the shore and started digging under the boat and dug out a bag of marijuana.
>
> It was the first time I found drugs, and people all the way up the road heard me praising Jackson for the find.[12]

Soon, Jackson established his usual routine of finding drugs where other police had already searched and found nothing. Baynes enjoyed watching officers' shocked faces when Jackson showed up on exercises. "When they first see him, they're like, 'Wait, nah, that's your pompek you brought from home?' But when they see him work, they say, 'Nah, boy.' They can't believe it. He's one of the most popular dogs among police officers over here in Tobago. And when he's not working, he loves playing at the beach and running up and down in the sand," said Baynes.

With crime in Tobago on the rise, the canine section has expanded, and now also has kennels at the Roxborough police station. "Firearm-related robberies are growing in Tobago. Bailable offences too. They're doing more robberies to pay the lawyers," said Baynes. "We don't want to think this place is getting like Trinidad, but sometimes it seems so," said James. "Development caused that. We have people from all over the world now wanting a piece of paradise, so they come here to live. Questionable characters see how Tobagonians live carefreely and laid back, and take advantage of that."

The Tobago Canine Section is relatively new. On October 11, 2000, four officers from Tobago and PC Premnanth Maharaj, stationed there, joined the canine section and came to Trinidad to train. They returned to Tobago in April 2001. There was no rotation of Trinidad officers again—except for corporals to supervise the Tobago canine section. Its founding members included PC Anthony Duke, PC Paul Romeo, PC Darnel Melville, PC Evans Gray, and PC Premnath Maharaj. Before that, Trinidad canine officers did short-term stints in Tobago.

Duke remembered his career with a twinge of nostalgia.

> I had a Belgian Malinois named Duke, bought and donated by the Tobago House of Assembly [the governing body of Tobago]. We were Duke and Duke.
> The oldest dog I ever had, Odessa, my first German Shepherd, would bark and run up and down the whole day if I didn't come to work. She had the most heart. At 12, she went to work. I'd have to lift her out of the vehicle and I'd say, "Girl, you ready to work?" and she would smile, like, "Let we go."[13]

Memories of working in Trinidad were far different for Duke.

> We worked in nightmarish conditions in Trinidad.
> In one case, we walked through some bush looking for a marijuana field. We saw bottles on the ground; the man had wet the field with Gramoxone the day before so the insects wouldn't eat the marijuana.
> If you see all the toxic chemicals around what people smoke. They'd pee in buckets and hide the drugs in faeces and stale pee. Sometimes they put guns in cellophane wrap and push them down into the sewer. Cpl. Keon James's Labrador Sunny found drugs under a manhole cover. Drug dealers put fish hooks in concrete slabs and set up trap guns to injure police....
> We worked in extreme conditions.[14]

Ultimately, Duke resigned from the police. "I miss being in canine. My reason for leaving wasn't a nice one. I just didn't want to choose going to Trinidad to train over staying with my family again. It's hard to live in a Trinidad police station, but if they call me back, I'd go," said Duke. He never got his wish. On March 27, 2020, he died of a heart attack in Tobago.

Sad stories and problems aside, Cpl. Deon Mapp couldn't imagine working anywhere in the police service but the Canine Section. "Other officers don't understand that bond between you and your dog, so you have to get that feeling of satisfaction from inside

Chapter 25. Tobago Tales

yourself. The dog and I can cover for each other better than another officer can protect me."[15]

In 2016 Mapp worked with WPC Andrews' former dog, Skeeto. Mapp remembered:

> I got the talk about Skeeto's skin problems before they sent him over. I didn't take it on. I saw it as something workable. Whatever dog they send, we work with them.
>
> After a while, we bonded. I rubbed him down with coconut oil and took him out as much as possible. I came on off days to be with him and make him as comfortable as possible. I tried not to bawl up on him too much. I'm not too boisterous or too physical with him.
>
> In more than five years I haven't taken a single sick day. Even if I don't feel good, I come to work to see my dog. All I want is for canine could be housed in some place better than this.[16]

Mapp also worried about the rising crime problem.

> Crime is going to get worse in Tobago. We had five murders for the year by April 2017, four of them gun-related, so that tells you crime is changing. The first three murders were drug-related; the last shooting was a robbery. A fourteen-year-old girl had her throat slit, and we don't know why.
>
> When I first started in the police service, narcotics made up most of the crimes. I believe drugs are coming from illegal boats and the ferry from Trinidad. Vehicles go on ferries unchecked for guns. Why don't they do something in Trinidad? Why do we have to go on the port to look for drugs coming from Trinidad?[17]

But nothing has ever frustrated Mapp enough to make him consider leaving Canine. "I will retire in Canine. I've been here so long, and it's just the dogs, the dogs, the dogs. I love the dogs. I always say, 'If Canine burns down, look for me in the ashes, because I ent goin' anywhere.'" Mapp remained true to his word. In August 2022, he was promoted to sergeant. He died a month later, on September 5. He was 44 years old.

"For the last five years, he held one of the highest crime-detection rates on the island," said Cpl. Baptiste. "Sgt. Mapp was an honest and trustworthy officer whose commitment to duty was unmatched."[18]

Chapter 26

Starring:
The "M" Dogs

Film director Michael Mooledhar and producer Christian James strolled through the police canine kennels in Cumuto searching for police dogs that matched the description of three dogs in the novel *Green Days by the River*, by Michael Anthony. They settled on Fando, a brindle Dutch Shepherd; Cif, a black German Shepherd; and Bak, a tan Belgian Malinois with a smudge of black on his mouth, to star in the movie based on the Trinidad classic. Filming the dog scenes took place over six days, and the movie opened at MovieTowne, Port of Spain, on September 27, 2017.[1]

Fando retired after the film. Cif, the dog who doesn't bark much, returned to Tobago to perform his tactical/narcotics work with PC Delroy James, and Bak accompanied Cpl. Neil Samaroo on many memorable exercises.[2] Samaroo remembered:

Once Bak searched a grocery store where we had information about someone selling drugs. Constable Hosein and I walked in with Bak and Eddie. Three guys were sitting together.
Bak ran up to one of the men and indicated on his waist. I thought he had a firearm, so I drew my weapon. Everyone put their hands in the air. I continued to task Bak, asking, "Where is it?"
He pushed his nose on the man's stomach and froze. When police officers came to search him, he had a quantity of marijuana in his crotch.[3]

Even in a pack of exemplary dogs like Bak, there are always a couple of memorable dogs who define an era. Maverick was one of those legendary dogs, who pops up in many officers' conversations about the most memorable dogs in the Canine Section.

PC Enoch Romeo, a soft-spoken giant of a man, who also trained

Chapter 26. Starring: The "M" Dogs

as a boxer, and his canine partner, Maverick, drove to police exercises like no other canine officers and their dogs. Too big to fit in a plastic portable kennel in the back of an air-conditioned police vehicle, Maverick sat in the back seat of a police car, with a paw resting on Romeo's shoulder. As they drove, Maverick scanned the roads for his favorite sight: a police car's flashing lights. Once he saw those lights, Maverick got excited.[4]

On one exercise in 2015, Maverick and Romeo headed south, to Gasparillo, near Pointe-à-Pierre and the Petrotrin oil refinery. When they arrived, Romeo stopped the car, Maverick jumped into the front seat, leapt out of the door and ran for the bush, where he discovered a camp. Romeo spotted a man sleeping on a cushion outside a wooden shack. Maverick crept forward, hovered over the man sleeping on the ground, and sniffed him. Groggy with sleep, the suspect stirred and raised his head to see Maverick standing over him. Trapped and terrified, he surrendered. Maverick had apprehended a man wanted for assault, robbery and attacking a police officer.[5]

"Maverick earned officers' respect and made them laugh," said Romeo. "He's a big dog with a high-pitched, female bark, so they call him the donkey dog."[6] Romeo and Maverick were the perfect match, but they nearly didn't become police partners. Romeo had been training with Strike, and when he went on leave, Winn took over Strike.

Romeo recalled:

> When I left for boxing, Cpl. Jason Donawa told me, "I will organise something special for you when you return to the Canine Section."
> On the day I returned to work, Donawa called me to a police vehicle and said, "Look."
> I watched inside the police vehicle and saw Maverick.
> We connected immediately. Maverick quickly distinguished himself as a dog willing to go anywhere. He went places I didn't think he could go: up mountains—anywhere.
> In San Fernando, Maverick found cocaine buried by the roots of a fig tree.
> Then Maverick began finding weapons—guns, ammunition, buried shotguns and AKA rifles.[7]

Perfect timing had brought Romeo and Maverick together. Had Romeo not returned to work when he did, Maverick would have been another officer's dog. Together Maverick and Romeo worked on the kinds of police exercises you see in the movies—like the night they headed north for Wharf Trace, in the steep mountains surrounding Maracas Valley.

Romeo said:

> I'll never forget that day: 1:30 a.m. and a mountain to climb again. Maverick picked up a track. We came to a clearing and saw a piece of galvanized iron on the ground in the center of the clearing.
>
> I whispered to the police officer with us, "Don't mash the galvanized. It could be an alarm." The house sat on stilts, right on the side of the mountain.
>
> The next thing I know, the officer stepped on the galvanized iron by mistake.
>
> From the corner of my eye, I saw a guy throw his frame [body] outside of the house. He went tumbling through the bush and over the precipice.
>
> Maverick and I walked to the precipice. We stood there, looking over the edge—and the piece of ground we were standing on broke away from the side of the cliff. I grabbed for a tree that had long picka (thorns) on it. We slid down this precipice and headed for a riverbank.
>
> I grabbed Maverick and placed him on my stomach while we were falling so he wouldn't get hurt. I ended up lying there on my back on a rock in a riverbed.[8]

Stunned, Romeo noticed the water rushing around him. He looked around, and Maverick was gone. "Maverick took off after the suspect. The police came after me and said, 'Go get Maverick.' He had the guy up a palm tree, and the suspect wouldn't come down."[9]

On another day in March 2015, Romeo and Maverick headed up a mountain with officers from the Western Division to find 12 armed men who had narcotics and firearms. Romeo remembered:

> The information wasn't 100 percent. We walked up a river bed and walked around two mountains.
>
> Like these guys knew we were coming. The closer we got, the more they moved. At one point, we had to use a rope to go up the mountain.
>
> In a clearing, we saw clothes and a child's knapsack full of marijuana and ammunition. They opened fire. We took cover.
>
> Maverick still wanted to go after them.
>
> By the end of the exercise, I noticed something wrong. Maverick's back legs collapsed. I had to lift him out of there on my back. His legs couldn't take the mountains any more.[10]

Chapter 26. Starring: The "M" Dogs

Maverick retired to the canine kennels. Romeo hoped Maverick's retirement papers would be processed swiftly, and he could take the dog to his home in Tobago, where he has a big yard. But the bureaucracy that requires police dogs to be written off by the same committee that writes off tables and chairs in the Ministry of Finance restricted Maverick to a sad life of confinement for over two years. Romeo made Maverick as comfortable as he could. He took accrued vacation leave so he wouldn't have to work a new dog and could spend time visiting Maverick in Caroni. Maverick and Romeo had climbed mountains, chased criminals and tumbled off a precipice together. Now Maverick sat on the grass outside the Caroni kennels, where he chewed a deflated soccer ball. In December 2017, Romeo finally got to take Maverick home.

From 2014–2020, many canine officers singled out Marko, a working German Shepherd trained in firearm/narcotic/tactical work, as an era-defining dog. Marko's coat resembled a patchwork quilt of black-and-tan ragged squares. His eyebrows had turned grey to match the grey inside his ears and along his nose. "He looks like a dog I could have in my yard," I said the first time a canine officer showed me Marko. "Good luck with that," he said.

Almost all of Marko's finds stunned his handler, PC Leon Lopez. He often discovered buried contraband. At the search of one man's house, Marko took off for a nearby river and found a shotgun buried far from the designated search. His drug finds made him a popular request for police exercises. For three years, Marko had the most finds in the Canine Section.[11]

"The instructors told me he is a once-in-a-lifetime dog. I had no idea he would turn out to be so special," said Lopez. On November 9, 2020, Marko had an emergency splenectomy after he was diagnosed with a tumor on his spleen. Marko didn't recover fully from the operation. He returned to the kennels, but wouldn't eat or drink. He died in Mt. Hope Hospital shortly after his surgery.

Another era-defining dog with a name beginning with "M" worked from 2015 to 2020 as a multi-purpose, tactical police dog trained to detect illegal drugs, firearms and ammunition. His handler did not want himself or his dog identified. (There are rumors of drug dealers putting hits on police dogs. Many canine officers said they believed Jackson was on a hit list for most of his career.)

The anonymous handler said:

> He enjoys finding people on tracking exercises, and he has an extremely high prey drive. He chases anything that moves, from birds to leaves or grass blowing in the wind, and destroys them or tries to kill them.
>
> He loves people, and he especially loves belly rubs from children. He is the perfect police dog, not afraid of anything—except turtles. His first encounter with a turtle was probably not a pleasant one. The way it approached him probably scared him.
>
> He is very intelligent and works without commands.
>
> His only problem is that he hates all male dogs and won't let any male dog come close to him.[12]

In 2014, "M" was hot on the trail of a man who had reportedly raped his companion. The canine officer said:

> A struggle ensued, and the woman stabbed the man several times. She was also injured.
>
> I noticed bloodstains leading to a broken fence. We followed the scent trail, found exactly where the man passed and reached a spot where the dog wasn't getting his scent any more.
>
> We interviewed some villagers nearby who told us they took the man to the hospital. One of the villagers accompanied the police to the hospital and positively identified the man. The police found him right where they had left him, waiting to see a doctor.
>
> Thank goodness for our slow health care system.

But the handler said M's most memorable assignment was a tracking exercise in the bush.

> Another canine officer and I received a report of a robbery in the Ravine Sable area of central Trinidad. We were informed that the perpetrators entered the victim's home. After relieving the victims—two men and a woman—of cash, jewelry and electronic items worth over $10,000, the three bandits escaped in a waiting vehicle with two other occupants.
>
> The two male victims went in pursuit of the bandits. On reaching an intersection at Ravine Sable Road, the victims, in a pickup, rear-ended the thieves, forcing them to crash into a concrete electric pole.
>
> Police officers who were responding to the home invasion came shortly after, but not fast enough. After the accident, the attackers ran into some nearby bushes.[13]

Chapter 26. Starring: The "M" Dogs

"M" arrived and police briefed his handler, telling him they had searched the area thoroughly, but couldn't find the men. The canine officer said:

> I gave the command "zoo" to my canine, and he commenced a tracking exercise, with the other canine officer following closely behind offering backup. We spent about an hour searching the bushes where the officers told us to check, but we came up empty-handed.
>
> The other officers were there for quite some time and had already searched a large forested area as well, so they returned to their vehicle and were about to drive off. They seemed exhausted.[14]

M's handler had parked close to the crashed getaway vehicle, and he too was heading back to leave, when M appeared to be getting the scent of something. He signaled to the other canine officer, and they both entered a bushy area close to the scene of the accident.

> The police officers were in their vehicles popping their horns for us to give up and leave.
>
> As I neared a riverbank with overgrown bushes, my dog became more excited and started to bark in a very aggressive manner. I knew a suspect was close. I shouted, "You there, in the bushes, come out! Come out, I say! I have a trained attack dog. Come out, or I will send him."
>
> My shouting made my dog more agitated. The officers in their cars heard me and quickly ran to our assistance. The dog pulled me through some thick grass, heading towards a patch of tall bushes on the riverbank.
>
> A slim-built, dark-skinned male stood up from the patch of bushes with both hands in the air and casually said, "Ok, he find meh."
>
> The officers quickly ran in and arrested the man, who had been a highly trained soldier dismissed from the army.[15]

"M" worked until 2022, retired early in 2023 and went home, where he chases his beloved ball all day.

His retirement leaves space for another era-defining dog to make his mark. One strong candidate is a multi-purpose tactical German Shepherd, Arci, who finds guns, ammunition and illegal drugs. "In Couva he had a big find on the edge of a mountain," said Arci's handler, PC Kerron Woodroffe. "Arci wanted to go over the mountain, and I had to decipher what was going on. There was a sharp drop and a hole over the edge with 877 grams of cocaine stuffed inside."[16]

With Arci, Woodroffe says, "Expect the unexpected."[17]

Police Dogs of Trinidad and Tobago

During a pitch-dark narcotic search at 4 a.m. in Couva, Arci, on a six-foot lead, took off and ran over a drain and into a valley filled with bull grass [slightly rough, tall clumps of grass] and no trees to hide behind.

Arci alone ran in that direction. I knew he was on a track, and I was encouraging him to do his thing.

Arci found an illegal immigrant stooping in the bush. I was just three feet away from this guy. I had my gun, so I escorted him out of the bush and put him in police hands.

That was an eye-opener. I was startled at how close he was to me. Adrenalin was pumping.[18]

Sometimes police dogs heading for a remarkable career end up following in the footsteps of Dog #2, Carlos, with careers cut unexpectedly short. Their handlers always wonder what might have been. In 2016, a small Belgian Malinois, just under 60 pounds, with a black snout and ears outlined in black, turned heads in the canine section. Like the red deer he was named after, Hart proved sure-footed and agile, climbing and leaping to get to find hidden contraband. He was smart and strong and never got sick, though he visited the vet twice after cutting his paw while searching. He would go places no other dog would go, squeezing himself into small spaces and crawling in confined places to find marijuana, cocaine, guns, and ammunition.[19] His handler, PC Sean Bailey, said:

Hart had no fear. He climbed up anything. Once he went down an embankment and wanted to walk on top of a log to get to drugs. He fell in the river, and I had to go down and pick him up.

Hart had many finds. One of my favorite ones was a Glock 30 and twenty-five rounds of ammunition that he found down in a hole covered with leaves inside of a bamboo patch.

He appeared on Insp. Roger Alexander's TV crime show *Beyond the Tape*, and found a firearm on camera.[20]

Sometime after Hart turned six, Bailey said he noticed a white film forming on Hart's eyes. He was going blind and under a vet's special care in Mt. Hope. "Hart kept working. He found a gun on a window ledge in a home. When his eyes got worse, he worked only in the airport," said Bailey. Hart retired at seven. At home, he loves to play fetch and act like a guard dog. "If he hadn't gone blind, Hart would still be working. His nose is still very good," said Bailey. "While he

Chapter 26. Starring: The "M" Dogs

Hart at work in the mountains in Carenage (photograph by Sean Bailey, March 14, 2019).

worked with me, I found Hart was number one. All the officers who worked alongside him said he had the heart of a champion."[21]

Kubo, a short-haired Dutch Shepherd with a black-and-brown

spotted coat, paired up with Zameer Mohammed in December 2015 for a succession of outstanding finds. Chosen by Cpl. Chase on a trip to buy dogs in Miami, Kubo was trained by Cpl. Swanson. His finds made Mohammed handler of the year in 2019 and officer of the month in January 2020.

Mohammed said:

> Kubo was on the small side for a tactical dog, but Cpl. Chase always said he was small in body, but big in mind.
>
> I still remember a 2 a.m. exercise we did in a three-story house in San Fernando. The police said the man in the house had given up the drugs, a small amount of marijuana.
>
> After that, Kubo went inside to search. In a cupboard he found a school bag with bullets. I rewarded the dog with his ball.
>
> He searched the grandmother's room and found an AK-47 on top of the wardrobe, a kilo of cocaine hidden in another bedroom and four kilos of marijuana tossed outside of a window. Kubo found about seven hundred rounds of bullets in the house.[22]

Nearly everywhere Kubo went, he had multiple finds. He was friendly with people. He loved bite work, and he did all the riot drills. Loud noise, music, firecrackers, chaos—nothing bothered him.

> He was my once-in-a-lifetime dog. Everyone in Canine told me, "You will never get another dog like him."
>
> You have to set yourself up for when your dog dies, but you are never prepared.
>
> I was driving down the highway when an officer called and said, "Pull to the side."
>
> He told me Kubo died.
>
> I went back to Caroni and sat there in his kennel and cried.
>
> Kubo died in November 2020 of tick fever. He was only six years old.
>
> I still have not recovered from the loss of that dog. I dream about him often and wake up depressed. I think about him running free in a field somewhere and waiting for me.[23]

The race for the era-defining dogs always has some unexpected turns. In the long run, it will be won by a nose. As Cpl. Chase always says, "Nearly all the police dogs operate on an equal footing now. They are separated only by degrees of drive."[24]

Chapter 27

Training Days

Cpl. Shane Chase was a moving target on a huge field on the Camp Cumuto army compound. He patted his arm and ran with heavy, exaggerated steps. Felix, a hefty German Shepherd, focused on Chase's zig-zag movements. He barked and strained against his lead. "Stop him!" Felix's handler yelled as he unclipped the dog's leash. Felix made a mad dash for Chase, leapt through the air and latched onto Chase's arm, which was covered with a padded sleeve. He wrapped his paws around Chase's leg.[1]

Tracking and bite work can be traced back to the first four police dogs: Bruno, Carlos, Shah, and Winston. The multi-purpose tactical dogs of today are trained to find illegal drugs, guns, ammunition, and suspects. In Thomas's era, the dogs' only purpose was to catch fleeing suspects or missing persons. "The dogs love bite work," said Chase. "It releases tension for them. But dogs can't be forced to do bite work. Training only enhances the traits that are already there for some dogs."[2] Chase also instructs handlers in the most challenging part of bite work: teaching dogs to let go on command.

Chase joined the police service in 1998 after working from 1994 to 1998 at the Emperor Valley Zoo in Port of Spain, where he cared for the reptiles and quarantined animals, including an orphaned baby owl, a baby ocelot, injured birds of prey, and a rare Brazilian otter found on the beach and brought to the zoo as a nine-pound baby. He said this work prepared him for his work in the canine section, where he transferred in 2002.[3]

> I learned a lot at the zoo. Working with the reptiles helped me later as a police dog trainer when I had to lay tracks inside the forest and come across mapepire [deadly, poisonous snakes].
>
> On one tracking exercise, I came across a whole, perfect snakeskin—

Police Dogs of Trinidad and Tobago

Retired police dog trainer Cpl. Shane Chase and police dog Felix do bite work training in Cumuto (photograph by Miquel Galofré, March 10, 2021).

diamond-shaped head skin and all. I knew the snake had just shed its skin and was nearby, so I shoved the snakeskin in my pocket and left the area before the dog training that day came to me and encountered the snake on the way.[4]

Being outdoors and working as a police dog handler, and then a police dog trainer, suited Chase. "I had wanted to join the army—not the police, because I like being outdoors. I always liked animals. That's who I was at the time, and that is who I still am."[5] His wry wit and frankness fortify a steely façade, but Chase balances professional detachment with a love for dogs visible in his enthusiasm when a dog performs well. "I don't get attached to any dog. I train them. They're not mine. ... To be a good trainer, you have to be dedicated to it and have imagination. ... While the dogs are with you, you're going to create boundaries and a learning environment. Dog training is patience and problem-solving, an understanding of how to turn theory into something practical."[6]

He wanted police dogs who are tenacious and brave—dogs who won't quit searching. Those characteristics jump out when he

Chapter 27. Training Days

remembers some of his favorite dogs. "One of my earliest experiences was with Zuco, a locally donated Belgian Malinois I trained in SAUTT." He recalls Jackson and his working dog Meg, a black Labrador, whom he spotted on a trip to England to buy four explosive detection dogs just before the Summit of the Americas was held in Trinidad in 2009.

> Meg was a whiz. I never saw another dog yet who had her work ethic. She wouldn't quit. If she didn't find something, she didn't want to come back.
>
> She was obedient, so if I called her, she would come to me, but she didn't want to. She'd go far away from me to search.
>
> During that trip to buy the dogs, two of us had to work four dogs we never saw before. We just interchanged them. Those dogs were Jed, Penny, Meg, and Missy.
>
> Meg was very headstrong. She would growl and try to bite you if you put her in the crate and she had her ball.
>
> At the time we got Meg, I had a firearm dog in SAUTT, and the instructor said, "Who will we give Meg to? She needs a strong handler, because she will dominate any other person." He said, "Why don't you take her?" and I said, "Because I already have a dog."
>
> He said, "Work two dogs."[7]

And Chase did exactly that, which rarely happens. "An army officer in SAUTT worked two dogs also, Penny and his firearms dog.[8] I used to run Meg and my other dog, Dasdy, a German Shepherd, together on the field for exercise, and when they tried to size each other up, I'd step in and say, 'None of that.' Dasdy died in the Cumuto kennels and I found Meg a home on a farm," said Chase.

After SAUTT, when he returned to work in the canine section as a police dog trainer, other memorable dogs passed through Chase's training courses.

"I selected Marko on a trip to buy police dogs in Miami. ... Marko came out to do bite work. He moved from the end of the line, sat down and waited for the guy to come in for the exercise. I was impressed with that. ... Cpl. Bernard's dog, Cezar, is exceptional at tracking."[9]

Chase explained,

> As a trainer, the joy is taking a green dog and giving him a purpose in terms of our work—watching him come from a place where he is

scratching his butt to doing something that benefits the police service. When you see the dogs using their noses and finding a gun or something, that's an achievement. You feel proud to see them come from nothing to something, from a normal dog to a police dog.[10]

In 2020, when the Covid 19 pandemic plunged the world into isolation, Cpl. Chase would find a new purpose on this Cumuto police training compound where police officers become canine officers. Here, it's all about the dog, and that is a transforming experience.

Saadiq Hosein's bond with his dog came naturally in training, and offered a feeling of accomplishment he'd never felt before.[11]

> Growing up, I felt confused about what I wanted to do. At sixteen, I attended the University of Trinidad and Tobago and pursued civil engineering for one year, then didn't continue. I signed up at the University of the West Indies in South to do criminology. I didn't finish that either.
>
> One morning my mom saw an ad in the newspaper to join the police service. I joined at nineteen and worked in the Task Force doing high-risk patrols, executing search warrants, working coastal patrols—a lot of outdoor things.[12]

Seeing Maverick at work on a police exercise in February 2010 changed the trajectory of Hosein's career.

> At 2 a.m. on that rainy morning in Fyzabad, Maverick, with PC Enoch Romeo, leapt out of a police vehicle and ran straight up to a guy who had some narcotics hidden in his underwear. Maverick started poking him with his nose.
>
> For the rest of that morning, I followed them just to see Maverick work.
>
> That same day we went to a swampy area in Oropouche. Maverick dived in the dirty water, swam about fifteen feet through the mangrove and all those tree roots, started barking and found an automatic firearm wrapped in plastic.
>
> I thought, "Wow, I didn't know it had dogs capable of that."
>
> We would plan police exercises for a month ahead, and if Canine couldn't make it, we'd cancel.[13]

Hosein transferred to the canine section. When he arrived, there were no dogs for new officers to train, so for about six months he groomed and exercised all the retired dogs waiting to go home. Then ten new dogs bought by the U.S. Embassy arrived, training

Chapter 27. Training Days

began, and three months after training, he got assigned to Eddie, a tan-and-black Belgian Malinois/German Shepherd mix.

"He's a little larger than most police dogs, and he has huge ears. During training, he got in a fight in Cumuto with a dog, so he is missing a piece of his ear. ... He's very intelligent and determined, not aggressive, and good at tracking. ... He's a bit goofy," said Hosein.[14]

In 2015, Eddie and Hosein had to find a man who had just killed someone and was hiding in the forest. They had to take a chopper to the scene. Eddie began searching on a 20-foot leash. Hosein recalled:

> He lost the track a couple of times when we had to cross rivers. We lost my police support and the Task Force support.
> I wondered if I should put myself and his life in danger by going on.
> I stopped, gave him a rest and some water. Eddie wanted to continue working, so we pushed forward, and Eddie found the guy hiding in some bushes, behind a farm.
> He held the guy and responded to my command "Speak!" which means, "Bark." Eddie will bark, show teeth and play the part, and look very menacing. He doesn't want to, but he'll do it for his ball.
> I told Eddie, "Watch him," meaning "Focus on the suspect." I held the suspect, handcuffed him and called for backup.
> Then the suspect got to hear my high-pitched voice tell Eddie, "Good boy!" and see Eddie play with his ball [his reward for apprehending the suspect].
> I escorted the handcuffed man out of the bush.[15]

Looking back on Eddie's many exercises, PC Hosein said, "Eddie and I work hand in hand. It could never be him or me alone making the decisions. I trust in his instincts and what he's feeling to do, and based on that, I make my decisions." It's a sentiment all canine police offers express. Police-dog training has changed and evolved since the first police dogs arrived in Trinidad in 1952, but nothing has ever replaced the foundation of that bond between officer and dog. At the heart of their relationship is an unshakeable feeling of trust, which canine officers claim transcends any experience they ever had with a human police partner.

CHAPTER 28

WHAT THE FUTURE HOLDS

SILENCE ENGULFED THE CARONI CANINE Section in April 2020 as Trinidad and Tobago settled into a stay-at-home government directive during the Covid-19 pandemic. Much had changed between the time I returned in April 2015 and the pandemic. Maharaj's dogs Bouncy, Buddy, and Beny were gone. On August 28, 2016, Bouncy died in her kennel. Her necropsy revealed an undetected tumor on her spleen had ruptured. Maverick retired in December 2017, went home and died in his kennel at Romeo's home on March 22, 2019, while Romeo was at work.

When PC Cedeno died in a car accident on Carnival Monday, February 27, 2017, Jed became noticeably droopy. But he bounced back to become Cpl. Maharaj's partner. Together they worked through the first half of 2018. In May, Maharaj found Jed listless in his kennel and rushed him to the Mt. Hope veterinarian hospital. Jed had an emergency splenectomy and returned to work. The police finally retired Jed a year later. He languished in a kennel and died of cancer in July 2019.

Maharaj signed Buddy's retirement papers, he went home and appeared in Cathy Ella's 2018 Carnival video "Mama Yo."[1] Buddy, the last of the Golden Retrievers, died peacefully on the morning of July 22, 2019. In Cumuto, Beny underwent rehabilitation for his aggression. But he bit Cpl. Swanson twice and was euthanized by the canine section's vet Dr. Anil Ramnanan on November 8, 2019.

Penny retired in 2017 after PC Kiff Singh migrated to the U.S. where he is now a sergeant in the U.S. army. In December 2020, when Joe Biden won the U.S. presidential election, Trinidad and Tobago's

Chapter 28. What the Future Holds

Puppies from the D litter meet the horses they will work with some day. From left: WPC Tekisha Hamilton-Figuero with Drago; PC Leon Lopez with Dana and Cpl. Premnath Maharaj with Deja (photograph by Angelo Marcelle, *Trinidad & Tobago Newsday*, November 21, 2021).

TV6 news featured Penny's role in protecting Biden on his 2013 trip to Trinidad. She lived with veterinarian Dr. Kriyan Singh in southern Trinidad, where she chased a ball to her heart's content. Penny died on November 30, 2022.

Jackson retired in September 2018, returned to Trinidad and went home with canine officer PC Joseph Gomez.

By 2022, PC Texeira had settled into working with Skok, an aggressive Belgian Malinois narcotics/firearm detection and tactical dog with an all-black face and chest.

Here, in Caroni, many memories reside in these empty kennels, and the ones occupied by new dogs spinning in circles as they anxiously await their chance to work. A canine officer's job is immeasurably rewarding, and equally as sad. Officers know they will toss many balls in celebration of work well done; they know they will face the loss of loyal partners. There is never enough time; there are always too many tears.

Maharaj reflected on decades of memories with his explosive-detection dogs. "I miss Woody," said Maharaj. "My memory always comes back to him. I always boasted that I could give Woody the command 'Stay,' and he would wait in that same spot until I returned."[2]

Theophilus Thomas had told the same story about Bruno. "Bouncy was sweet. She loved attention, and she had this fragile way about her. Buddy was so laid-back. Jed was a butterball of joy," said Maharaj.

The Canine Section recorded some uplifting moments in the year before Covid-19 closed down the country. On August 31, 2019, police dogs appeared in the Independence Day parade for the first time in 15 years.

"We're going to steal the show," promised Cpl. Akil Bernard,[3] and they did. Cezar and Romeo's new dog Riko, a Dutch Shepherd, weaved between their handlers' legs and performed complicated moves as the canine officers marched through the Queen's Park Savannah.

No one watching the parade would have guessed just how much those police dogs had accomplished. Cezar had recently found guns, ammunition, and drugs stuffed in a hole in a tree and marijuana concealed in a duffel bag at the airport. He had run through a pavilion less than half a mile west of the La Horquetta police station, trotted through an open doorway and indicated continuously on government workers' uniforms stuffed with marijuana. Cezar retired and went home with Bernard on October 21, 2022. He now runs along the beach—just as Bernard always imagined.[4]

In December 2019, Supt. Joseph appointed Bernard, Cpl. Samaroo, and me to draft an update to the canine police Standing Order and insert its first retirement policy, which calls for dogs to retire as police officers directly under the police commissioner, rather than government property to be written off through a long bureaucratic procedure via the Ministry of Finance. The retirement policy was finally approved by the commissioner of police in November 2023.

Chapter 28. What the Future Holds

The retirement issue is the biggest source of stress for canine officers—especially for Tobago officers, whose dogs often end up in the Caroni kennels after retirement.

"Even if they are sick or dying, we want to spend their last days with them," said Cpl. Caruth. "But it's too late for me now."[5] Caruth's dog, Cordon, died in Trinidad in 2020.

Remarkably, Theophilus Thomas's influence can still be seen and felt decades after he departed from the Dog Section. Thomas had interviewed and accepted Cpl. Dunstan Harry into the canine section on June 6, 1981, when Harry requested a transfer there. At 55, Harry retired on May 6, 2013, but returned as a special reserve officer on November 4 of that year to manage the canine section's fleet of response vehicles. Harry, who once worked with dog Zak, still worked in the Canine Section in 2022, and he told younger canine officers about their history.

In January 2021, the Canine Section refurbished six kennels and canine officers' dormitories in the Point Fortin police station with a grant facilitated by the Wishing for Wings Foundation through the U.S. Embassy and the National Gas Company. The kennels signal a return to decentralization, reminiscent of Thomas's days, when dogs worked out of police stations.

In 2022, a crime that first made the police dogs' files in 1958 made headlines. Copper wire thieves had disrupted telephone and cable lines.[6]

As PC Romeo studied how to turn his fondest memories of Maverick into new experiences for himself and Riko, Maharaj waited to see what the future would bring for him. "I never thought I would be without a dog," he said, "and I never wish I had done anything else in life other than work in canine."[7]

In 2020, decades after their retirement, Hector Lewis and Khairool Khan still relived their former glory days with Carlo, Rex, and Daemon. Winston Matthews, who had travelled to St. Vincent with Khan and Daemon and reached the rank of Assistant Commissioner of Police before he retired, died alone in his Freeport home on March 25, 2020. I broke that news to Lewis. "Another one of us is gone," said Lewis. "I must call Khan now and speak to him."[8] Lewis died in 2022.

Police Dogs of Trinidad and Tobago

In its history, the canine section discovered an unexpected benefit of this specialized police service: dogs humanize police officers in a profession stereotyped by its rough, callous, much-maligned image. Canine officers always have to be upbeat and animated for their dogs. They can't bring their worries, anger and sadness to work. They always talk about how their feelings "travel down the leash."

No canine officer ever forgets his once-in-a-lifetime dog. Kenny Winn, retired now, keeps a framed picture of Jango in his living room and pictures of his top dog, Strike, on his cellphone.[9]

"They brought me joy. I think of them all the time. I remember the spiritual connection I had with Strike on the night he died. Our whole life together flashed before my eyes while he was dying," said Winn. "There is one perfect dog, and you always search for a dog to match that perfect dog you once had," said Romeo.[10] Thomas knew that feeling too. No dog ever lived up to Bruno's legacy.

In today's volatile world, filled with terrorists, illegal drugs, and every crime imaginable, the bond between police officers and their working dogs grows ever stronger. No one knows exactly what the future will hold, but this seems certain: Maharaj will get another dog and other canine officers will discover their once-in-a-lifetime dogs.

During the pandemic, completely closed borders in Trinidad and Tobago made it impossible for new police dogs to enter the country, so Police Commissioner Gary Griffith and Supt. Hospedales resurrected one of Thomas's solutions to police-dog shortages: raise puppies. In 2020, the Canine Section began raising German Shepherd, Belgian Malinois and short haired German Pointer puppies.

On October 10, 2020, WPC Gibson's dog Brixa gave birth to 11 Belgian Malinois puppies in Cumuto. They all caught parvovirus, one died, and Ati, the smallest, fought for her life. A team of canine officers including PC Hosein, WPC Caren Moreau and Cpl. Maharaj worked 24-hour shifts, dispensing medication and hydrating the puppies orally with a syringe every single hour. Two months later, on Christmas Day, WPC Narine's German Shepherd Adina, had an emergency Caesarean section. Dr. Ramnanan delivered eight puppies (three were stillborn). In January, the mostly black butterballs known as the B puppies listened to Mozart and other soothing

Chapter 28. What the Future Holds

WPC Caren Moreau holds Ati from the A litter (photograph by Roger Jacob, *Trinidad & Tobago Newsday*, March 10, 2021).

Police Dogs of Trinidad and Tobago

Cpl. Titus Worrell holds two German Shepherd puppies from the B litter (photograph by Roger Jacob, *Trinidad & Tobago Newsday*, March 10, 2021).

Chapter 28. What the Future Holds

A puppy from the A litter in training (photograph by Miquel Galofré, February 5, 2021).

classical music piped into their enclosed, air-conditioned, fly-proof kennels. Adina's puppies became the B litter.

By October 2020, the C litter of shorthair German Pointers had been born, followed by the D, E, F, and G litters. Chase and Lopez were the puppies' trainers.[11]

In the first week of 2021, the A puppies, all brown with black faces—except for one all-black puppy, Ashes—began basic puppy training. PC Lopez carried Anya to the training room, where she confidently climbed steep steps and jumped into a box filled with noisy, empty plastic water bottles.[12]

One by one the puppies headed for a wooden frame on the floor. They stood inside like a three-dimensional picture, responded to commands for "Sit" and "Down," and collected chow for their rewards. The males, Apollo, Ammo, Alpha, Arrow, and Axel, and the females, Aniva, Ashes, Ava, and Anya, worked with hand signals and the sound of a clicker when they completed a task. Ati was on sick leave as she recovered from the parvovirus.[13] All the officers have a soft spot for Ati. They all noted how she would grab the water hose and try to shake it in her weakened state. "She has attitude," said Moreau.[14] "She had so much fight," Maharaj said, with Ati in his arms. "She will make it as a police dog."[15]

Maharaj took Ati for long walks to strengthen her legs. No one could have imagined that in one and a half years, Ati, paired with Maharaj and Beast, working with Sgt. Antoine, would be the two dogs chosen for Sgt. Donawa's cadaver-dog training program. In March 2023, Dani, the only working cadaver dog, went home to live with Donawa. He died three months later.

On the morning of February 5, 2021, canine officers carried all Brixa's puppies to run on the grass for the first time. As the puppies gamboled across the field with a view of the Northern Range, I recalled ANZAC, Andy, and Adolph's files. I remembered Action, Aura, and Ace, tails wagging, running across the grass to Dyer at the Caroni kennels. The A-litter puppies led by Ammo and Apollo tumbled, fell, scrambled to their feet and ran away. Canine police officers laughed and dreamed of the future.

It was easy to imagine Theophilus Thomas smiling.

Appendix A: Thomas's Final Report on Bruno

July 26, 1960

I have to report for your information that at around 2:40 p.m. on Tuesday, 26 July, 1960 Police dog Bruno died at his Kennel at the Mounted Branch. The Veterinary officer Dr. Khan had not long left. He had given him two injections and taken a sample of his blood for tests. The doctor was unable at the time of examination to diagnose his complaint. He had left a bottle of medicine with instructions to give the dog a dose at once and another at 9 p.m.. He stated he would be back early on the morning of 27 July, but was not happy about Bruno's condition.

Immediately after his departure, I set about giving Bruno his medicine. Some slime was running from his mouth. It was while wiping this off he died. Bruno had been a very healthy and active dog until during February 1959, shortly after he assisted me to arrest Phedillo Lammorell who had struck him with a piece of cane on his left side of his head. He was operated on 25 February, 1959 for a swollen left ear, a haematoma. His dew claws were removed then. I have had cause to consult the veterinary officer about him before but for minor complaints.

Since after the operation, he had been seen by the Vet on six occasions each time by Dr. Gonzales for different complaints, once for an infected left ear, another for a swelling by the neck. During that period I observed he bled from his nose, about which I spoke to Dr. Gonzales. He told me he thought it was due to heat and told me

Appendix A

not to be worried about it. It will soon subside. It did after a couple of days. I did not think it serious because (the vet) seemed not bothered.

Early in the month of June 1960, I observed the nose bleeding again. This time only the left nostril and shortly after the left eye became bloodshot and he had no vision from that eye. Dr. Gonzales was consulted. He saw Bruno on 13 June, 1960. He stated that it was due to a strain or overwork. He also considered age which he thought to be fairly advanced. He prescribed an ointment which worked very well. The eye cleared and the vision returned.

Bruno, however, appeared listless and lost appetite. I discussed this with Dr. Gonzales by telephone. He suggested that I give him milk on mornings and Vetazyme tablets daily, which I did. He picked up, but hadn't the energy of before. I did patrols with him at Four Roads police area during that time and each time he showed signs of being very fatigued when done.

On 9 July, 1960, I took him to Maracas Bay where I joined a search party for the wanted man Bruno Mendez. We left the kennels at 4:15 am and returned at 9:15 p.m., he had a rough day. That night he did not eat and was very tired. From then on he again became listless and just picked his feed. I discussed this with you, Sir, about two days later, when you enquired about him. You agreed with me that he be put back on milk on mornings and biscuits instead of chow on evenings again his condition improved.

On Friday, 22 July, 1960, I took him to the bushes at the back of the old Pistol range to do a seek practice with No. 5190 PC Cuthbert. He worked satisfactorily but not with the zest he is accustomed to. That evening he did not eat. Neither did he on the following day. This was not strange because he sometimes stayed off his food without any ill effects. When he did not eat on Sunday evening, I became worried because I then observed that he was having great difficulties to do his numbers and appeared to be getting weak.

On Monday, 25 July, 1960 I took him to the home of Dr. Gonzales and told him of my observations, he looked him over and said that it could be chronic constipation and instructed me to give him a warm enema. Composition: a rum bottle full of soap water with about 2 ounces of liquid paraffin and to put him on soft foods, no chew or biscuits but minted meat. He further stated that he had to leave for Jamaica on the following day and should I have the necessity for a vet, to consult Dr. Khan who will be holding on in his absence. Sgt. Bridgeman assisted me to administer the prescribed enema. Bruno was very weak at the time and his general condition was not at all good. He did not take the milk at all that day. I tried putting some down his throat. He took about half a pint, but vomited in less than half an hour.

On 26 July, 1960, I spoke to Dr. Khan by telephone asking him to visit Bruno, he said that he couldn't before 1:30 p.m. and that he had no transportation. Insp. Redhead went for him. I again tried feeding Bruno some milk. He took a small bit and again vomited. I also observed the he was suffering badly and was groaning and was restless. When Dr. Khan came I told him of my observations.[1]

APPENDIX B:
PANTHER'S VETERINARY REPORT

Ministry of Agriculture
San Fernando
August 10, 1965

On Friday, August 6, at about 1 p.m., I was called to the Mon Repos Police Station by Constable Figaro. Police dog Panther was lying on his side panting vigorously. Just as I arrived at the kennel, he had a very violent fit with convulsions. I gave him a tranquillizer and treated him with about 500 ccs of 10 per cent glucose intravenously. His temperature was at this time, 106.2 degrees F. We applied cold packs to his head area and over his body, and by 2:00 p.m. his temperature had returned to normal.

At about 5 p.m. on the same day, I revisited the animal and his temperature had dropped to below normal, about 100 degrees F. He was passing bloody fluid from his rectum. I then decided to take him to Dr. Kanhai's Clinic for further treatment.

Upon consultation with Dr. Kanhai we again treated him with about 500 ccs of a Ringers lactate solution intravenously. We both agreed that the prognosis was very poor. The animal died at midnight the same day.

A post-mortem was performed by Dr. Kanhai in the presence of Sgt. Thomas, Constable Figaro and myself. The signs seen indicated a poisoning or some sort of heat stroke. They were identical with those of police dog Carlo. Samples of liver, heart, lung, spleen and kidney were forwarded to the Government Chemist for analysis.

In my opinion, this animal died of either (a) Poisoning or (b)

Panther's Veterinary Report

Heat stroke, but I withhold a definite diagnosis until the laboratory report is completed.[1]

Ralph VG De Gannes
Veterinary Officer (South)

Appendix C: Privy Council Summary of Junior "Spirit" Cottle Case

Weekly Law Reports (ICLR)/1976/Volume 3 /COTTLE AND ANOTHER APPELLANTS AND THE QUEEN RESPONDENT– [1976] 3 WLR 209

[1976] 3 WLR 209

COTTLE AND ANOTHER APPELLANTS
AND THE QUEEN RESPONDENT

[PRIVY COUNCIL]

1976 April 5; May 11

Lord Diplock, Viscount Dilhorne and Lord Simon of Glaisdale

West Indies—Saint Vincent—Crime—Evidence—Capital and non-capital offences wrongly charged in one indictment—Whether evidence relevant to non-capital charge admissible on capital charge—Duty to weigh probative value against risk of prejudice— Jury Ordinance (Laws of St. Vincent, 1966 rev., c. 5) (as amended), ss. 12, 13

On May 11, 1973, in Kingstown, St. Vincent, in two separate shootings R was killed and wounded. The defendants were charged jointly in one indictment with the murder (a capital offence) of R (count 1), attempted murder of G (count 2) and discharging a loaded firearm with intent to cause grievous bodily harm to G (count 3). The trial was by a jury of 12. No objection was taken to the joinder of

Summary of Junior "Spirit" Cottle Case

the counts nor to the admissibility on count I of evidence relating to counts 2 and 3. By unanimous verdicts the jury convicted the defendants on counts I and 3 and acquitted them on count 2. The defendants appealed. The Court of Appeal decided that under the Jury Ordinance it was unlawful for capital and non-capital offences to be tried together and that the non-capital offences should have been tried by a jury of 9. Accordingly it quashed the convictions on count 3 and dismissed the appeals on count 1. Neither the trial judge nor the Court of Appeal considered whether the evidence against the defendants on counts 2 and 3 was prejudicial in relation to count 1.

On appeal by the defendants to the Judicial Committee:—

Held, allowing the appeal, that the Court of Appeal rightly concluded that by virtue of the Jury Ordinance capital and

[1976] 3 WLR 209 at 210

non-capital offences could not be tried together; that the admission of evidence at the trial tending to show that the defendants had committed offences other than that charged in count 1 was a material irregularity unless it could be shown that the evidence was admissible in relation to that count; that if it were so admissible, it was the duty of the trial judge to decide (and appropriate for the decision only of judges familiar with local conditions) whether the probative value of such evidence outweighed the risk of prejudice to the defendants; accordingly notwithstanding that some of the evidence in relation to counts 2 and 3 might have been admissible on count 1, since it was prejudicial to the defendants and neither the trial judge nor the Court of Appeal had considered the question of prejudice, there was a serious risk that the jury's verdict was unsafe and unsatisfactory; it was not appropriate for the Judicial Committee to substitute their discretion for a discretion not exercised by either the trial judge or the Court of Appeal and the conviction should be quashed.

Decision of the Court of Appeal of the West Indies Associated States Supreme Court reversed.

Appendix C

The following case is referred to in the reasons of their Lordships:

Practice Direction (Homicide: Indictment) [1964] 1 W.L.R. 1244; [1964] 3 All E.R. 509, C.C.A.

The following additional cases were cited in argument:

Latham v. The Queen (1864) 5 B. & S. 635.

Reg. v. Boardman [1975] A.C. 421; [1974] 3 W.L.R. 673; [1974] 3 All E.R. 887, H.L.(E.).

Reg v. Fuidge (1864) 1 Le. & Ca. 390.

Reg. v. Kray (Ronald) [1970] 1 Q.B. 125, [1969] 3 W.L.R. 831; [1969] 3 All E.R. 941, C.A.

Reg. v. Ludlow [1971] A.C. 29; [1970] 2 W.L.R. 521; [1970] 1 All E.R. 567; H.L.(E.).

APPEAL (No. 27 of 1975) of Junior Cottle, otherwise known as Spirit, and Lorraine Laidlow from a judgment and order (May 20, 1974) of the Court of Appeal of the West Indies Associated States Supreme Court (Lewis Ag. C.J., St. Bernard J. and Peterkin Ag.J.) dismissing their appeal against conviction and sentence before Berridge J. and a jury of 12 on October 17, 1973, of murder contrary to section 71 of the Indictable Offences Ordinance.

The facts are stated in the judgment of their Lordships.

C. F. Fletcher-Cooke Q.C. and Eugene Cotran for the defendants.

(only of judges familiar with local conditions) whether the probative value of such evidence outweighed the risk of prejudice to the defendants; accordingly notwithstanding that some of the evidence in relation to counts 2 and 3 might have been admissible on count 1, since it was prejudicial to the defendants and neither the trial judge nor the Court of Appeal had considered the question of prejudice, there was a serious risk that the jury's verdict was unsafe and unsatisfactory; it was not appropriate for the Judicial Committee to substitute their discretion for a discretion not exercised by either the trial judge or the Court of Appeal and the conviction should be quashed.

Summary of Junior "Spirit" Cottle Case

Decision of the Court of Appeal of the West Indies Associated States Supreme Court reversed.

The following case is referred to in the reasons of their Lordships:

Practice Direction (Homicide: Indictment) [1964] 1 W.L.R. 1244; [1964] 3 All E.R. 509, C.C.A.

The following additional cases were cited in argument:

Latham v. The Queen (1864) 5 B. & S. 635.

Reg. v. Boardman [1975] A.C. 421; [1974] 3 W.L.R. 673; [1974] 3 All E.R. 887, H.L.(E.).

Reg v. Fuidge (1864) 1 Le. & Ca. 390.

Reg. v. Kray (Ronald) [1970] 1 Q.B. 125, [1969] 3 W.L.R. 831; [1969] 3 All E.R. 941, C.A.

Reg. v. Ludlow [1971] A.C. 29; [1970] 2 W.L.R. 521; [1970] 1 All E.R. 567; H.L.(E.).

APPEAL (No. 27 of 1975) of Junior Cottle, otherwise known as Spirit, and Lorraine Laidlow from a judgment and order (May 20, 1974) of the Court of Appeal of the West Indies Associated States Supreme Court (Lewis Ag. C.J., St. Bernard J. and Peterkin Ag.J.) dismissing their appeal against conviction and sentence before Berridge J. and a jury of 12 on October 17, 1973, of murder contrary to section 71 of the Indictable Offences Ordinance.

The facts are stated in the judgment of their Lordships.

C.F. Fletcher-Cooke Q.C. and Eugene Cotran for the defendants.[1]

Chapter Notes

Preface

1. Reuters, "Trinidad and Tobago Declares State of Emergency as Covid cases rise," May 15, 2021. https://www.reuters.com/world/trinidad-tobago-declares-state-emergency-covid-19-cases-surge-2021-05-15/.
2. Destination Trinidad and Tobago, "Birdwatching," 2023. https://www.destinationtnt.com/to-do-and-see/eco-adventure/birdwatching/#:~:text=Trinidad%20and%20Tobago%20is%20a,470%20recorded%20species%20of%20birds.
3. Carole Simm, "The History of the Pitch Lake in Trinidad," *USA Today*, McLean, Virginia, March 15, 2018. https://traveltips.usatoday.com/history-pitch-lake-trinidad-58120.html.
4. Jonathan Ali, "The Return of King Cocoa," *Caribbean Beat Magazine*, Port of Spain, Trinidad, May/June 2011. https://www.caribbean-beat.com/issue-109/return-king-cocoa#axzz80ya0aels.
5. Emily Salmon and John Salmon, "Tobacco in Colonial Virginia," in *Encyclopedia Virginia*, February 13, 2022. https://encyclopediavirginia.org/entries/tobacco-in-colonial-virginia.
6. National Archives of Trinidad and Tobago, "The Merikins: Our heritage, our faith, our future," Port of Spain. http://www.natt.gov.tt/sites/default/files/images/NATT%20Merikin%20Collection%20GuideREV2021.pdf.
7. Ministry of Energy, "Historical Facts on the Petroleum Industry of Trinidad and Tobago," Ministry of Energy and Energy Industries, Port of Spain, 2023. https://www.energy.gov.tt/historical-facts-petroleum/.
8. H. Williams, "Postcolonial Structural Violence: A Study of School Violence in Trinidad and Tobago," *International Journal of Peace Studies* 18, no. 2, 43–70, Port of Spain, 2023.

Introduction

1. Leonard Dyer, Personal interview, May 3, 1992, Caroni.
2. Debbie Jacob, "Drug Lord's Worst Enemy," *Trinidad Express*, Port of Spain, May 12, 1992, 1.

Chapter 1

1. The terms "Alsatian" and "German Shepherd" are used interchangeably. After World War II, "Alsatian" became the preferred term in Britain. The terms in this book are used according to what is written in the dogs' files or what was said in interviews.
2. Grady Norton, "Hurricanes of 1952," Monthly Weather Review, Miami Weather, Miami, January 12, 1953, 12.
3. Description of officers and dogs landing in Trinidad taken from a police photo in the Trinidad and Tobago Police Museum, Central Police Station, Port of Spain, and from a report in Bruno's file number 1.
4. Grady Norton, "Hurricanes of 1952," Miami, January 12, 1953, 14.
5. Theophilus Thomas, "Royal Gaol [Port of Spain] Prison Breakout" canine police report, Bruno's file 1, Depot kennels, St. James, December 19, 1952.

Chapter Notes

6. Thomas, canine police report, Bruno's file 1, St. James, December 19, 1952.
7. *Ibid.*

Chapter 2

1. Theophilus Thomas, "Robbery in Belmont," canine police report, Bruno's file 1, January 4, 1953.
2. Thomas, "Robbery in San Juan," canine police report, Bruno's file 1, March 21, 1953.
3. Thomas, "Theft at tobacco factory in Champs Fleurs," canine police report, Bruno's file 1, August 3, 1953.
4. Thomas, "Theft at tobacco factory in Champs Fleurs," August 3, 1953.
5. Thomas, "Shooting with intent, Cunupia," canine police report, Bruno's file 1, August 19, 1953.
6. Thomas, "House break-in, Couva," canine police report, Bruno's file 1, October 7, 1953.
7. Thomas, "Beating and robbery, Cunupia," canine police report, Bruno's file 1, November 21, 1953.

Chapter 3

1. Kim Johnson, "The history of steel pan: sounds like steel," clip 1, Chas Shepherd, YouTube, April 20, 2023. "https://www.youtube.com/watch?v=iN3YOFu_yIM.
2. Johnson, "The history of steel pan," April 20, 2023.
3. Johnson, "The history of steel pan," April 20, 2023.
4. Johnson, "Steelband clashes," phone interview, January 6, 2021.
5. Theophilus Thomas, "Bruno scatters gamblers in Laventille," canine police report, Bruno's file 2, March 9, 1955.
6. Thomas, "Bruno apprehends thief in Port of Spain," canine police report, Bruno's file 2, March 23, 1955.
7. Thomas, "Bruno pursues car part thieves in Caroni," canine police report, Bruno's file 2, October 5, 1955.
8. Thomas, "Summary of multiple canine police reports," Bruno's file 2, 1955–1956.
9. Thomas, "Summary of multiple canine police reports, Bruno's file 2, 1955–1956.
10. Thomas, "Pursuit of suspicious-looking man, St. Joseph," canine police report, Bruno's file, November 25,1956.
11. Thomas, "Bruno apprehends wanted murderer from Grenada," canine police report, Bruno's file, November 25,1956.
12. Thomas, "Summary of Bruno's cases," canine police reports, Bruno's file 3, 1957–1958.
13. Thomas, "Bruno's commendations," canine police reports, Bruno's file 3, 1958–1959.
14. Thomas, "Summary of Bruno's cases," canine police reports, Bruno's file 3, 1959.
15. Thomas, "Bruno's health report," canine police reports, Bruno's file 3, September 24, 1959.
16. Thomas, "Report of Bruno's death," canine police report, Bruno's file 3, July 26, 1960.

Chapter 4

1. Summary of several reports found in Carlos's file, 1952.
2. George Alexis, "Carlos tracks down suspect, La Seiva," canine police report, Carlos's file, no date.
3. Carlos's death is recorded on the cover of his file, as all police dogs' deaths were recorded at the time.
4. A written description of Shah is found in his first file, September 1952.
5. Hector "Pee Wee" Lewis, personal interview, Port of Spain, March 2, 2009.
6. Theophilus Thomas, "Thomas's report to senior officers on Shah apprehending suspect," canine police report, Shah's file, November 1954.
7. Obtaining a police vehicle was often a problem, so canine officers used their personal cars.
8. Hamilton Bridgeman, "Wanted men stop police in unmarked car," canine police report, Shah's file, August 22, 1955.
9. Winston Matthews, personal interview, Freeport, April 12, 2012.

Chapter Notes

10. Matthews, personal interview, Freeport, April 12, 2012; Hector Lewis, personal interview, Port of Spain, March 2, 2009; Leonard Dyer, personal interview, Caroni, May 3, 1992; Khairool Khan, personal interview, Caroni, May 3, 1992.
11. Hamilton Bridgeman, "Shah apprehends thief in Couva," canine police report, Shah's file, November 14, 1956.
12. Newspaper clipping found in Shah's file.
13. Hamilton Bridgeman, "Shah bites civilian," canine police report, Shah's file, October 14, 1957.
14. Hamilton Bridgeman, "Shah pursues gamblers," canine police report, Shah's file, November 12, 1957.
15. Hamilton Bridgeman, "First report of copper wire theft," canine police report, Shah's file, July 15, 1958. (Copper wire theft continues to be a problem in Trinidad and in the U.S. It can disrupt the flow of electricity, telecommunications, transport, water supply, heating, and security and emergency services).
16. Hamilton Bridgeman, "Shah finds money," canine police report, Shah's file, August 16, 1958. (Shah was not trained as a currency dog. He would have been following the trail of the suspect when he discovered the money.)

Chapter 5

1. Dogs' background, forwarded from the commissioner's office, appears in Theophilus Thomas's administrative files, Depot kennels, 1955–1957.
2. George Alexis, "Rex's chicken chasing escapades," police canine report, Rex's file, June 17, 1957.
3. ASP Duke, "Letter of complaint," Rex's file, August 23, 1957.
4. Copy of letter from depot kennels in Thomas's administrative files, August 26, 1957.
5. George Alexis, "Rex solves a chicken case," police canine report, Rex's file, October 19, 1959.
6. Thomas often editorialized in the dogs' files.

7. Thomas kept detailed reports on what the puppies and dogs ate. He followed the puppies' progress and recorded which puppies succeeded as police dogs.
8. Notes found in Thomas's administrative files for 1959.
9. Dunstan Harry, "Recollections on Theophilus Thomas," personal interview, Caroni, April 23, 2019.
10. Thomas, "Dobermans in the police service," personal note in Thomas's administrative file for 1959.
11. Horace Hicks, "Jett catches suspect in the forest," canine police report, Jett's file, July 10, 1960.
12. Hicks, "Letter of complaint," canine police report, Jett's file, July 11, 1960.
13. Thomas, "Letter addressing Hick's complaint," canine police report, Jett's file, September 30, 1960.
14. Note on Chag's behaviour appears in Thomas's administrative file and is corroborated by Khairool Khan.
15. Cromwell St. Louis, "Letter requesting police dogs," Thomas's administrative file, March, 10,1961.
16. Thomas, "Letter of regret," correspondence file, March 15, 1961.

Chapter 6

1. Theophilus Thomas, "Decision to not use Dobermans," note in Thomas's administrative file, no date.
2. WF Handy, *The K-9 Corps: The Use of Dogs in Police Work* (Chicago: Northwestern University, 1961), 300.
3. Khairool Khan, personal interview, Trincity, May 8, 2010; Hector Lewis, personal interview, Port of Spain, April 10, 2009.
4. Michael Roban, personal interview, Westmoorings, November 9, 2019.
5. Clayton Chandler, telephone interview, October 13, 2021.
6. Charles Duhigg, *Power of Habit: Why We Do What We Do in Life and in Business* (New York: Random House, 2012), 108–109.
7. Debbie Thomas, phone interview, March 17, 2022.
8. Thomas, "Jestine West murder,"

Chapter Notes

canine police report, Jett's file, November 9, 1959.
9. PC Charles, "Jett solves murder case in Blanchisseuse," canine police report, Jett's file, November 8, 1959.
10. PC Charles, "Jett tracks down thief in Curepe," canine police report, Jett's file, February 15, 1963.
11. Note in Thomas's administrative file. No source given.
12. Alexandra Horowitz, *Being a Dog: Following the Dog into a World of Smell* (New York: Scribner, 2016), 9.
13. Thomas, administrative reports, December 1963.
14. Thomas, "Dog's food," administrative reports, November 22, 1963.
15. Thomas, "Letter to APC Claud May," administrative reports, April 19, 1965.

Chapter 7

1. Sheba's kennel card, Sheba's file.
2. Theophilus Thomas, Letter to superintendent, administrative file, depot kennels, July 8, 1965.
3. PC Narace, "Theft, St Augustine," canine police report, Sheba's file, January 6, 1968.
4. Narace, "Larceny of fowls, Arima," canine police report, Sheba's file, December 23, 1968.
5. Narace, "Threat and attempted suicide, Curepe," canine police report, Sheba's file, December 27, 1968.
6. Narace, "Theft, St. Joseph," canine police report, Sheba's file, March 11, 1969.
7. Thomas, letter requesting Sheba's retirement, canine police report, Sheba's file, June 8, 1970.
8. Winston Matthews, letter to Thomas, administrative file, September 25, 1973.
9. Matthews, letter to Thomas, administrative file, October 29, 1973.
10. Thomas, letter to senior officers, administrative file, November 30, 1973.
11. Crawford Williams, phone interview, July 7, 2022.

Chapter 8

1. Hector Lewis, personal interview, Port of Spain, March 2, 2009.
2. Lewis, personal interview, March 2, 2009.
3. Lewis, personal interview, March 2, 2009.
4. Lewis, personal interview, March 2, 2009.
5. Lewis, personal interview," March 2, 2009.
6. Michel Jean Cazabon, "Trinidad from the North Post," lithograph, 1851, https://www.artnet.com/artists/michel-jean-cazabon/canon-north-post-diego-martin-trinidad-X6WubZLeXP46r2-f66ihKw2.
7. Lewis, "Tracking police officer lost in the forest, Diego Martin," canine police report, Carlo's file, August 6, 1962.
8. Lewis, personal interview, March 2, 2009.
9. Angelo Bissessar, "The East Dry River Birthplace of Legends and Stories," *Trinidad Guardian*, Port of Spain (no date). https://www.guardian.co.tt/article-6.2.396474.8609c85271. The East Dry River was once the St. Ann's River that flowed from the upper reaches of Fondes Amandes in St. Ann's through the burgeoning town of Port of Spain, flooding the area every year. When the Spanish moved the capital from St. Joseph to Port of Spain in 1783, they diverted the river to the east, just below the Laventille hills and to the sea.
10. Lewis, personal interview, March 2, 2009.
11. Gérard Besson, "Conrad Frederick Stollmeyer," The Caribbean History Archives, Paria Publishing, November 8, 2011. http://caribbeanhistoryarchives.blogspot.com/2011/11/conrad-frederick-stollmeyer.html.
12. Lewis, personal interview, March 2, 2009.
13. Lewis, personal interview, March 2, 2009.
14. Lewis, personal interview, March 2, 2009.
15. Lewis, personal interview, March 2, 2009.
16. Raffique Shah, "Stealing Elections

Chapter Notes

by Any Vote Necessary," *Independent*, November 15, 2000. http://www.trinicenter.com/Raffique/Nov/byanyvote.htm.

17. Lewis, personal interview, March 2, 2009.
18. Lewis, "Stabbing in Cocoyea Village," Carlo's file, February 23, 1965.
19. Lewis, personal interview, March 2, 2009.
20. Lewis, personal interview, March 2, 2009.

Chapter 9

1. Hector Lewis, personal interview, Port of Spain, November 11, 2009.
2. Lewis, personal interview, November 11, 2009.
3. Hamilton Bridgeman, "Letter informing senior officers of Panther's arrival," canine police report, Panther's file, July 18, 1962.
4. Lewis, personal interview, November 11, 2009.
5. Theophilus Thomas, "Panther officially presented to police seniors," canine police report, Panther's file, July 19, 1962.
6. Bridgeman, "Update on Panther's progress and police number requested," canine police report, Panther's file, November 21, 1962.
7. Bridgeman, "Panther apprehends suspects in the Beetham," canine police report, Panther's file, January 10, 1963.
8. Thomas, "Request to take dogs to the beach," correspondence file, February 1, 1963.
9. Thomas, "Correspondence to Yearwood," correspondence file, February 4, February 5, 1963.
10. Lewis, "Panther's death," canine police report, Panther's file, August 7, 1965.
11. Thomas, "Preserving Panther's body for necropsy," canine police report, Panther's file, August 7, 1965.
12. Thomas ensured a copy of all correspondence regarding Panther's death was inserted in Panther's file.

Chapter 10

1. Matthews, personal interview, April 20, 2008.
2. Saturday Express, "212 years of the police service, 1798–2010," *Trinidad Express*, November 27, 2010. https://trinidadexpress.com/news/local/212-years-of-the-police-service/article_9434f0e6-2561-52d9-a41a-77af4d3c71cf.html.
3. Matthews, personal interview, April 20, 2008.
4. Matthews, personal interview, April 20, 2008.
5. Keith McNeal, "Miracle Mother—Siparee Mai, La Divina Pastora," *Caribbean Beat* 54 (March/April 2002), Maraval. https://www.caribbean-beat.com/issue-54/siparee-mai-miracle-mother#axzz7zdfM08iY.
6. Matthews, personal interview, April 20, 2008.
7. Matthews, personal interview, April 20, 2008.
8. The balisier is a flower in the heliconia family. It is the symbol of the PNM party.
9. Matthews, personal interview, April 20, 2008.
10. Matthews, personal interview, April 20, 2008.
11. Matthews, personal interview, April 20, 2008.
12. Matthews, personal interview, April 20, 2008.
13. Matthews, "Abduction in Arouca," canine police report, ANZAC's file, April 19, 1966.
14. PC Mohammed, "ANZAC's second case," canine police report, ANZAC's file, April 19, 1966.
15. Matthews, personal interview, April 20, 2008.
16. Mohammed, "Larceny of stumps," canine police report, ANZAC's file, March 25, 1967.
17. Mohammed, "Malicious wounding," canine police report, ANZAC's file, December 7, 1967.
18. Mohammed, "Copper wire thieves," canine police report, ANZAC's file, November 20, 1968.
19. Theophilus Thomas, "Malicious

Chapter Notes

damages, San Fernando," canine police report, Adolph's file, December 25, 1969.
20. Thomas, "Murder, Moruga," canine police report, Adolph's file, January 4, 1969.
21. Matthews, "Stabbing, Princes Town," canine police report, January 19, 1969.
22. PC Sifontis, "ANZAC changes handlers," canine police report, ANZAC's file, 1970–1974.
23. Matthews, "Stolen purse, Point Fortin," canine police report, 2008 Bullet's file, January 24, 1969; personal interview April 20, 2008.
24. Matthews, personal interview, April 20, 2008.
25. Matthews, personal interview, April 20, 2008.
26. Bhadase Mahabir, "Sentry's report on Bullet," administrative file, November 6, 1970.
27. Matthews, "Bullet's death," canine police report, Bullet's file, November 1, 1970.
28. Bullet's cause of death listed on file cover.
29. Dennis Figaro, "Juno's death," canine police report, Juno's file, May 6, 1971.
30. Amy A. Hosein, "ANZAC's treatment," veterinary report, ANZAC's file, April 3, 1973.
31. Hosein, "ANZAC's death," veterinary report, ANZAC's file, March 20, 1974.

Chapter 11

1. Noel James, "Assault case, Port of Spain," police canine report, Trigger's file 2, November 4, 1972.
2. James, "Assault case," November 4, 1972.
3. PC Feracho, "Trigger's background," police canine report, Trigger's file 1, 1964–1966.
4. Lystra D. Lewis, Letter offering Trigger to police, administrative file, 1965.
5. Theophilus Thomas, "Trigger enlisted," canine police report, Trigger's file 1, December 2, 1965.

6. Winston Matthews, personal interview, Freeport, April 20, 2008. (Trinidad police dogs worked throughout the Caribbean, particularly in St. Lucia, Belize and St. Vincent.)
7. James, "Trigger's cases," canine police reports, Trigger's files 1, 2, 1968–1973.
8. James, "Theft, Chaguanas," canine police report, Trigger's file 2, February 24, 1971.
9. James, "Tracking in Manzanilla forest," canine file 2, police report, Trigger's March 14, 1972.
10. James, "Suspects' responses to Trigger," canine police reports, Trigger's files, 1, 2, 1968–1973.
11. James, "Theft, Sangre Grande," canine police report, Trigger's file 2. April 15, 1972.
12. James, "Case of cow killed, Sangre Grande," canine police report, Trigger's file 2, June 14, 1972.
13. James, "Trigger's cases," canine police reports, Trigger's police file 2, 1971–1973.
14. James, "Theft Sangre Grande canine police report," Trigger's file 2, July 5, 1972.
15. James, "Theft, Sangre Grande," July 5, 1972.
16. James, "Theft, St Joseph," canine police report, Trigger's file 2, January 24, 1973.
17. James, "Theft, St Joseph," January 24, 1973.
18. James, "Rape, Port of Spain," canine police report, Trigger's file, November 26, 1968.
19. James, "Rape, Port of Spain," November 26, 1968.

Chapter 12

1. Dylan Kerrigan, "Bobol as a Transhistorical Cultural Logic," *Caribbean Quarterly* 66, May 20, 2020. https://www.tandfonline.com/doi/abs/10.1080/00086495.2020.1759231.
2. Police dog files often alluded to police searching homes of known drug dealers several times and finding nothing until dogs like Shep were brought to search them.

Chapter Notes

3. Leonard Dyer, personal interview, May 3, 1992, Caroni.
4. Theophilus Thomas, administrative file, Depot Kennels, 1974.
5. Marcellus Grant, "Shep's first premise search," canine police report, Shep's file, August 17, 1974.
6. Grant, "Arrest of Dole Chadee," canine police report, Shep's file, April 23, 1975.
7. Winston Matthews, Note on back of Chadee arrest report, Shep's file, April 30, 1975.
8. Thomas, "Report to Supt. Yearwood," Shep's file, May 7, 1975.
9. Rupert Yearwood, "Reply to Thomas on Chadee arrest," Shep's file, May 14, 1975.
10. Grant, "Shep's work in drug detection," canine police reports, Shep's file, 1975–1976.
11. Grant, "Shep's first underground find," canine police report, Shep's file, March 19, 1977.
12. Grant, "Shep euthanized," canine police report, Shep's file, April 1, 1980.

Chapter 13

1. UPI, "Caribbean News Briefs," UPI Archives, 1984. https://www.upi.com/Archives/1985/04/08/Caribbean-News-Briefs/3577481784400/.
2. Winston H.E. Suite, "Who is the man Makandal Daaga?" *The Caribbean Camera*, August 18, 2016. https://thecaribbeancamera.com/who-is-the-man-makandal-daaga/.
3. Photograph of Eric Williams at Woodford Square appears on the cover of *Massa Day Done: A Masterpiece of Political and Sociological Analysis* (Port of Spain: PNM, 1961). http://ufdcimages.uflib.ufl.edu/uf/00/00/16/20/00001/binder1.pdf.
4. V.S. Naipaul, "The Baker's Story," *A Flag on the Island* (London: Penguin, 1993).
5. Raffique Shah, "Readying a nation for battle," Trinicenter, 2000. http://www.trinicenter.com/1970/Blackpower2.htm.
6. Shah, "Readying a nation for battle," Trinicenter, 2000.
7. Khairool Khan, personal interview, Westmoorings, February 2, 2020.
8. Khan, personal interview, February 2, 2020.
9. Shah, phone interview, March 20, 2021.
10. Khan, "Police dogs track NUFF," canine police dog reports, Daemon and Rex's files, 1970–1972.
11. Khan, personal interview, February 2, 2020.
12. Theophilus Thomas, correspondence files, 1970–1972.
13. Thomas, correspondence file, 1973.
14. Supt Yearwood, Thomas's correspondence file, 1973.
15. Yearwood, "Shortages," correspondence file, 1973.
16. Thomas, Thomas's correspondence file, 1973.
17. Thomas, "Matthews leaves for training," September 24, 1972.
18. Khan, personal interview, February 2, 2020.
19. Khan, personal interview, February 2, 2020.
20. Khan, personal interview, February 2, 2020.
21. Khan, personal interview February 2, 2020.
22. Thomas, "Daemon's first report," canine police report, Daemon's file, February 11, 1969.
23. Khan, personal interview, February 2, 2020.
24. Paul, "Apprehension of suspect, St. Joseph," canine police report, Daemon's file, June 17, 1962.
25. Septimus Paul, "Murder suspect in Las Lomas," canine police report, Daemon's file, September 27, 1969.
26. Paul and Thomas, "Daemon's behaviour and commendations," canine police report and police commissioner's official reports, 1969–1972.
27. Khan, personal interview, February 2, 2020.
28. Paul, "Tracking NUFF, San Fernando," canine police report, Daemon's file, June 6, 1972.
29. Khan, personal interview, February 2, 2020.

Chapter Notes

Chapter 14

1. Winston Matthews, personal interview, Freeport, April 20, 2008.
2. Khairool Khan, personal interview, Trincity, May 8, 2010.
3. Karl Hudson-Phillips, personal interview, Port of Spain, April 12, 2012.
4. Khan, personal interview, Trincity, May 8, 2010.
5. Matthews, personal interview, Freeport, April 20, 2008.
6. Matthews and Khan, personal interviews, April 20 and May 8, 2010.
7. Matthews, personal interview, April 20, 2008.
8. Matthews, personal interview, April 20, 2008.
9. Khan, personal interview, May 8, 2010.
10. Matthews and Khan, personal interviews, April 20 and May 8, 2010.
11. Theophilus Thomas, "Report on Daemon's death," Daemon's file, June 8, 1973.
12. Hendren Brown, "Brutus at work," canine police reports, Brutus's files, 1970–1973.
13. Khan, personal interview, March 18, 2020. (If Khan's recollection is correct, this would mean Brutus was walking on the wrong side of his handler.)
14. Khan, personal interview, May 8, 2010.
15. Kenneth John, "Gun Talk," *The Vincentian*, April 21, 2017. https://thevincentian.com/gun-talk-p13047-108.htm.
16. John, "Gun Talk," *The Vincentian*, 2017.
17. Patrick Junior "Spirit" Cottle, phone interview, January 23, 2021.
18. Cottle, phone interview, January 23, 2021.
19. Cottle, phone interview, January 23, 2021.
20. Cottle, phone interview, January 23, 2021.
21. Cottle, phone interview, January 23, 2021.
22. Cottle, interview, phone January 23, 2021.
23. Khan, phone interview, January 25, 2021.

Chapter 15

1. Leonard Dyer, personal interview, Caroni, March 3, 1992; Winston Matthews, personal interview, Freeport, April 20, 2008.
2. Dyer, personal interview, March 3, 1992.
3. Dyer, personal interview, March 3, 1992.
4. Dyer, personal interview, March 3, 1992.
5. Dyer, personal interview, March 3, 1992.
6. Donna Mae Tam, phone interview, October 16, 2021.
7. PC Samuel, "Kidnapping case, Gasparee island," canine police report, Rover's file, February 25, 1982.
8. Clayton Chandler, phone interview, October 16, 2021.
9. Chandler, phone interview, October 16, 2021.
10. Dyer, phone interview, March 3, 1992.
11. Dyer, phone interview, March 3, 1992.
12. Dyer, phone interview, March 3, 1992.
13. Khan, interview, February 2, 2020.

Chapter 16

1. Premnath Maharaj, personal interview, Caroni, April 8, 2015.
2. Maharaj, personal interview, April 16, 2015.
3. Maharaj, personal interview, April 22, 2015.
4. Maharaj, personal interview, Caroni, April 8, 2015.
5. Debbie Jacob, personal observation, August 17, 2017.
6. Maharaj, personal interview, April 8, 2015.
7. Maharaj, personal interview, April 8, 2015.

Chapter 17

1. Winn, personal interview December 1, 2016.

Chapter Notes

2. Caribbean Elections, "Trinidad and Tobago Election Centre," Year in review, 2019. http://www.caribbeanelections.com/tt/elections/tt_results_2001.asp.
3. "The end of an era: Guardian 50 moments that made T&T history," *Trinidad Guardian*, Port of Spain, July 31, 2003. https://www.guardian.co.tt/article-6.2.427024.0889b4f0a1.
4. Central Statistical Office, "Population of Trinidad 2018–2022," Port of Spain, 2020. https://www.populationu.com/trinidad-and-tobago-population.
5. BBC News, "Thousands March on Trinidad crime," October 23, 2005. http://news.bbc.co.uk/2/hi/americas/4368582.stm.
6. World Bank, Trinidad and Tobago crime statistics, 2000–2022. https://data.worldbank.org/indicator/VC.IHR.PSRC.P5?locations=TT.
7. Winn, personal interview, December 1, 2016.
8. Winn, personal interview, December 1, 2016.
9. Winn, personal interview, December 1, 2016.
10. Winn, personal interview, December 1, 2016.
11. Winn personal interview, December 1, 2016.
12. Winn, personal interview, December 1, 2016.
13. Winn, personal interview, December 1, 2016.
14. Winn, personal interview, December 1, 2016.
15. Winn, personal interview, December 1, 2016.

Chapter 18

1. Anthony Piegaro, Letters from U.S. embassies and U.S. companies, CSI website, and phone interview, October 14, 2019. http://www.csiemergencyservice.com/. Michael Roban, personal interview, November 9, 2019.
2. Piegaro, Letters from clients and newspaper clippings, CSI website. http://www.csiemergencyservice.com/.
3. Raphael Mohammed, personal interview, August 3, 2018.
4. Piegaro, phone interview, October 14, 2019.
5. Piegaro, phone interview, October 14, 2019.
6. Lindsay Clutterbuck and Richard Warnes, "References," in *Exploring Patterns of Behaviour in Violent Jihadist Terrorists: An Analysis of Six Significant Terrorist Conspiracies in the UK* (Santa Monica: RAND Corporation, 2011), 57–62. http://www.jstor.org/stable/10.7249/tr923ant.11.
7. Francis Joseph, "Bomb in the City," *Trinidad & Tobago Newsday*, July 12, 2005, 3.
8. Nalinee Seelal, (no headline), *Trinidad Newsday*, Port of Spain, July 12, 2005. http://www.csiemergencyservice.com/.
9. No one can pinpoint when the police began to use Canine Section rather than Dog Section, but by the 1990s, it was called the Canine Section.
10. Piegaro, phone interview, October 14, 2019.
11. Piegaro, phone interview, October 14, 2019.
12. Premnath Maharaj, phone interview, November 20, 2022.
13. Lenford Blades, phone interview, March 3, 2016.
14. Piegaro, phone interview, March 3, 2016.
15. Roban, personal interview, November 9, 2019.
16. Roban, personal interview, November 9, 2019.
17. Roban, personal interview, November 9, 2019.
18. Shane Chase, personal interview, Cumuto, March 18, 2021.
19. Roban, personal interview, November 9, 2019.
20. Roban, personal interview, November 9, 2019.
21. Jason Donawa, personal interview, Cumuto, December 11, 2019.
22. Donawa, personal interview, Cumuto, December 11, 2019.

Chapter 19

1. Premnath Maharaj, personal interview, Caroni, August 23, 2017.

Chapter Notes

2. Maharaj, personal interview, August 23, 2017.
3. Maharaj, personal interview, August 23, 2017.
4. Maharaj, personal interview, August 23, 2017.
5. Maharaj, personal interview, August 23, 2017.
6. Maharaj, personal interview, August 23, 2017.
7. Rawle Ryan, personal interview, Cumuto, February 3, 2019.
8. Ryan, personal interview, February 3, 2019.
9. Ryan, personal interview, February 3, 2019.
10. Nalinee Seelal, "Operation Anaconda: National Crime Plan," *Trinidad & Tobago Newsday*, February 21, 2002. http://www.trinidadandtobagonews.com/forum/webbbs_config.pl?md=read;id=221.
11. Nalinee Seelal, "Operation Anaconda: National Crime Plan," *Trinidad and Tobago Newsday*, February 21, 2002.
12. Ryan, personal interview, February 3, 2019.
13. Ryan, personal interview, February 3, 2019.
14. Ryan, personal interview, February 3, 2019.
15. Ryan, personal interview, February 3, 2019.
16. Ryan, personal interview, February 3, 2019.
17. Ryan, personal interview, February, 3, 2019.
18. Ryan, personal interview, February 3, 2019.
19. Ryan, personal interview, February 3, 2019.
20. John Phillips, personal interview, Caroni, April 6, 2017.
21. Phillips, personal interview, April 6, 2017.
22. Phillips, personal interview, April 6, 2017.
23. Phillips, personal interview, April 6, 2017.
24. Neil Perez, phone interview, January 6, 2021.
25. Perez, phone interview, January 6, 2021.
26. Perez, phone interview, January 6, 2021.
27. Perez, phone interview, January 6, 2021.
28. Reynold Bahadoor, personal interview, Cunupia, February 28, 2020.
29. Bahadoor, personal interview, February 28, 2020.
30. Bahadoor, personal interview, February 28, 2020.

Chapter 20

1. Kirt Antoine, personal interview, Chaguaramas, April 5, 2016.
2. Antoine, personal interview, April 5, 2016.
3. Antoine, personal interview, April 5, 2016.
4. Antoine, personal interview, April 5, 2016.
5. Because of the dogs' tracking speed, canine police often get separated from other police on assignments.
6. Antoine, personal interview, April 5, 2016.
7. Akil Bernard, personal interview, Cumuto, September 14, 2021.
8. Bernard, personal interview, September 14, 2021.
9. Bernard, personal interview, September 14, 2021.
10. Antoine, personal interview, April 5, 2016.
11. Antoine, personal interview, April 5, 2016.
12. Dina Temple-Raston, "Police Tackle Kidnapping Surge in Trinidad," National Public Radio, New York, August 17, 2007.
13. C.J. Williams, "Kidnappings send a chill through Sunny Trinidad," *Los Angeles Times*, January 2, 2005. https://www.latimes.com/archives/la-xpm-2005-jan-02-fg-kidnap2-story.html.
14. An anonymous source spoke about SAUTT's canine participation in anti-kidnapping exercises. SAUTT operations are classified.
15. Reynold Bahadoor, personal interview, Cunupia, February 28, 2020.
16. Bahadoor, personal interview, February 28, 2020.

Chapter Notes

17. Bahadoor, personal interview, February 28, 2020.
18. Bahadoor, personal interview, February 28, 2020.
19. Bahadoor, personal interview, Februrary 28, 2020.
20. Bahadoor, personal interview, February 28, 2020.
21. Bahadoor, personal interview, February 28, 2020.
22. Bahadoor, personal interview, February 28, 2020.
23. Bernard, personal interview, September 14, 2021.

Chapter 21

1. Renrick Texeira, personal interview, Chaguaramas, May 12, 2017.
2. Texeira, personal interview, May 12, 2017.
3. Shane Chase, personal interview, March 9, 2020.
4. Kiff Singh, personal interview, Caroni, June 20, 2015.
5. Singh, personal interview, June 20, 2015.
6. Renrick Texeira, personal interview, Chaguaramas, May 12, 2017.
7. Sherwin Cedeno, personal interview, Caroni, May 5, 2015.
8. Kiff Singh, person interview, Caroni, April 5, 2015.
9. Sherwin Cedeno, personal interview, May 2, 2015.
10. Ashram Pariagsingh, police canine reports, Caroni, Condor's files, 1990–1992.

Chapter 22

1. Debbie Jacob, personal observations, Port of Spain Prison, September 2018–July 2021.
2. Anonymous prison guard, "Personal description of events during prison breakout," Port of Spain, October 20, 2022.
3. Anonymous prison guard, "Description of prison breakout," October 20, 2022.
4. Ryan Hamilton-Davis, "Frederick Street prison break questions still unanswered six years later," *Trinidad & Tobago Newsday*, Port of Spain, July 26, 2021. https://newsday.co.tt/2021/07/26/frederick-street-prison-break-questions-still-unanswered-6-years-later/?fbclid=-IwAR3XB-5B6jnFmZxnugTqb_V2m-.
5. Ryan Hamilton-Davis, "Frederick Street prison break questions still unanswered six years later," *Trinidad & Tobago Newsday*, Port of Spain, July 26, 2021.
6. Premnath Maharaj, personal interview, Caroni, May 11, 2019.
7. Sherwin Cedeno, personal interview, May 20, 2015.
8. Central Statistical Office, "Population Statistics," Ministry of Planning, Port of Spain, 2011. https://cso.gov.tt/subjects/population-and-vital-statistics/population/.
9. Emma Graham-Harrison and Joshua Surtees, "Trinidad's jihadis: how tiny nation became ISIS recruiting ground," *The Guardian*, London, February 2, 2018. https://www.theguardian.com/world/2018/feb/02/trinidad-jihadis-isis-tobago-tariq-abdul-haqq.
10. Simon Cottee, "Isis in the Caribbean," *Atlantic*, Washington, D.C., December 8, 2016. https://www.theatlantic.com/international/archive/2016/12/isis-trinidad/509930/.
11. Premnath Maharaj, personal interview, May 11, 2019.
12. Sharlene Rampersad, "Jacobs: Country has 134 gangs accounting for most daily crimes," *The Guardian*, Port of Spain, May 11, 2022. https://www.guardian.co.tt/news/jacobs-country-has-134-gangs-accounting-for-most-daily-crimes-6.2.1491608.eb12e2bf32.
13. Ryan Hamilton-Davis, "Frederick Street prison break questions still unanswered six years later," *Trinidad & Tobago Newsday*, Port of Spain, July 26, 2021.
14. Premnath Maharaj, personal interview, Caroni, May 11, 2019.
15. Ryan Hamilton-Davis, "Frederick Street prison break questions still unanswered six years later," *Trinidad & Tobago Newsday*, Port of Spain, July 26, 2021.

Chapter Notes

Chapter 23

1. Personal observations, Cumuto, June 21, July 3 and July 28, 2018.
2. Stephen Swanson, personal interview, Caroni, July 2, 2018.
3. Swanson, personal interview, July 2, 2018.
4. Debbie Jacob, "Hard-working dog," *Trinidad & Tobago Newsday*, Port of Spain, July 16, 2018. https://newsday.co.tt/2018/07/16/hard-working-dog/.
5. World Bank, "Trinidad and Tobago Homicide Rates, 2000–2023." https://www.macrotrends.net/countries/TTO/trinidad-and-tobago/murder-homicide-rate.
6. Indarjit Seuraj, "Morvant URP man killed," *Trinidad Guardian*, July 2006.
7. Debbie Jacob, "Hard-working dog," *Trinidad & Tobago Newsday*, July 16, 2018.
8. Debbie Jacob, "Hard-working dog," *Trinidad & Tobago Newsday*, July 16, 2018.
9. Debbie Jacob, "Hard-working dog," *Trinidad & Tobago Newsday*, July 16, 2018.
10. Debbie Jacob, "Hard-working dog," *Trinidad & Tobago Newsday*, July 16, 2018.
11. Stephen Swanson, letter to Supt. Geoffrey Hospedales, Chaguaramas, May 26, 2020.
12. Geoffrey Hospedales, Letter to police commissioner, Mounted Branch, administrative files, St. James, May 29, 2020.
13. Swanson, letter to superintendent, May 26, 2020.
14. Swanson, letter to superintendent, May 26, 2020.
15. Hospedales, letter to police commissioner, May 29, 2020.
16. Swanson, letter to superintendent, May 26, 2020.
17. Hospedales, letter to police commissioner, May 29, 2020.
18. Loop News, "Police officer dies, autopsy ordered," June 22, 2020. https://tt.loopnews.com/content/police-officer-dies-autopsy-ordered.

Chapter 24

1. Donna Mae Tom, phone interview, October 16, 2021.
2. Malissa Narine, phone interview, April 3, 2020.
3. Narine, phone interview, April 3, 2020.
4. Personal observations and conversations, 2017–2022.
5. Jiselle Andrews, personal interview, Caroni, March 13, 2016.
6. Andrews, personal interview, March 13, 2016.
7. The National Trust of Trinidad and Tobago, "The Pointe-à-Pierre Wild Fowl Trust," 2023. https://nationaltrust.tt/home/location/pointe-a-pierre-wild-fowl-trust/?v=df1f3edb9115. The Pointe-à-Pierre Wild Trust has more than 40 tree species including Flamboyant trees, Red Blossoms, Pink Pouis, Crepe, and Myrtle trees, and 86 protected avian species including Black-bellied Whistling Tree Duck, White-cheeked Pintail, Wild Muscovy Duck, Fulvous Whistling Duck, Blue and Gold Macaw, and the Scarlet Ibis.
8. Andrews, personal interview, March 13, 2016.
9. Andrews, personal interview, March 13, 2016.
10. Andrews, personal interview, March 13, 2016.
11. Andrews, personal interview, March 13, 2016.

Chapter 25

1. Delroy James and Deon Mapp, personal interviews, Tobago, April 18, 2016.
2. Anthony Duke, personal interview, Tobago, April 22, 2016.
3. Duke, personal interview, April 22, 2016.
4. Andrew Lawler, "Invaders nearly wiped out Caribbean's first people long before Spanish came, DNA reveals," *National Geographic*, Washington, D.C., December 23, 2020.
5. John Paul Jones, "Letter to Benjamin Franklin," Philadelphia, March 6, 1770, in Reginald De Koven (Mrs.), *The*

Chapter Notes

Life and Letters of John Paul Jones (New York: Charles Scribner's Sons, 1913), Vol. II, pp. 440–444.
6. Royal Museums, Greenwich, "Robinson Crusoe," 2023. https://www.rmg.co.uk/collections/objects/rmgc-object-63975.
7. Darren Baptiste, personal interview, Tobago, April 19, 2016.
8. Darren Baptiste, "A Day in the Life of Riko, Trinidad and Tobago's Only Tactical/Explosive Detection Dog," *Trinidad and Tobago Newsday*, May 28, 2023. https://newsday.co.tt/2023/05/28/a-day-in-the-life-of-riko-trinidad-and-tobagos-only-explosive-detection-dog/.
9. Ronnie Caruth, personal interview, Tobago, April 18, 2016.
10. Caruth, Mapp, personal interviews, Tobago, April 18, 2016.
11. Kenon Baynes, personal interview, Tobago, April 17, 2016.
12. Baynes, personal interview, April 17, 2016.
13. Anthony Duke, personal interview, Tobago, April 22, 2016.
14. Duke, personal interview, April 22, 2016.
15. Mapp, personal interview, April 18, 2016.
16. Mapp, personal interview, April 18, 2016.
17. Mapp, personal interview, April 18, 2016.
18. Baptiste, phone interview, September 9, 2022.

Chapter 26

1. Debbie Jacob, "Canine Stars of Green Days," *Trinidad & Tobago Newsday*, September 17, 2017. https://newsday.co.tt/2017/09/17/canine-stars-of-green-days/.
2. Neil Samaroo, personal interview, Caroni, September 10, 2017.
3. Samaroo, personal interview, September 10, 2017.
4. Enoch Romeo, personal interview, Caroni, August 2, 2015.
5. Romeo, personal interview, August 2, 2015.
6. Romeo, personal interview, Caroni, August 9, 2015.

7. Romeo, personal interview, August 9, 2015.
8. Romeo, personal interview, Caroni, September 15, 2015.
9. Romeo, personal interview, September 15, 2015.
10. Romeo, personal interview, September 15, 2015.
11. Leon Lopez, personal interview, Cumuto, April 3, 2020.
12. Anonymous dog handler, phone interview, March 29, 2020.
13. Anonymous dog handler, phone interview, March 29, 2020.
14. Anonymous, dog handler, phone interview, March 29, 2020.
15. Anonymous, dog handler, phone interview, March 29, 2020.
16. Kerron Woodroffe, phone interview, November 22, 2022.
17. Woodroffe, phone interview, November 22, 2022.
18. Woodroffe, phone interview, November 22, 2022.
19. Sean Bailey, phone interview, April 9, 2023.
20. Bailey, phone interview, April 9, 2023.
21. Bailey, phone interview, April 9, 2023.
22. Zameer Mohammed, phone interview, April 14, 2023.
23. Mohammed, phone interview, April 14, 2023.
24. Shane Chase, personal interview, Cumuto, October 3, 2022.

Chapter 27

1. Debbie Jacob, personal observations, Cumuto, May 7, 2021.
2. Shane Chase, personal interview, Cumuto, September 27, 2021.
3. Chase, personal interview, September 27, 2021.
4. Chase, personal interview, September 27, 2021.
5. Chase, personal interview, Cumuto, October 3, 2021.
6. Chase, personal interview, October 3, 2021.
7. Chase, personal interview, Cumuto, October 10, 2021.

Chapter Notes

8. Chase, personal interview, October 20, 2021.
9. Chase, personal interview, October 20, 2021.
10. Chase, personal interview, October 20, 2021.
11. Saadiq Hosein, personal interview, Caroni, April 17, 2017.
12. Hosein, personal interview, April 17, 2017.
13. Hosein, personal interview, April 17, 2017.
14. Hosein, personal interview, April 17, 2017.
15. Hosein, personal interview, April 17, 2017.

Chapter 28

1. Cathy Ella, "Mama Yo," Visual Arts Production, St. Ann's, 2018.
2. Premnath Maharaj, personal interview, Cumuto, April 13, 2020.
3. Akil Bernard, personal interview, Cumuto, April 14, 2020.
4. Bernard, personal interview, April 14, 2020.
5. Ronnie Caruth, phone interview, December 28, 2019.
6. Loop News, "Close to 200 Detained for Copper Theft," Port of Spain, May 23, 2022. https://tt.loopnews.com/content/close-200-detained-copper-theft.
7. Maharaj, personal interview, April 13, 2020.
8. Hector Lewis, phone interview, March 27, 2020.
9. Kenny Winn, phone interview, April 9, 2020.
10. Enoch Romeo, phone interview, April 10, 2020.
11. Debbie Jacob, "Raising a hard-working police dog," *Trinidad & Tobago Newsday*, Port of Spain, March 10, 2021. https://newsday.co.tt/2021/03/10/raising-a-hard-working-police-dog/.
12. Debbie Jacob, "Raising a hard-working police dog," *Trinidad & Tobago Newsday*, Port of Spain, March 10, 2021.
13. Debbie Jacob, "Raising a hard-working police dog," *Trinidad & Tobago Newsday*, Port of Spain, March 10, 2021.
14. Debbie Jacob, "Raising a hard-working police dog," *Trinidad & Tobago Newsday*, Port of Spain, March 10, 2021.
15. Maharaj, personal interview, Cumuto, March 4, 2021.

Appendix A

1. Theophilus Thomas, "Bruno's final report," canine police report, Bruno's file 3, Caroni, July 26, 1960.

Appendix B

1. Ralph V.G. De Gannes, "Panther's veterinarian report," Panther's file, Caroni, August 10, 1965.

Appendix C

1. Lord Diplock, Viscount Dilhorne and Lord Simon, "Privy Council Summary of Junior 'Spirit' Cottle Case," *Weekly Law Reports* 3 (1976).

Bibliography

Books

Duhigg, Charles. *Power of Habit: Why We Do What We Do in Life and in Business*. New York: Random House, 2012.
Handy, W.F. *The K-9 Corps: The Use of Dogs in Police Work*. Chicago: Northwestern University, 1961.
Horowitz, Alexandra. *Being a Dog: Following the Dog into a World of Smell*. New York: Scribner, 2016.
Jones, John Paul. Letter to Benjamin Franklin, Philadelphia, March 6, 1770. In (Mrs.) Reginald De Koven, *The Life and Letters of John Paul Jones*. New York: Charles Scribner's Sons, 1913, Vol. II.
Naipaul, V.S. "The Baker's Story." *A Flag on the Island*. London: Penguin, 1993.
Williams, Eric Eustace. *Massa Day Done: A Masterpiece of Political and Sociological Analysis*. Port of Spain: PNM, 1961.

Personal Interviews

All personal and phone interviews done by the author

Andrews, Jiselle. "Challenges of a woman police officer." Caroni, March 13, 2016.
Antoine, Kirt. "Ambushed." Chaguaramas, April 5, 2016.
Bahadoor, Reynold. "Kidnapping and Dog Jack." Cunupia, February 28, 2020.
Baptiste, Darren. "Crime and police dogs in Tobago." Tobago, April 19, 2016 and September 9, 2022.
Baynes, Keon. "Becoming a Tobago police officer." Tobago, April 17, 2016.
Bernard, Akil. "Canine Cezar,." Cumuto, April 14, 2020 and September 14, 2021.
Caruth, Ronnie. "Canine Cordon and crime in Tobago." Tobago, April 18, 2016.
Cedeno, Sherwin. "Canine Jed and Port of Spain Prison breakout." Caroni, May 2, 5, 20, 2015.
Chase, Shane. "Police dog training." March 9, 2020, September 27, October 3, October 10, October 20, 2021, and October 23, 2022.
Donawa, Jason. "Anthony Piegaro's training." Cumuto, December 11, 2019.
Duke, Anthony. "Working and training in Trinidad." Tobago, April 22, 2016.
Dyer, Leonard. "History of Police Canine, A-puppies and canine police in the 80s." Caroni, May 3, 1992.
Harry, Dunstan. "Recollections of Theophilus Thomas, and Canine Zak." Caroni, April 23, 2019.
Hinds, Vincent. "Cadaver dog Red." Chaguaramas, December 8, 2016.
Hosein, Saadiq. "Canine Eddie." Caroni, April 17, 2017.
Hudson-Phillips, Karl. "Murder in St. Vincent of acting attorney General." Port of Spain, April 12, 2012.
James, Delroy. "Crime and police dogs in Tobago." Tobago, April 18, 2016.

Bibliography

Khan, Khairool. "Police dogs in the 60s and 70s and the Role of Police Dogs in the Black Power Movement." Caroni, May 3, 1992; Trincity, May 8, 2010; Westmoorings, March 18, 2020.
Lewis, Hector. "Police Dogs in the 60s and Canine Carlo." Port of Spain, March 2 and 11, April 10, November 11, 2009.
Lopez, Leon. "Canine Marko." Cumuto, April 3, 2020.
Maharaj, Premnath. "Dustbin bombings and Canine puppies." Caroni, April 8, 26, 22, 2015, August 23, 2017, May 11, 2019, April 13, 2020, and Cumuto, March 4, 2021.
Mapp, Deon. "Crime in Tobago." Tobago, April 18, 2016.
Matthews, Winston. "Police dogs in the 60s." Freeport, April 20, 2008, and May 12, 2012.
Phillips, John. "Anthony Piegaro's training." Caroni, April 6, 2017.
Roban, Michael. "Canine history and the Piegaro era." Westmoorings, November 9, 2019.
Romeo, Enoch. "Canine Maverick." Caroni, August 2, 2015.
Ryan, Rawle. "Piegaro's training." Cumuto, February 3, 2019.
Samaroo, Neil. "Canines Bak and Boyca." Caroni, September 10, 2017.
Singh, Kiff. "Canine Penny." Caroni, April 5 and June 20, 2015.
Swanson, Stephen. "Cadaver dog training." Caroni, July 2, 2018.
Texeira, Renrick. "Canine Jackson." Chaguaramas, May 12, 2017.
Winn, Kenny. "Canines Jango and Strike." December 1, 2016.

Phone Interviews

Bailey, Sean. "Canine Hart." April 9, 2023.
Blades, Lenford. "Anthony Piegaro's influence on police canine." March 3, 2016.
Caruth, Ronnie. "Tobago canine." December 28, 2019.
Chandler, Clayton. "Purchasing police dogs." October 13 and 16, 2021.
Cottle, Patrick Junior. "Assassination of acting St. Vincent attorney general." January 23, 2021.
Dyer, Leonard. "Request for air-conditioned canine police vehicles." May 3, 1992.
Lewis, Hector. "Police canine in the 1960s." March 27, 2020.
Maharaj, Premnath. "Training with Anthony Piegaro." November 20, 2022.
Mohammed, Raphael. "Anthony Piegaro." August 3, 2018.
Mohammed, Zameer. "Canine Kubo." April 14, 2023.
Narine, Malisa. "Challenges and contributions of women canine police." April 3, 2020.
Perez, Neil. "Training under Anthony Piegaro." January 6, 2021.
Piegaro, Anthony J. "Training in Trinidad." October 14, 2019.
Romeo, Enoch. "Police dogs Maverick and Riko." April 10, 2020.
Thomas-Austin, Deborah. "Theophilus Thomas." March 17, 2022.
Tom, Donna Mae. "Women in the canine police." October 16, 2021.
Williams, Crawford. "Canine in the 80s." July 7, 2022.
Winn, Kenny. "Jango and Strike." April 9, 2020.
Woodroffe, Kerron. "Canine Arci." November 22, 2022.

Police Canine Section Correspondence

Bridgeman, Hamilton. "Letter informing senior officers of Panther's arrival." Canine police report, Panther's file, July 18, 1962.
De Gannes, V.G. "Panther's Veterinary Report." Canine correspondence file, Caroni, August 10, 1965.
Duke (no first name). "Letter of complaint about Rex." Canine police administrative file (and Rex's file), Caroni, August 26, 1957.

Bibliography

Hicks. "Letter of complaint." Canine police report, Jett's file, Caroni, July 11, 1960.
———. "ANZAC's treatment." Veterinary report, ANZAC's file, Caroni, April 3, 1973.
Hospedales, Geoffrey. "Letter to police commissioner." Mounted and Canine Branch administrative files, St. James, May 29, 2020.
Lewis, Lystra D. "Letter offering Trigger to police." Canine police administrative file, Caroni, 1965.
Mahabir, Bhadase. "Sentry's report on Bullet's death." Canine police administrative file, Caroni, November 6, 1970.
Matthews, Winston. "Letter to Theophilus Thomas re: purchase of dogs." Canine police administrative file, Caroni, September 25, 1973.
———. "Letter to Theophilus Thomas re: purchase of dogs." Canine police administrative file, Caroni, October 29, 1973.
St. Louis, Cromwell. "Letter requesting police dogs' services." Canine police administrative file, Caroni, March, 10, 1961.
Swanson, Stephen. "Letter to Supt. Geoffrey Hospedales." Mounted and Canine Branch administrative files, St. James, May 26, 2020.
Thomas, Theophilus. "Correspondence to Supt. Yearwood." Correspondence file, Caroni, February 5, 1963.
———. "Dobermans in the police service." Personal note in canine administrative file, Caroni, 1959.
———. "Dogs' food." Administrative reports, Caroni, November 22, 1963.
———. "Final report on Bruno." Bruno's file, Caroni, July 26, 1960.
———. "Letter addressing Hicks's complaint about station police." Canine police report, Jett's file, Caroni, September 30, 1960.
———. "Letter from Thomas on purchase of Shep." Administrative file, Caroni, 1974.
———. "Letter of regret." Canine correspondence file, Caroni, March 15, 1961.
———. "Letter requesting Sheba's retirement." Canine police report, Sheba's file, Caroni, June 8, 1970.
———. "Letter to APC Claud May." Administrative reports, Caroni, April 19, 1965.
———. "Letter to senior officers." Administrative file, Caroni, November 30, 1973.
———. "Letter to superintendent." Administrative file, Caroni, July 8, 1965.
———. "Matthews leaves for training." Administrative file, Caroni, September 24, 1972.
———. "Panther officially presented to police seniors." Canine police report, Panther's file, Caroni, July 19, 1962.
———. "Preserving Panther's body for autopsy." Canine police report, Panther's file, August 7, 1965.
———. "Report to Supt. Yearwood." Shep's file, Caroni, May 7, 1975.
———. "Request to take dogs to the beach." Correspondence file, Caroni. February 1, 1963.
———. "Thomas's report to senior officers on Shah apprehending suspect." Canine police report, Shah's file, Caroni, November 1954.
Yearwood, Rupert. "Shortages." Canine correspondence file, Caroni, 1973.
———. "Letter in reply to Thomas on Chadee arrest." Shep's file, May 14, 1975.

Police Dog Files

Alexis, George. "Carlos tracks down suspect, La Seiva." Canine police report, Carlos's file, no date.
———. "Rex solves a chicken case." Police canine report, Rex's file, October 19, 1959.
———. "Rex's chicken-chasing escapades." Police canine report, Rex's file, June 17, 1957.
Bridgeman, Hamilton. "First report of copper wire theft." Canine police report, Shah's file, July 15, 1958.
———. "Shah apprehends thief, Couva." Canine police report, Shah's file, November 14, 1956.

Bibliography

———. "Shah bites civilian." Canine police report, Shah's file, October 14, 1957.
———. "Shah finds money." Canine police report, Shah's file, August 16, 1958.
———. "Shah pursues gamblers." Canine police report, Shah's file, November 12, 1957.
———. "Update on Panther's progress and police number requested." Canine police report, Panther's file, November 21, 1962.
———. "Panther apprehends suspects, Beetham." Canine police report, Panther's file, January 10, 1963.
———. "Wanted men stop police in unmarked car." Canine police report, Shah's file, August 22, 1955.
Brown, Hendren. "Brutus at work." Canine police reports, Brutus's files, 1970–1973.
Charles (no first name). "Jett solves murder case, Blanchisseuse." Canine police report, Jett's file, November 8, 1959.
———. "Jett tracks down thief, Curepe." Canine police report, Jett's file, February 15, 1963.
Feracho (no first name). "Trigger's background." Police canine report, Trigger's file 1, 1964–1966.
Figaro, Dennis. "Juno's death." Canine police report, Juno's file, May 6, 1971.
Grant, Marcellus. "Arrest of Dole Chadee." Canine police report, Shep's file, April 23, 1975.
———. "Shep euthanized." Canine police report, Shep's file, April 1, 1980.
———. "Shep's first premise search." Canine police report, Shep's file, August 17, 1974.
———. "Shep's first underground find." Canine police report, Shep's file, March 19, 1977.
———. "Shep's work in drug detection." Canine police reports, Shep's file, 1975–1976.
Hicks, Horace. "Jett catches suspect in the forest." Canine police report, Jett's file, July 10, 1960.
James, Noel. "Assault case, Port of Spain." Police canine report, Trigger's file 2, November 4, 1972.
———. "Case of cow killed, Sangre Grande." Canine police report, Trigger's file 2, June 14, 1972.
———. "Rape, Port of Spain." Canine police report, Trigger's file, November 26, 1968.
———. "Suspects' responses to Trigger." Canine police reports, Trigger's files, 1, 2, 1968–1973.
———. "Theft, Chaguanas." Canine police report, Trigger's file 2, February 24, 1971.
———. "Theft, Sangre Grande." Canine police report, Trigger's file 2, April 15, 1972.
———. "Theft, Sangre Grande." Canine police report, Trigger's file 2, July 5, 1972.
———. "Theft, St. Joseph." Canine police report, Trigger's file 2, January 24, 1973.
———. "Tracking, Manzanilla forest." Canine police report, Trigger's file 2, March 14, 1972.
———. "Trigger's cases." Canine police report, Trigger's police file 2, 1971–1973.
———. "Trigger's cases." Canine police reports, Trigger's files 1, 2, 1968–1973.
Khan, Khairool. "Police dogs track NUFF." Canine police dog reports, Daemon and Rex's files, 1970–1972.
Lewis, Hector. "Murder, Morvant." Carlo's file, February 23, 1965.
———. "Panther's death." Canine police report, Panther's file, August 7, 1965.
Matthews, Winston. "Abduction, Arouca." Canine police report, ANZAC's file, April 19, 1966.
———. "Bullet's death." Canine police report, Bullet's file, November 1, 1970.
———. "Stabbing, Princes Town." Canine police report, January 19, 1969.
———. "Stolen purse, Point Fortin." Canine police report, Bullet's file, January 24, 1969.
Mohammed (no first name). "ANZAC's second case." Canine police report, ANZAC's file, April 19, 1966.
———. "Copper wire thieves." Canine police report, ANZAC's file, November 20, 1968.
———. "Larceny of tree stumps." Canine police report, ANZAC's file, March 25, 1967.
———. "Malicious wounding." Canine police report, ANZAC's file, December 7, 1967.

Bibliography

Narace (no first name). "Larceny of fowls, Arima." Canine police report, Sheba's file, December 23, 1968.

———. "Theft, St. Augustine." Canine police report, Sheba's file, January 6, 1968.

———. "Theft, St. Joseph." Canine police report, Sheba's file, March 11, 1969.

———. "Threat and attempted suicide, Curepe." Canine police report, Sheba's file, December 27, 1968.

Pariagsingh, Ashram. "Kiki." Police canine report, Condor's files, 1990–1992.

Paul, Septimus. "Apprehension of suspect, St. Joseph." Canine police report, Daemon's file, June 17, 1962.

———. "Murder suspect, Las Lomas." Canine police report, Daemon's file, September 27, 1969.

———. "Tracking NUFF, San Fernando." Canine police report, Daemon's file, June 6, 1972.

Paul, Septimus, and Thomas Theophilus. "Daemon's behaviour and commendations." Canine police report and police commissioner's official reports, 1969–1972.

Samuel (no first name). "Kidnapping case, Gasparee island." Canine police report, Rover's file, February 25, 1982.

Sifontis (no first name). "ANZAC changes handlers." Canine police report, ANZAC's file, 1970–1974.

Thomas, Theophilus. "Beating and robbery, Cunupia." Canine police report, Bruno's file 1, November 21, 1953.

———. "Bruno apprehends thief, Port of Spain." Canine police report, Bruno's file 2, March 23, 1955.

———. "Bruno apprehends wanted murderer from Grenada." Canine police report, Bruno's file, November 25, 1956.

———. "Bruno pursues car part thieves, Caroni." Canine police report, Bruno's file 2, October 5, 1955.

———. "Bruno scatters gamblers in Laventille." Canine police report, Bruno's file 2, March 9, 1955.

———. "Bruno's commendations." Canine police reports, Bruno's file 3, 1958–1959.

———. "Bruno's health report." Canine police reports, Bruno's file 3, September 24, 1959.

———. "Daemon's first report." Canine police report, Daemon's file, February 11, 1969.

———. "House break-in, Couva." Canine police report, Bruno's file 1, October 7, 1953.

———. "Jestine West murder." Canine police report, Jett's file, November 9, 1959.

———. "Malicious damages, San Fernando." Canine police report, Adolph's file, December 25, 1969.

———. "Murder, Moruga." Canine police report, Adolph's file, January 4, 1969.

———. "Pursuit of suspicious-looking man, St. Joseph." Canine police report, Bruno's file, November 25, 1956.

———. "Report of Bruno's death." Canine police report, Bruno's file 3, July 26, 1960.

———. "Robbery, Belmont." Canine police report, Bruno's file 1, January 4, 1953.

———. "Robbery, San Juan." Canine police report, Bruno's file 1, March 21, 1953.

———. "Royal Gaol [Port of Spain] Prison Breakout." Canine police report, Bruno's file 1, Depot kennels, St. James. December 19, 1952.

———. "Shooting with intent, Cunupia." Canine police report, Bruno's file 1, August 19, 1953.

———. "Summary of Bruno's cases." Canine police reports, Bruno's file 3, 1957–1958.

———. "Summary of Bruno's cases." Canine police reports, Bruno's file 3, 1959.

———. "Summary of multiple canine police reports." Bruno's file 2, 1955–1956.

———. "Theft at tobacco factory, Champs Fleurs." Canine police report, Bruno's file 1, August 3, 1953.

———. "Trigger enlisted." Canine police report, Trigger's file 1, December 2, 1965.

Bibliography

Newspaper and Journal Articles and Privy Council Summary

Grady, Norton. "Hurricanes of 1952." Monthly Weather Review, Miami Weather, January 12, 1953.
Jacob, Debbie. "Drug Lord's Worst Enemy." *Trinidad Express*, Port of Spain, May 12, 1992.
Joseph, Francis. "Bomb in the City." *Trinidad & Tobago Newsday*, July 12, 2005.
Privy Council. "Privy Council Summary of Junior 'Spirit' Cottle Case." *Weekly Law Reports* 3 (1976).

Newspapers, Magazines, Journals and Other Articles Online

Ali, Jonathan. "The Return of King Cocoa." *Caribbean Beat Magazine*, May/June 2011, Maraval, Trinidad. https://www.caribbean-beat.com/issue-109/return-king-cocoa#axzz80ya0aels.
BBC News. "Thousands March on Trinidad crime." October 23, 2005. http://news.bbc.co.uk/2/hi/americas/4368582.stm.
Besson, Gérard. "Conrad Frederick Stollmeyer." The Caribbean History Archives, Paria Publishing, November 8, 2011. http://caribbeanhistoryarchives.blogspot.com/2011/11/conrad-frederick-stollmeyer.html.
Caribbean Elections. "Trinidad and Tobago Election Centre: Year in Review." Caribbeanelections.com, 2019. http://www.caribbeanelections.com/tt/elections/tt_results_2001.asp.
Central Statistical Office. "Population of Trinidad 2018–2022." Port of Spain, 2020. https://www.populationu.com/trinidad-and-tobago-population.
———. "Population Statistics." Ministry of Planning, Port of Spain, 2011. https://cso.gov.tt/subjects/population-and-vital-statistics/population/.
Clutterbuck, Lindsay, and Richard Warnes. "References." *Exploring Patterns of Behaviour in Violent Jihadist Terrorists: An Analysis of Six Significant Terrorist Conspiracies in the UK*. Santa Monica: RAND Corporation, 2011, 57–62. http://www.jstor.org/stable/10.7249/tr923ant.11.
Cottee, Simon. "Isis in the Caribbean." *Atlantic*, Washington, D.C., December 8, 2016. https://www.theatlantic.com/international/archive/2016/12/isis-trinidad/509930/.
Cultural Mix, Carnival Music and Arts. "Steel Pan History." UK Education Resources, 2023. https://culturemixarts.co.uk/education/resources/history-of-steel-pan/.
Destination Trinidad and Tobago, Ltd. "Birdwatching." 2023. https://www.destinationtnt.com/to-do-and-see/eco-adventure/birdwatching/#:~:text=Trinidad%20and%20Tobago%20is%20a,470%20recorded%20species%20of%2Birds.
Ella, Cathy. "Mama Yo." Imij World Studios, Port of Spain, 2019. https://www.youtube.com/watch?v=l4q-0dsXO6k.
"The end of an era: Guardian 50 moments that made T&T history." *Trinidad Guardian*, Port of Spain, July 31, 2003. https://www.guardian.co.tt/article-6.2.427024.0889b4f0a1.
Graham-Harrison, Emma, and Joshua Surtees. "Trinidad's jihadis: How tiny nation became ISIS recruiting ground." *The Guardian*, London, February 2, 2018. https://www.theguardian.com/world/2018/feb/02/trinidad-jihadis-isis-tobago-tariq-abdul-haqq.
Hamilton-Davis, Ryan. "Frederick Street prison break questions still unanswered six years later." *Trinidad & Tobago Newsday*, Port of Spain, July 26, 2021. https://newsday.co.tt/2021/07/26/frederick-street-prison-break-questions-still-unanswered-6-years-later/?fbclid=IwAR3XB-5B6jnFmZxnugTqb_V2m-.

Bibliography

Jacob, Debbie. "Canine Stars of Green Days." *Trinidad & Tobago Newsday*, September 17, 2017. https://newsday.co.tt/2017/09/17/canine-stars-of-green-days/.

———. "Hard-working dog." *Trinidad & Tobago Newsday*, Port of Spain, July 16, 2018. https://newsday.co.tt/2018/07/16/hard-working-dog/.

———. "Raising a hard-working police dog." *Trinidad & Tobago Newsday*, Port of Spain, March 10, 2021. https://newsday.co.tt/2021/03/10/raising-a-hard-working-police-dog/.

John, Kenneth. "Gun Talk." *The Vincentian*, April 21, 2017. https://thevincentian.com/gun-talk-p13047-108.htm.

Johnson, Kim. "The history of steel pan: Sounds like steel." Clip 1, Chas Shepherd, YouTube, April 20, 2023. https://www.youtube.com/watch?v=iN3YOFu_yIM.

Kerrigan, Dylan. "Bobol as a Transhistorical Cultural Logic." *Caribbean Quarterly* 66, May 20, 2020. https://www.tandfonline.com/doi/abs/10.1080/00086495.2020.1759231.

Lawler, Andrew. "Invaders nearly wiped out Caribbean's first people long before Spanish came, DNA reveals." *National Geographic*, Washington, D.C., December 23, 2020.

Loop News. "Close to 200 Detained for Copper Theft." Port of Spain, May 23, 2022. https://tt.loopnews.com/content/close-200-detained-copper-theft.

———. "Police officer dies, autopsy ordered." Port of Spain, June 22, 2020. https://tt.loopnews.com/content/police-officer-dies-autopsy-ordered.

McNeal, Keith. "Miracle Mother—Siparee Mai, La Divina Pastora." *Caribbean Beat* 54 (March/April 2002), Maraval. https://www.caribbean-beat.com/issue-54/siparee-mai-miracle-mother#axzz7zdfM08iY.

Ministry of Energy. "Historical Facts on the Petroleum Industry of Trinidad and Tobago." Ministry of Energy and Energy Industries, Port of Spain, 2023. https://www.energy.gov.tt/historical-facts-petroleum/.

The National Archives of Trinidad and Tobago. "The Merikins: Our heritage, our faith, our future." National Archives, Port of Spain. http://www.natt.gov.tt/sites/default/files/images/NATT%20Merikin%20Collection%20GuideREV2021.pdf.

The National Trust of Trinidad and Tobago. "The Pointe-à-Pierre Wild Fowl Trust." 2023. https://nationaltrust.tt/home/location/pointe-a-pierre-wild-fowl-trust/?v=df1f3edb9115.

Piegaro, Anthony J. "Letters from US embassies and US companies." CSI International website, October 14, 2019. http://www.csiemergencyservice.com/.

Rampersad, Sharlene. "Jacob: Country has 134 gangs accounting for most daily crimes." *Trinidad Guardian*, Port of Spain, May 11, 2022. https://www.guardian.co.tt/news/jacobs-country-has-134-gangs-accounting-for-most-daily-crimes-6.2.1491608.eb12e2bf32.

Reuters. "Trinidad and Tobago Declares State of Emergency as Covid cases rise." May 15, 2021. https://www.reuters.com/world/trinidad-tobago-declares-state-emergency-covid-19-cases-surge-2021-05-15/.

Royal Museums, Greenwich. "Robinson Crusoe." 2023. https://www.rmg.co.uk/collections/objects/rmgc-object-63975.

Salmon, Emily, and John Salmon. "Tobacco in Colonial Virginia." *Encyclopedia Virginia*, February 13, 2023. https://encyclopediavirginia.org/entries/tobacco-in-colonial-virginia.

Saturday Express. "212 years of the police service, 1798–2010." *Trinidad Express*, November 27, 2010. https://trinidadexpress.com/news/local/212-years-of-the-police-service/article_9434f0e6-2561-52d9-a41a-77af4d3c71cf.html.

Seelal, Nalinee. "Operation Anaconda: National Crime Plan." *Trinidad & Tobago Newsday*, Port of Spain, February 21, 2002. http://www.trinidadandtobagonews.com/forum/webbbs_config.pl?md=read;id=221.

———. (No headline). *Trinidad and Tobago Newsday*, Port of Spain, July 12, 2005. http://www.csiemergencyservice.com/.

Bibliography

Shah, Raffique. "Readying a nation for battle." Trinicenter, 2000. http://www.trinicenter.com/1970/Blackpower2.htm.

―――. "Stealing Elections by Any Vote Necessary." *Independent*, November 15, 2000. http://www.trinicenter.com/Raffique/Nov/byanyvote.htm.

Simm, Carole. "The History of the Pitch Lake in Trinidad." *USA Today*, McLean, Virginia, March 15, 2018. https://traveltips.usatoday.com/history-pitch-lake-trinidad-58120.html.

Suite, Winston, H.E. "Who is the man Makandal Daaga?" The Caribbean Camera, Inc., August 18, 2016. https://thecaribbeancamera.com/who-is-the-man-makandal-daaga/.

Temple-Raston, Dina. "Police Tackle Kidnapping Surge in Trinidad." National Public Radio, New York, August 17, 2007. https://www.npr.org/2007/08/17/12649870/police-tackle-kidnapping-surge-in-trinidad.

UPI. "Caribbean News Briefs." UPI Archives, 1984. https://www.upi.com/Archives/1985/04/08/Caribbean-News-Briefs/3577481784400/.

Williams, C.J. "Kidnappings send a chill through Sunny Trinidad." *Los Angeles Times*, January 2, 2005. https://www.latimes.com/archives/la-xpm-2005-jan-02-fg-kidnap2-story.html.

Williams, H. " Postcolonial Structural Violence: A Study of School Violence in Trinidad and Tobago." *International Journal of Peace Studies* 18, no. 2 (2023), 43–70.

World Bank. "Trinidad and Tobago homicide rates, 2000–2023." https://www.macrotrends.net/countries/TTO/trinidad-and-tobago/murder-homicide-rate.

―――. "Trinidad and Tobago crime statistics, 2000–2022." https://data.worldbank.org/indicator/VC.IHR.PSRC.P5?locations=TT.

Index

Abu Bakr, Yasin 111, 137
aiding escaped prisoner 56
Al Qaeda 110
Alexander-Clifford, Rosamund 145
Alexis, George 11–12, 28, 34–36, 42, 54, 65
Alsatian 11, 13, 29, 36, 37, 40, 44, 46, 49, 54, 65, 73–74, 79, 85–86, 98, 100, 103, 114, 119, 122–123, 129, 132, 151, 158, 160, 163, 165, 169, 171, 173, 175, 178. 180–181, 193; *see also* German Shepherd
Andrews, Jiselle 148–149, 159,
Anglican 4
anonymous handler 164–165
Anthony, Michael 160
Anthony, Sylvester "Zandolee" 65
anthropology 1, 2, 9
Antoine, Kirt 125–127, 182
Applejackers 55
Arab Oil Embargo 78
Arena Forest 3
Arima, Trinidad 142
armed robbery 20, 26, 38, 56
arthritis 47, 104, 134; *see also* lame
assassination 90, 94
assault (indecent assault) 73
assault with intent to rob 31
attempted murder 38
attempted suicide 50
Atwell, Hassan 136, 138

Baboolal, Deo 67
Baboolal, Hamilton 67
Baboolal, Monica 67
Baboolal, Rookmin 67
Bahadoor, Reynold 107, 110, 118, 123–124, 128–130
Bailey, Sean 166–167
Bailey, Winston "Shadow" 78
Bamboo Settlement 109
Baptiste, Darren 152–155, 159
Barbados 64
Bascombe (no first name) 91–92, 95
Battle of Waterloo 64
Baynes, Kenon 156, 157
Beadon, Eric Hammet Fairfax 12, 34

Beetham 61, 138
"Behind the Bridge" 22
Belgian Malinois 106, 108, 119, 125, 140, 158, 160, 166, 171, 173, 178
Belmont, Trinidad 14, 16, 56, 66, 71, 73, 76
Bernard, Akil 104, 126–127, 131, 176
Bernard, Eustace 12
Besson Street 30, 32, 55–56, 61–62, 65
Biche 80
Biden, Joe 134, 174–175
Bissessar, Ryan 106, 121, 132
Black Power 80, 81–83, 85, 93–96, 137
Blackman, Garfield "Lord Shorty" 78
Blades, Lenford 107, 113, 116, 121
Blake (no first name) 51
Blakie, Carlton "Lord Blakie" 21
bobol (corruption) 78
Bolivar, Simón 5
bomb 93, 107, 111–113, 116, 118, 137, 154; *see also* grenade
Botanical Gardens 118, 125
Breadon, Eric Hammet Fairfax 12, 34
breaking and entry 69–70
Bridgeman, Hamilton 11–13, 17, 28–33, 35, 41–42, 54, 60–61, 185
Brown, Hendren 93
Bruno (Dog 1) 10–27, 33–34, 37–38, 44, 169, 176, 183–185
Burroughs, Randolph 66, 98

cadaver dog 112, 115, 140–142, 144, 182
Calderon, Luisa 64
calypso: "Iron Man" 65; "Money Is No Problem" 78; "The Puppy" 93; "Steelband Clash" 21; "Woman Police" 65
cane (canefield, cane fires) 19, 23, 28, 31, 55, 57, 68, 70, 183
Canine Academy 113
canine police dogs: Adina 147, 178; Arci 5, 165; Atos 115, 120, 122–123; Bak 160; Bear 148; Beast 182; Ben 38, 54, 114; Beny 101–102, 104, 174; Biest 103, 105, 121; Bobby 38, 74; Bonnie 7–9, 99, 114; Bouncy 101–102, 104, 137–139, 174, 176; Brixa 178; Bruce 33–34, 38; Bruno (Dog

215

Index

1) 10–27, 33–34, 37–38, 44, 169, 176, 183–185; Bruno (Tobago) 154; Bruno (II) 49; Brutus 93; Buddy 102, 104, 115, 154, 174, 176; Bullet 64, 70–72; Caesar 38; Carlo 37–38, 53–59, 63, 66, 177, 186; Carlos 11–13, 28, 32–34, 55, 84, 166, 169; Cezar 126–127, 171, 176; Chag 38, 40; Charlie 103, 114, 116–117; Chico 121; Cif 160; Condor 134; Cordon 155–156, 177; Daemon 81, 83, 85–93, 96, 177; Dani 140–144, 182; Dasdy 171; Duke 158; Eddie 104, 160, 173; Fando 157, 160; Felix 169–170; Hart 166–167; Jack (cadaver dog) 140; Jack (tactical dog) 113, 122–124, 129–131; Jackson 132–135, 157, 164, 175; Jango 105–107, 121, 178; Jed 103–104, 133–139, 171, 174, 176; Jett 38–41, 44–45, 47–49, 57, 93; Kiki 114; Kim 54, 59, 66; Kubo 167–168; Lady 98, 145–147; "M" dog 163–165; Marko 163, 171; Maverick 160–163, 172–174, 177; Max 110; Meg 171; Minnie 33–34, 36; Nero 126–127; Nissan 115, 120; Panther (Panta, Punch) 38, 57, 60–63, 186; Penny 133–134, 171, 174–175; Prince 33, 36, 38; Princess 42, 54; Queenie 46; Ralph 33–35, 38, 41, 54, 65; Red 112, 115, 142; Rex (Khan's dog) 85, 87–88; Rex (Ryan's dog) 115; Rex Dog # 8 33–39; Ringo 74; Rover 98; Sam 99; Satan 33, 36, 40–41; Shah 11–13, 17, 20, 28–41, 58, 82–83, 169; Shane 97–98; Sheba (Estha) 49–52; Sheba (second) 51–52; Shep 78–80; Skeeto 149, 159; Strike 105, 107–109; Sunny 115, 158; Tess 109; Toby 93; Trigger 73–77; Viking 90–91; Viper 154; Wesley 99; Wilson 125–126; Winston 11–13, 28, 30–31, 33, 37, 169; Woody 104, 116–117, 176; Yeyo 132; Zak 177; Zando 151–152

canine police officers: Alexander-Clifford, Rosamund 145; Alexis, George 11–12, 28, 34–36, 42, 54, 65; Andrews, Jiselle 148–149, 159; anonymous handler 164–165; Antoine, Kirt 125–127, 182; Bahadoor, Reynold 107, 110, 118, 123–124, 128–130; Bailey, Sean 166–167; Baptiste, Darren 152–155, 159; Baynes, Kenon 156, 157; Bernard, Akil 104, 126–127, 131, 176; Bissessar, Ryan 106, 121, 132; Blades, Lenford 107, 113, 116, 121; Blake (no first name) 51; Bridgeman, Hamilton 11–13, 17, 28–33, 35, 41–42, 54, 60–61, 185; Brown, Hendren 93; Caruth, Ronnie 155–156, 177; Cedeno, Sherwin 103–104, 113, 133–135, 138, 177; Chandler, Clayton 43, 45, 99, 121; Charles, McDonald 54, 57; Chase, Shane 114, 126–127, 132–133, 168–172, 181; Donawa, Jason 103, 107, 111, 114, 116–118, 144, 161, 182; Douglas, George 90–91, 93; Duke, Anthony 151–152, 158; Dyer, Leonard 7, 8–10, 79, 97–99, 145 182; Feracho (no first name) 73–74; Figaro, Israel Dennis 34, 56–57, 59–63, 71–73, 186; Gomez, Joseph 175; Grant, Marcellus 79; Gray, Evans 120, 158; Harry, Dunston 37, 177; Hicks, Horace 39, 40, 65; Hinds, Vincent 142; Hosein, Saadiq 160, 172–173, 178; James, Delroy 151, 157, 160; James, Noel 73–77; Khan, Khairool 8, 30, 40, 43, 83, 85, 87–88, 90–93, 96–97, 177; Lewis, Festus "Spider" 25–26, 37; Lewis, Hector 29–30, 43, 54–66, 74, 83, 177; Lopez, Leon 163, 175, 181; Mahabir, Stephen 7, 9, 99; Maharaj, Premnath 100–104, 107, 111–113, 116–118, 137–139, 154, 157–158, 174; Mapp, Deon 149, 151, 158–159; Matthews, Winston 30, 51–52, 63–71, 74, 79, 83, 85, 90–92, 96, 145, 177–178, 182; Melville, Darnel 158; Miller, Racine 156; Mohammed, Raphael 140, 149; Mohammed, Rasheed 129; Mohammed, Zameer 168; Moreau, Caren 178–179, 182; Narace (no first name) 50; Narine, Malissa 147–148; Pariagsingh, Ashram 134–135; Paul, Septimus 86–88; Perez, Neil 107, 110, 118, 122–123; Phillips, John 107, 110, 118, 121–122; Piggott, Carlyle 11, 12, 30, 68; Roban, Michael 9, 43, 106, 107, 110, 112–115, 132; Romeo, Enoch 154, 155, 160–163, 172, 174, 177–178; Romeo, Paul 158; Ryan, Rawle 107, 110, 113, 118–120, 122; Sifontis (no first name) 70, 72; Singh, Kiff 133–134, 174–175; Swanson, Stephen 140–144, 168, 174; Texeira, Renrick 132–133, 175; Thomas, Theophilus 11–18, 20–24, 26–32, 36–49, 52, 54, 61–65, 67, 72, 74, 80, 83–85, 92, 176–178; Tom, Donna Mae 145–146; Williams, Crawford 52, 106; Winn, Kenny 105–109, 115, 156, 161, 178, 182; Woodroffe, Kerron 165

canine police puppies: Ace 8; Action 8, 10; Adolph 64, 66, 67–72; Adonis 66; Ajax 66; Alpha 181; Ammo 181–182; Andy 66, 84, 182; Aniva 181; Anya 181; ANZAC 64, 66–72 182; Apollo 181–182; Arrow 181; Ashes 181; Ati 178–179, 181–182; Aurora 8, 10; Ava 181; Axel 181; Beast 182; Gino 105–106

Capildeo, Rudranath 58
Caribbean Kennel Club 49, 93
Carmichael, Stokely 81; *see also* Kwame Ture
Carnival 3, 21, 128, 174
Caroni (1975) Ltd. 105
Caroni, Trinidad 1–3, 7, 9, 23, 27–30, 54,

216

Index

68, 98, 100, 105, 107, 110, 114, 120, 134–135, 138, 146, 148, 153–154, 163, 168, 174–175, 177, 182
Caruth, Ronnie 155–156, 177
Castara, Tobago 157
Catholicism 66
Caura, Trinidad 82
Cedeno, Sherwin 103–104, 113, 133–135, 138, 177
Cedula of Population 153
Chadee, Dole (Boodram, Nankissoon) 66, 79
Chaguanas, Trinidad 28, 31–32, 74, 129, 142
Chaguaramas, Trinidad 151
Champs Fleur, Trinidad 17
Chandler, Clayton 43, 45, 99, 121
Charles, Joseph (Makmadeen, Serjad) 80
Charles, McDonald 54, 57
Chase, Shane 114, 126–127, 132–133, 168–172, 181
Civil Rights Movement 81
cocaine 8, 99, 120, 124, 149, 154, 161, 165, 166, 168
cocoa 4, 56, 61, 80, 87
cocoa estate robbery 56
Cocobel 4
Cocoyea Village, Trinidad 57, 59
colonialism 81–82, 94, 106, 153
Columbus, Christopher 4
corruption (bobol) 78
Cottee, Simon 137
Cottle, Patrick, Jr. "Spirit" 90, 93–95, 188–191
Couva, Trinidad 19, 31, 54, 165–166
Covid-19 pandemic 3, 172, 174, 176
Cox-Modeste, Helen 99–100
crime: aiding escaped prisoner 56; armed robbery 20, 26, 38, 56; assassination 90, 94; assault (indecent assault) 73; assault with intent to rob 31; attempted murder 38; attempted suicide 50; breaking and entry 69–70; cocaine 8, 99, 120, 124, 149, 154, 161, 165, 166, 168; cocoa estate robbery 56; factory break-in and larceny 61; gambling 22, 50, 78; gun violence 5; heroin 122; house break-in 17, 19, 24, 28, 50, 86; kidnapping 96, 128–129, 136; larceny 16, 20, 23–24, 37–38, 50, 69, 75; malicious damage 45; marijuana 8, 66, 75, 79–80, 99, 108, 120, 122–124, 134, 145, 149, 156–158, 160, 162, 166, 168, 176; money (currency) detection 133; murder 26, 30, 44, 58, 61, 67, 87, 90, 93–94, 108, 136, 142, 173, 188, 190; opium 66; possession of offensive weapon 55; praedial larceny 55, 59, 61; prison escape 13, 68, 135–137; rape 77; robbery 71, 88, 94, 123, 159, 161, 164; shooting with intent 38, 40, 56–57, 68, 125, 129, 159; stolen property 28, 37–38; unlawful possession of a bicycle 50, 76; whe whe 32; wounding with intent 50
crime statistics 106, 128, 142, 159
Crown Point, Tobago 154, 156
CSI International 116
Cumuto, Trinidad 2–3, 5, 126, 130, 132–133, 141, 143, 147, 156, 160, 169, 170–174, 178
Cunupia, Trinidad 18–20, 28, 55, 87
Curepe, Trinidad 24, 26, 45, 50
Czechoslovakia 52

Darwent, Walter 5
Death March 106
Democratic Labour Party 58
Depot kennels 16, 27, 37, 72, 74, 79, 80
Desperadoes 21
Diego Martin, Trinidad 55, 60, 66, 125, 142
Divina Pastora (Siparee Mai) 66
Doberman Pinscher 36–38, 42–43, 54
dog deaths: heat exhaustion/heat stroke 72; twisted intestine 114
dog diseases: arthritis 47, 104, 134; cancer 28, 154, 174; distemper 63
Dog Section 12–13, 28, 29–31, 33–34, 36–38, 40–43, 45–46, 51–52, 54, 59, 61, 63, 65–66, 70–72, 79, 83–86, 90, 92, 97, 112, 177
dog training 85, 114–116, 141, 151, 169–172, 182
Donawa, Jason 103, 107, 111, 114, 116–118, 144, 161, 182
Douglas, George 90–91, 93
drug dealers 8, 78–79, 120, 124
Duke, Anthony 151–152, 158
dustbin bombings 104, 111, 116, 137
Dutch Shepherd 155, 160, 167, 176
Dyer, Leonard 7, 8–10, 79, 97–99, 145 182

East Dry River 23, 71, 74, 138
election fraud 58, 78; see also gerrymandering
English Springer Spaniel 99, 104, 132–135, 157
escape (dog) 40, 119–120
ethnicity (Trinidad) 106
explosives-detection dog 171
Exxon 110

factory break-in and larceny 61
FBI (Federal Bureau of Investigation) 128
Feracho (no first name) 73–74
Figaro, Israel Dennis 34, 56–57, 59–63, 71–73, 186
Flying Squad 98

Index

forest exercises 38, 44, 55, 57, 67–68, 70, 75, 83, 87–88, 126–127, 129–130
Freeport, Trinidad 66, 71, 98, 129, 177
Fyzabad, Trinidad 88, 172,

gambling 22, 50, 78
Gasparee island 98
Gasparillo, Trinidad 161
German Shepherd 65, 73, 79, 85, 100, 103, 114, 119, 122–123, 129, 132, 151, 158, 163, 165, 169, 171, 178, 181
German Short-Haired Pointers 181
gerrymandering 58, 78
Golden Grove Prison 58, 93, 159
Golden Retriever 102, 112, 154
Gomez, Joseph 175
Granger, Geddes 81
Grant, Marcellus 79
Gray, Evans 120, 158
Green Days by the River 157, 160
Grenada 25–26
grenade 134, 137–138
Griffith, Gary 143, 178
guarding duties: escorting inmates 28; President and Prime Minister's residence 67, 98–99; voting machines 58–59, 93
gun violence 5
guns: AK 47 168; pistol 19; rifle 92; sawed-off shotgun 30, 87

Harewood-Christopher, Erla 65
Harry, Dunston 37, 177
heroin 122
Hicks, Horace 39, 40, 65
Hinds, Vincent 142
Hindu 4, 100
Horowitz, Alexandra 45
Hosay 3–4
Hosein, Saadiq 160, 172–173, 178
Hospedales, Geoffrey 143–144
house break-in 17, 19, 24, 28, 50, 86
Hudson-Phillips, Karl 90
Hume, Cecil "Maestro" 78
Hurricane Dog 12

illegal gambling: cards 22, 94; whe whe 32
immersion journalism 9
indentureship 4, 106, 137
independence 12, 54, 65, 81
Independence Square 111
ISIS (Islamic State of Iraq and Syria) 137, 138
Islamiya 110

jailbreak 13, 104, 136–137
Jamaat al Muslimeen 137
James, Christian 160
James, Delroy 151, 157, 160

James, Noel 73–77
John, Kenneth 93
Johnson, Kim 21–22
Jones, John Paul 153
Joseph, Patsy 101, 137
journalism 1, 2

Kerrigan, Dylan 78
Khan, Khairool 8, 30, 40, 43, 83, 85, 87–88, 90–93, 96–97, 177
kidnapping 96, 128–129, 136

La Brea, Trinidad 4, 69
labor unions 21, 31, 50, 82
Labrador 7–8, 38, 54, 60–61, 93, 102, 104, 114–117, 148, 158, 171
Laidlow, Lorraine "Blackie" 90, 93–94, 190–191
lameness 47
Lapeyrouse cemetery 5
larceny 16, 20, 23–24, 37–38, 50, 69, 75
Las Lomas, Trinidad 87, 123
Laventille, Trinidad 22, 31, 51, 77, 119
Lawbreakers 55
Lewis, Festus "Spider" 25–26, 37
Lewis, Hector 29–30, 43, 54–66, 74, 83, 177
Lopez, Leon 163, 175, 181

MacIntosh, Llewellyn "Short Pants" 78
Mahabir, Stephen 7, 9, 99
Maharaj, Premnath 100–104, 107, 111–113, 116–118, 137–139, 154, 157–158, 174
malicious damage 45
Manning, Patrick 105, 112, 132
mapepire (snake) 3, 83, 169
Mapp, Deon 149, 151, 158–159
Maracas, Trinidad 56, 162, 184
Maraval, Trinidad 56, 123, 142
marijuana 8, 66, 75, 79–80, 99, 108, 120, 122–124, 134, 145, 249, 156–158, 160, 162, 166, 168, 176
Martin, Allan; "Scanny" 136,
Marxist/Leninist movement 82, 96
Matthews, Winston 30, 51–52, 63–71, 74, 79, 83, 85, 90–92, 96, 145, 177–178, 182
Mavrogordato, A.V. 64
Mayaro, Trinidad 79
Melville, Darnel 158
Merikins 5
Merrimac 5
Metropolitan Police (England) 11, 85
Miller, Racine 156
Mohammed, Raphael 140, 149
Mohammed, Rasheed 129
Mohammed, Zameer 168
Mon Repos, Trinidad 62–63, 66, 70, 85, 87–88, 186

218

Index

money (currency) detection 133
Monkey Town, Trinidad 140
Montano, Machel 4
Mooledhar, Michael 160
Moreau, Caren 178–179, 182
Moruga, Trinidad 67, 69
Morvant, Trinidad 58, 119, 142
Mounted and Canine Branch 2, 37, 99, 101, 137, 143, 149; superintendents (Cox-Modeste, Helen 99–100; Hospedales, Geoffrey 143–144; Joseph, Patsy 101, 137)
Mounted Section 2, 13, 16, 27, 37, 40, 41, 43, 52, 61, 65, 80, 83–85, 99, 101, 183
murder 26, 30, 44, 58, 61, 67, 87, 90, 93–94, 108, 136, 142, 173, 188, 190
Muslim 3, 4, 137
mutiny 58, 81–82

Naipaul, V.S. 1, 82, 142
Naipaul-Coolman, Vindra 142
Narace (no first name) 50
Narine, Malissa 147–148
National Crime Plan 118
National Joint Action Committee (NJAC) 81–82, 95
necropsy 27, 63, 109, 174
North Post Road 55, 125
NUFF (National United Freedom Fighters) 81–83, 87, 95

oil: drums (steel pans) 21; history 4, 5; production and economy 8, 69, 76, 110, 128, 161
oil companies: Exxon 110; Merrimac 5; Petrotrin 148–149, 161; Shell 38, 67, 69; Texaco 40, 49, 83
Operation Anaconda 118
opium 66
Organized Crime and Narcotics Bureau (OCNB) 108
Oropuche, Trinidad 172

Padmore, Overand 83
Panday, Basdeo 105
Pariagsingh, Ashram 134–135
patois 21, 56
patrols 8, 22, 28, 39–40, 45, 75, 98, 107, 118, 127, 172, 184,
Paul, Septimus 86–88
Penal, Trinidad 140
People's National Movement (PNM) 58, 105, 132
People's Partnership Coalition 132
Perez, Neil 107, 110, 118, 122–123
Perry, Oliver 5
Persad-Bissessar, Kamla 132
Petrotrin 148–149, 161
Philbert, James 9

Phillips, John 107, 110, 118, 121–122
picong (satire) 82
Picton, Thomas 64
Piegaro, Anthony 103, 107–108, 110–124, 142
Piggott, Carlyle 11, 12, 30, 68
Piparo, Trinidad 67, 79
Pitch Lake 4–5
Point Fortin 67, 70, 177
Pointe-à-Pierre, Trinidad 40, 148–149, 161
police commissioners: Breadon, Eric Hammet Fairfax 12, 34; Burroughs, Randolph 66, 98; Griffith, Gary 143, 178; Harewood-Christopher, Erla 65; Mavrogordato, A.V. 64; Philbert, James 9; Williams, Stephen 101
police dog (breeds): Alsatian (German Shepherd) 11, 29, 36, 37, 40, 44, 46, 49, 54, 65, 73–74, 79, 85–86, 98, 100, 103, 114, 119, 122–123, 129, 132, 151, 158, 160, 163, 165, 169, 171, 173, 175, 178. 180–181, 193; Belgian Malinois 106, 108, 119, 125, 140, 158, 160, 166, 171, 173, 178; Doberman Pinscher 36–38, 42–43, 54; Dutch Shepherd 155, 160, 167, 176; English Springer Spaniel 99, 104, 132–135, 157; German Short-Haired Pointers 181; Golden Retriever 102, 112, 154; Labrador 7–8, 38, 54, 60–61, 93, 102, 104, 114–117, 148, 158, 171; Rottweiler 97
police dog in court 68
politics (Trinidad) 105
Port of Spain 1, 5, 7, 11, 12–14, 21–23, 29–30, 32, 35–36, 39–40, 54–57, 61–65, 69, 73–74, 81, 98, 106, 111, 116–120, 122, 125, 128, 136–139, 142, 145, 160, 169
Port of Spain Prison 136, 138; see also Royal Gaol
possession of offensive weapon 55
poverty 5, 95
Power of Habit 43
praedial larceny 55, 59, 61
Princes Town, Trinidad 70
prison escape 13, 68, 135–139
Privy Council 94, 188
Protestants (Presbyterians) 4

Raleigh, Sir Walter 4
rape 77
Rasta City (gang) 138
Rastafarian 4
Rawle, Cecil Eric 90
Red House 81
religions: Anglican 4; Catholic 66; Hindu 4, 100; Muslim 3, 4, 137; Protestants (Presbyterians) 4; Rastafarian 4; Seven Day Adventists 4; Shouter/Spiritual Baptist 4

Index

retirement (Dogs) 104, 163, 165, 174, 176–177
Rio Claro, Trinidad 140
Roban, Michael 9, 43, 106, 107, 110, 112–115, 132
robbery 71, 88, 94, 123, 159, 161, 164
Robinson, NR, Arthur 105
Romeo, Enoch 154, 155, 160–163, 172, 174, 177–178
Romeo, Paul 158
Rottweiler 97
Rowley, Keith 3
Royal Gaol 13, 136; *see also* Port of Spain Prison
Ryan, Rawle 107, 110, 113, 118–120, 122

St. James, Trinidad 69, 104, 111, 117, 118, 125, 137
St. Joseph, Trinidad 22, 24, 29, 38–41, 50, 54, 61, 66, 72, 76, 81, 86; police station 24, 38–40, 61, 86
St. Lucia 74
St. Vincent 83, 89–95
San Fernando, Trinidad 35, 56–57, 59, 69, 72, 87, 144, 161, 168, 186
San Juan All Stars 21
San Juan, Trinidad 14, 17, 21, 29, 32, 80, 128
Sangre Grande, Trinidad 66, 75–76, 140
Santa Cruz, Trinidad 56
SAUTT (Special Anti-crime Unit) 106, 121, 128–129, 132–133, 140, 171
scandal 47
Scarborough, Tobago 155–156
scent identification 57
Sea Lots, Trinidad 56
Secret Service 134
Seelal, Nalinee 111, 118
Seven Day Adventists 4
Shah, Raffique 58, 82–83
Shell 38, 67, 69
shoes (at crime scene) 25, 28, 59, 67–68, 73
shooting with intent 38, 40, 56–57, 68, 125-, 129, 159
Shouter/Spiritual Baptist 4
Sifontis (no first name) 70, 72
Singh, Kiff 133–134, 174–175
Siparia, Trinidad 56–57, 66
slavery 4, 106
soca (music) 78
Solo beverage factory 80
State of Emergency 3, 82
steelband clashes 55; Applejackers 55; Desperadoes 21; Lawbreakers 55; San Juan All Stars 21
steelbands 3, 21–22, 30
Stewart, Sterling 100
stolen property 28, 37–38

Stollmeyer, Conrad Frederick 56
Stollmeyer Castle 56
Stollmeyer Cocoa Estate 56
Swanson, Stephen 140–144, 168, 174

Task Force 129, 142, 156, 172–173
terrorism 93, 110
Texaco 40, 49, 83
Texeira, Renrick 132–133, 175
theft: bull 61; copper wire 32, 68–69, 177; fowl (chickens) 35–36, 50–51; gun 75; money 19, 39, 56, 70–71, 73, 75, 78, 105, 120; motorcar parts 23, 29, 76; payroll 56, 87; purse/wallet 31–32, 38, 70; watch 74
Thomas, Debbie 43
Thomas, Theophilus 11–18, 20–24, 26–32, 36–49, 52, 54, 61–65, 67, 72, 74, 80, 83–85, 92, 176–178
tobacco 4, 17
Tobago 154–157
Tobago House of Assembly 154, 158
Toby, Quentyn "The Mighty Toiler" 93
Tom, Donna Mae 145–146
tracking: criminals 128; illegal immigrant 126–127; kidnappers 128
Trincity, Trinidad 108, 133
Trinidad Chronicle 31
Trinidad ethnic groups 106
Trinidad towns: Arima 142; Belmont 14, 16, 56, 66, 73, 76; Caroni 1–3, 7, 9, 23, 27–30, 54, 68, 98, 100, 105, 107, 110, 114, 120, 134–135, 138, 146, 148, 153–154, 163, 168, 174–175, 177, 182; Caura 82; haguanas 28, 31–32, 74, 129, 142; Chaguaramas 151; Champs Fleur 17; Cocoyea Village 57, 59; Couva 19, 31, 54, 165–166; Cumuto 126, 130, 132–133, 141, 143, 147, 156, 160, 169, 170–174, 178; Cunupia 18–20, 28, 55, 87; Curepe 24, 26, 45, 50; Diego Martin 55, 60, 66, 125, 142; Freeport 66, 71, 98, 129, 177; Fyzabad 88, 172,; Gasparillo 161; La Brea 4, 69; Las Lomas 87, 123; Laventille 22, 31, 51, 77, 119; Maracas 56, 162, 184; Maraval 56, 123, 142; Mayaro 79; Mon Repos 62–63, 66, 70, 85, 87–88, 186; Monkey Town 140; Moruga 67, 69; Morvant 58, 119, 142; Oropuche 172; Penal 140; Piparo 67, 79; Point Fortin 67, 70, 177; Pointe-à-Pierre 40, 148–149, 161; Princes Town 70; Rio Claro 140; St. James 69, 104, 111, 117, 118, 125, 137; St. Joseph 22, 24, 29, 38–41, 50, 54, 61, 66, 72, 76, 81, 86; San Fernando 35, 56–57, 59, 69, 72, 87, 144, 161, 168, 186; San Juan 14, 17, 21, 29, 32, 80, 128; Sangre Grande 66, 75–76, 140; Santa Cruz 56; Sea Lots 56; Siparia 56–57, 66;

Index

Trincity 108, 133; Tunapuna 50; Valsayn 36, 48, 59; Wallerfield 26
Tunapuna, Trinidad 50
Ture, Kwame (Stokely Carmichael) 81

United National Congress (UNC) 105
US Embassy 110, 172, 177
University of Woodford Square 81
unlawful possession of a bicycle 50, 76

Valsayn, Trinidad 36, 48, 59
Venezuela 1, 3–5, 66, 78, 98, 156
voting machines 58–59, 93

Wallerfield, Trinidad 26
West Germany 49, 52, 83, 106, 107
West Indies Federation 37
whe whe 32
Williams, Crawford 52, 106
Williams, Eric 78, 81–83
Williams, Stephen 101
Winn, Kenny 105–109, 115, 156, 161, 178, 182
Woodroffe, Kerron 165
wounding with intent 50

www.ingramcontent.com/pod-product-compliance
Ingram Content Group UK Ltd.
Pitfield, Milton Keynes, MK11 3LW, UK
UKHW041951140426
5217IPUK00015B/748